"WARNING: If, like most Americans calling themselves Christian, you prefer the comfort of acquiescing to the official version of 9/11 and the imperial wars it facilitated, DROP THIS BOOK NOW. But if you are open to the grace of honest inquiry and the risk of following the historical Jesus in confronting the evils of empire, this rigorously argued book is a MUST READ."

—Ray McGovern, CIA veteran analyst now with Tell the Word, a project of the
ecumenical Church of the Saviour, Washington, D.C.

"David Griffin has previously made the case for the Bush administration's complicity in 9/11 and the cover-up of this evidence by the 9/11 Commission. Here, in this important book, he puts these shocking realities in the context of Christian theology and the challenge to the churches. In a profound exploration of the nature and history of the demonic, Griffin suggests that American empire is a culmination of human demonic alienation from God."

—Rosemary Radford Ruether, emeritus scholar, Claremont Graduate University
and Claremont School of Theology

"Do American Christians want the United States to act like the New Rome, invading other countries to impose its imperial rule and its control of other peoples' resources? That is just what the U.S. is doing, increasingly so since 9/11, explains David Griffin. In this gripping summary of evidence for the truth behind 9/11 and the 9/11 Commission report, Griffin makes a compelling case that the imperial practices of the American government have become a destructive force in the world. And he clarifies the biblical and theological basis for Christians to challenge the resurgent American imperialism that often claims divine blessing on its destructive actions."

—Richard A. Horsley, Distinguished Professor of Liberal Arts and the Study of
Religion, University of Massachusetts, and author of *Jesus and Empire: The
Kingdom of God and the New World Disorder*

"Compelling reading. Here is a remarkably thorough presentation of facts regarding 9/11 events. Professor Griffin sets the events of 9/11 in a historical, religious, and philosophical context that is most enlightening. Although this context is also somewhat chilling, he holds out hope in his discussion of where we can go from here. I most highly recommend this book!"

—Steven E. Jones, Professor of Physics, Brigham Young University

CHRISTIAN FAITH AND THE TRUTH BEHIND 9/11

A Call to
Reflection and Action

David Ray Griffin

Westminster John Knox Press
LOUISVILLE • LONDON

Scripture quotations from the New Revised Standard Version of the Bible are copyright © 1989 by the Division of Christian Education of the National Council of the Churches of Christ in the U.S.A. and are used by permission.

Scripture quotations from *The Holy Bible, New International Version* are copyright © 1973, 1978, 1984 International Bible Society. Used by permission of Zondervan Bible Publishers.

Book design by Sharon Adams
Cover design by Eric Walljasper, Minneapolis, MN

First edition
Published by Westminster John Knox Press
Louisville, Kentucky

This book is printed on acid-free paper that meets the American National Standards Institute Z39.48 standard. ∞

PRINTED IN THE UNITED STATES OF AMERICA

06 07 08 09 10 11 12 13 14 15 — 10 9 8 7 6 5 4 3 2 1

Library of Congress Cataloging-in-Publication Data is on file at the Library of Congress, Washington, D.C.

ISBN-13: 978-0-664-23117-0
ISBN-10: 0-664-23117-9

Contents

"Those who can make you believe absurdities can make you commit atrocities."

—Voltaire

Preface

In the spring of 2003, near the end of my thirty-one-year teaching career at the Claremont School of Theology, I began writing a book about 9/11, which would be published as *The New Pearl Harbor: Disturbing Questions about the Bush Administration and 9/11*. I have often been asked why I, as a Christian theologian, would write such a book.

The answer is that one of our main tasks as theologians is to deal with current events in light of the fact that our first allegiance must be to God, who created and loves all people—indeed all forms of life. If we believe that our political and military leaders are acting on the basis of policies that are diametrically opposed to divine purposes, it is incumbent upon us to say so. This is especially the case if we live in a rich and powerful country, the policies of which affect the welfare of other peoples, even other species. Our mandate is all the more important if these leaders are claiming divine support for their policies, as did Vice President Cheney in sending out a Christmas card with the statement: "And if a sparrow cannot fall to the ground without His notice, is it probable that an empire can rise without His aid?"[1] Still another reason for me, as a Christian theologian, to speak out is that Christianity began as an anti-imperial movement; there can be no greater distortion of the original Christian message than the use of Christianity to support imperialism.

Accordingly, when I came to the conclusion that the Bush-Cheney administration had orchestrated 9/11 in order to promote this empire under the pretext of the so-called war on terror, I decided that I needed to say so by means of summarizing the evidence for this conclusion.

I am also often asked how I first came to this conclusion. I did not do so immediately. For about a year and a half after 9/11, I accepted the government's conspiracy theory, according to which the attacks resulted from a conspiracy between Osama bin Laden and other members of al-Qaeda. I also accepted the standard liberal view, according to which the attacks were "blowback" for U.S. foreign policy.[2] On that assumption, I began working on a book about the American empire.

In the course of my research, I learned that U.S. political and military leaders had, many times in the past, lied about or even created incidents that could be used as pretexts to go to war. Given this awareness, I might have immediately regarded the attacks of 9/11 as one more fabricated pretext. But when I first heard this allegation from a theological colleague about a year after 9/11, I replied that I did not think the Bush administration—*even* the Bush administration—would do such a heinous thing. I briefly examined some suggested Web sites but concluded that the evidence was not sufficiently convincing to overcome my *a priori* judgment that the allegation was unlikely.

A few months later, however, I was informed about a Web site containing a 9/11 timeline by Paul Thompson, which presented an enormous number of reports, all drawn from mainline sources, that contradicted the official story and thereby implied governmental complicity of some sort.[3] This discovery started a process that led me to publish *The New Pearl Harbor*, which summarized much of the evidence that had been discovered by previous researchers—evidence, I concluded, that provided a "strong *prima facie* case for official complicity."[4]

I wish to emphasize that it was evidence, of which I had previously been ignorant, that changed my mind. This statement is important for two reasons. First, there is a tendency among those who accept the official account of 9/11 to call all people who suspect official complicity "conspiracy theorists," the accusation implicit in this term being that they are people who, tending to see conspiracies everywhere, brought this predisposition to the issue of 9/11. But I, like many other people, did not reject the official story until I was—*against* my initial reaction—convinced by an abundance of evidence.

A second reason for emphasizing the importance of evidence is that there is a widespread tendency, especially by Americans, to reject the idea of official complicity on a purely *a priori* basis, without any examination of the evidence. Of the various *a priori* reasons for rejecting the idea of official complicity out of hand, the most prevalent seems to be the one that initially kept me from seriously looking to see what evidence might be available—namely, the assumption that our political leaders simply would not carry out, or even deliberately allow, such attacks. Yet only on the basis of the relevant evidence can an answer be given to the question of who orchestrated the attacks of 9/11—if it is to be a *responsible* answer. The relevant evidence, moreover, would include any historical information that either supports or undermines the assumption that U.S. officials would not have been complicit in 9/11.

It is widely assumed that the 9/11 Commission dealt with the question of who orchestrated the attacks of 9/11 and concluded that al-Qaeda did. However, as I showed in a follow-up book, *The 9/11 Commission Report: Omissions and Distortions*, the Commission did *not* ask this question. Rather, the Commission, being directed by a virtual member of the Bush-Cheney administration, simply presupposed the truth of this administration's conspiracy theory. In doing so, the Commission simply ignored—or in a few cases distorted—the various kinds of evidence that pointed to a different conclusion.

This book discusses the ideas touched on in these introductory comments in terms of four theses: (1) The historical record does *not* support the assumption that we can know *a priori* that American political and military leaders would not have orchestrated the attacks of 9/11. (2) Once the relevant evidence is examined apart from that *a priori* judgment, it strongly supports the twofold conclusion that members of the Bush administration and the U.S. military orchestrated the attacks of 9/11 and that they did so in order to advance their imperial aims. (3) Christians have especially strong reasons to oppose these imperial aims. (4) Because the recent efforts to fulfill these imperial aims have been justified by the official account of 9/11, Christians have especially strong reasons to expose the truth behind 9/11.

In June 2003, I was honored to deliver the Robert E. Brennan Lectures in Louisville, Kentucky, on behalf of the Episcopal Diocese of Kentucky. Chapters 7 and 8 and some of the ideas in Chapter 6 are based on lectures given on that occasion. I greatly appreciate the stimulus provided by that invitation to develop my thoughts on these subjects.

A slightly different version of chapter 3 was previously published in *The Hidden History of 9-11-2001,* Vol. 23 of *Research in Political Economy,* ed. Paul Zarembka (Amsterdam: Elsevier, 2006). It is based on a lecture delivered at the University of Vermont, Burlington, October 12, 2005, under the auspices of the Vermonters for a Fair Economy and Environmental Protection (VFEEP), and at St. Mark's (Episcopal Church) in the Bowery, New York City, October 16, 2005, under the auspices of New York 9/11 Truth. It has also been posted at 911Review.com.

Chapter 4 was previously published in *Global Outlook* 11 (Spring/Summer 2006). It is based on a lecture given in Montpelier, Vermont, October 12, 2005, on behalf of VFEEP. This chapter (under a different title) and chapter 2 have been posted at 911Truth.org.

I wish to thank Tod Fletcher for great help, both technical and substantive, in preparing the final form of the manuscript for this book. I am also grateful to Matthew Everett and Jim Hoffman for great assistance with chapters 2 and 3, respectively.

Finally, I would like to express my deep gratitude to Randy Coffin, the wife of William Sloane Coffin Jr., who conveyed the statement from him that is quoted on the back cover, and to Bruce Marshall and Jeanine Weir of Vermont Coalition for 9-11 Truth, who asked for a statement from him about my work on 9/11. Bill was one of the great Christians of the last century, so I hope that his statement, made shortly before his death, about the potential power of 9/11 truth will inspire the churches to take up this issue.

PART ONE
EVIDENCE THAT 9/11 WAS A FALSE-FLAG OPERATION

Chapter 1

9/11 and Prior False-Flag Operations

The official theory about 9/11 is that the attacks were planned and carried out entirely by Arab Muslims belonging to al-Qaeda. The main alternative theory, which is developed in this book, is that 9/11 was a "false-flag" attack, orchestrated by forces within the U.S. government who made it appear to be the work of Arab Muslims.

Originally, a false-flag attack was one in which the attackers, perhaps in ships, literally showed the flag of an enemy country, so that it would be blamed. But the expression has come to be used for any attack made to appear to be the work of some country, party, or group other than that to which the attackers themselves belong.

The evidence that the attacks of 9/11 were false-flag operations—orchestrated, at least in part, to marshal support for a "war on terror" against Muslims and Arabs—is very strong. However, many Americans who encounter this idea reject it on *a priori* grounds, thereby refusing even to examine the evidence. The most prominent *a priori* assumption is that America's political and military leaders simply would not commit such a heinous act. Many people will not be ready to look at evidence about 9/11 until they see that this assumption about U.S. political and military leaders is dubious.

This chapter presents some evidence that undermines this assumption. The first three sections provide some examples of false-flag attacks carried out by other countries, some examples of false accusations by the U.S. government to start wars, and some examples of U.S.-sponsored attacks on innocent citizens in friendly countries. The fourth section describes a Pentagon plan for the U.S. government to attack its own citizens as a pretext for war. The final section then takes a preliminary look at some facts suggesting that 9/11 was a false-flag operation to justify the resulting "war on terror."

FALSE-FLAG OPERATIONS BY OTHER COUNTRIES

From at least the time of the Roman Empire, imperialist and would-be imperialist powers have staged false-flag attacks to justify various types of action, such as "retaliatory" attacks on countries they wanted to conquer and the elimination of domestic opposition. Here we look at two such incidents from the previous century.

The Mukden Incident

In the early decades of the twentieth century, Japan, hoping to establish economic self-sufficiency, was exploiting resource-rich Manchuria. The chief instrument of this exploitation was the South Manchuria Railway. In 1930, Chiang Kai-shek's increasingly successful effort to unify China was causing Japanese leaders to fear that their position in Manchuria was threatened.

On September 18, 1931, Japanese army officers secretly blew up a portion of the railway's tracks near the Chinese military base in Mukden. Then, blaming the sabotage on Chinese solders, the Japanese army used this incident as a pretext for taking control of all of Manchuria. This military operation is considered by many historians to be the beginning of World War II. Therefore, the Mukden incident—which the Chinese call 9/18—was one of the most important false-flag incidents of the twentieth century.[1]

The Reichstag Fire

An equally fateful false-flag operation was the burning of the Berlin Reichstag, the home of Germany's parliament, on the night of February 27, 1933. The fire—which occurred less than a month after the Nazis took power—is now known to be have been orchestrated by Hermann Göring, the president of the Reichstag, and Joseph Göbbels, Hitler's propaganda minister, who had the fire started by members of the SA (Storm Troops).

The Nazis then blamed the arson on the German Communist Party, claiming that the fire was intended to be the signal for a Communist uprising. The only evidence the Nazis presented for this claim was the "discovery" on the site of Marinus van der Lubbe, a feeble-minded left-wing radical from Holland, who had evidently been brought to the site by the SA troops.[2]

The Reichstag fire then became "the excuse for a hitherto unparalleled persecution of Communist and Social Democratic workers, intellectuals and party leaders."[3] Thousands of people allied with the workers movement were arrested; all left-wing newspapers were shut down; and two so-called fire decrees annulled civil rights provided by the constitution of the Weimar Republic. These decrees "formed the pseudo-legal basis for the entire Nazi dictatorship."[4]

Operation Himmler

Nazi Germany attacked Poland on the morning of September 1, 1939. In Hitler's speech to the Reichstag later that day, he referred to twenty-one "border incidents" of the previous night in which Polish troops had allegedly initiated hostilities. The attack on Poland was hence presented as a defensive necessity. But this attack had been planned long before. The Nazis only needed a pretext, so that the war would not be strongly opposed by the German people and, hopefully, other nations.

After Heinrich Himmler came up with the basic idea for the pretext, the task of planning and directing it was assigned to Reinhard Heydrich (who would later be centrally involved in the "final solution") and Heinrich Müller, the head of the Gestapo. The plan, dubbed "Operation Himmler," was to have members of the Gestapo and the Security Service, dressed as Poles, stage various raids near the Polish-German border on the night of August 31.

The plan in some cases was to take some German convicts, dress them as Poles, give them fatal injections, take them to the sites, shoot them, then leave them there as proof that they had been killed while attacking German troops.

The most famous of these raids was the Gleiwitz incident, which was headed by Alfred Naujocks (who later testified at Nuremberg about all this activity). Naujocks had one of the convicts, who had been injected and shot, delivered to the German radio station at Gleiwitz. Then he and his men seized the station, broadcast a message in Polish urging Poles to attack Germans, and left. The body of the dead convict, "discovered" shortly thereafter, was used as proof that an attack by Poles had occurred.

The invasion of Poland on September 1 was the beginning of World War II, as France and the United Kingdom declared war on Germany two days later.[5]

These three false-flag operations—the Mukden Incident, the Reichstag Fire, and Operation Himmler—were all crucial events on the road to World War II. The fact that this war caused millions of deaths and enormous suffering illustrates how important it is that false-flag operations be exposed before the true perpetrators can use them as pretexts for carrying out their designs.

Many Americans may, to be sure, agree with this principle while assuming that U.S. leaders would never engage in such deadly deceit. But this assumption is contradicted by the historical record.

U.S. WARS BASED ON FALSE CHARGES OF ENEMY AGGRESSION

American leaders have in several cases knowingly used false charges of enemy aggression to start a war. I look here at four examples.

The Mexican-American War

One factor in the background to the Mexican-American War of 1846–1848 was a border dispute between Mexico and the Republic of Texas, after the latter had won its independence in 1836. According to Mexico and common understanding, the border was marked by the Nueces River, whereas the Texans placed the border much farther south, at the Rio Grande.

Another factor was American expansionism, especially that of President James Polk. Although he was mainly interested in acquiring California, Polk had committed himself to annexing Texas, promising to support its border claim.

In 1846, after being rebuffed in his attempt to purchase California, Polk ordered the U.S. Army to build a fort on the Rio Grande, about 150 miles south of the commonly accepted border. Facing humiliation as the only alternative, Mexico reportedly initiated hostilities. When the good news reached Polk, he told Congress that Mexico had "shed American blood upon the American soil." Polk's claim that Mexico had been the aggressor was called "the sheerest deception" by a congressman named Abraham Lincoln.[6]

In any case, Mexico, being outgunned, signed a peace treaty in 1848, ceding away what is now California, Arizona, Nevada, New Mexico, Utah, and part of Colorado. In compensation, the U.S. government paid $15 million, which was a paltry sum even in those days (the United States would later offer Spain $100 million for Cuba). The United States, in other words, used the trumped-up war to steal about half of Mexico.[7]

The Spanish-Cuban-American War

Through the nineteenth century, U.S. business, military, and political leaders lusted after Cuba, wanting to make this richly endowed island part of America's commercial system.[8] They had, accordingly, supported Spain's continued sovereignty over Cuba, not wanting Cuba to be liberated until the United States was ready to take it over.[9] During the Cubans' war of liberation in the 1890s, the United States refused to lend money or sell arms to them.[10] By 1898, however, it appeared that the Cubans might win anyway.[11] The administration of President William McKinley decided, against the wishes of the Cuban leaders, to intervene.[12]

In preparation, McKinley sent, without invitation, the battleship U.S.S. *Maine* to Havana Harbor. A few weeks later, it blew up and sank, killing some 260 men. Although Theodore Roosevelt, then assistant secretary of the navy, accused Spain of "an act of dirty treachery,"[13] Washington knew that the last thing the Spanish wanted was for America to have an excuse to enter the war. But U.S. newspapers inflamed the American public with the charge that Spain was responsible. The national slogan became "Remember the *Maine*, to hell with Spain." McKinley took advantage of this situation to get Congress to appropriate money for the war.[14]

Some critics of U.S. foreign policy have argued that the *Maine* was blown up by Americans themselves, which would make this incident a classic false-flag operation. But no clear evidence to support this charge has emerged. An investigation by the navy in 1976 concluded that the explosion was probably an accident resulting from ammunition stored too close to the engine. Whatever the real cause, however, U.S. leaders knowingly used a false accusation to enter the war in order to take control of Cuba and other Spanish colonies.

The U.S. War in the Philippines

The most important reason to go to war against Spain, from the point of view of U.S. imperialists such as Roosevelt, was to take control of the Philippine Isles, partly for their own sake, partly as a stepping-stone to the fabled China market.[15] The United States quickly overpowered the Spanish forces and then, at the peace talks, demanded and obtained the entire Philippine archipelago for the tiny sum of $20 million. The Filipinos, however, were not party to this agreement and claimed independence. As a result, the United States, in order to control the island nation, would have to go to war against the Filipinos, who had just recently been their allies against Spain.

In January 1899, General Arthur MacArthur—father of Douglas MacArthur—ordered all Filipino soldiers out of a village they had occupied for several months. Another U.S. general set up a sentry at a position in this disputed area known as the "pipeline," ordering the men to fire on any intruders. On the evening of February 4, the sentries, approached by four Filipino soldiers—who were probably drunk and unarmed—opened fire on them. U.S. troops, having been prepared for this "pipeline incident," then fired on Filipino positions for the next six hours. Few shots were fired in return by the Filipinos, but the war was on.

The U.S. secretary of war, giving the official version of what happened, said: "On the night of February 4th . . . , an army of Tagalogs . . . attacked, in vastly superior numbers, our little army . . . and after a desperate and bloody fight was repulsed in every direction." This statement was part of a more general "propaganda offensive to prove that the Filipino army started the war."

Years later, MacArthur and three U.S. officers who had been on the scene confessed that the whole battle was prearranged and that American troops had fired first.[16] By then, however, it did not matter much. The Philippines lost 250,000 people in this war, which was so dreadful that the usually ironic William James was provoked to say, "God damn the U.S. for its vile conduct in the Philippine Isles."[17]

The Vietnam War

In June 1964, advisors of President Lyndon Johnson discussed escalating the war in Vietnam by bombing North Vietnam. Pointing out that this escalation would require a congressional resolution, they counseled that without some "drastic change in the situation to point to," such as an "armed attack" by the North Vietnamese, it would be hard to pass this resolution. Shortly thereafter, a clandestine operation known as OPLAN 34A was formulated.[18]

In mid-July, the U.S. destroyer *Maddox* was sent to the Gulf of Tonkin to carry out electronic espionage. On July 30, South Vietnamese gunboats, with American advisors, made commando raids against North Vietnamese islands in the Gulf.[19] Then on August 2, the *Maddox* cruised near North Vietnamese islands that were under attack by the South Vietnamese gunboats. Three patrol boats of the North Vietnamese, who rightly believed that the *Maddox* and the gunboats were part of one operation, charged repeatedly at the *Maddox*, veering off at the last moment. The *Maddox* then opened fire on them. The gunboats fired torpedoes in return, but missed. On August 3, Secretary of State Dean Rusk sent a cable saying: "We believe that present Op Plan 34 A activities are beginning to rattle Hanoi."[20]

On the night of August 4, the *Maddox* and another destroyer fired their huge guns for several hours, having evidently been told by their sonarmen that torpedoes were headed at them. But no torpedoes hit them. A naval commander flying directly over the destroyers saw "nothing but black sea and American firepower." Commodore Herrick of the *Maddox*, realizing he might have been firing at nothing, sent a radio message saying, "Review of action makes many reported contacts and torpedoes fired appear very doubtful." The next morning, nevertheless, U.S. troops were given orders to "retaliate" against North Vietnamese targets. At the same time, President Johnson was telling congressional leaders that the North Vietnamese had made "unprovoked attacks" against American ships in international waters.[21]

Secretary of Defense Robert McNamara, when asked by Congress if we had done anything to provoke the attacks, declared that the attacks were "deliberate and unprovoked" against a ship on "routine patrol in international waters." When he was asked whether there was a connection between the *Maddox* and the South Vietnamese commando raids, he said, "Our Navy was not associated with, was not aware of, any South Vietnamese actions."[22]

Congress, accepting these lies, passed the Tonkin Gulf Resolution, which authorized the president "to take all necessary measures to repel any armed attack against the forces of the United States" and to help South Vietnam defend its freedom.[23] With that blank check in hand, the Johnson administration soon initiated a full-scale war, which would go on for another eight years and result in the deaths of over fifty-eight thousand Americans and some two million Vietnamese.

FALSE-FLAG ATTACKS IN EUROPE

Some Americans, being confronted with the preceding evidence of the willingness of U.S. leaders to provoke and lie about incidents to justify going to war, might reply, "I grant that American leaders have done such things to enemies, but they would not deliberately kill citizens of friendly countries for political reasons." That assumption, however, would be false. In a 2005 book entitled *NATO's Secret Armies: Operation Gladio and Terrorism in Western Europe*, Swiss historian Daniele Ganser has extensively documented the fact that during the Cold War, the United States sponsored false-flag terrorist incidents in many countries of Western Europe in order to discredit Communists. I begin with some historical background.

Historical Background

In 1947, the Truman administration successfully sponsored the National Security Act, which created the Central Intelligence Agency (CIA) and its overseer, the National Security Council (NSC). Existing primarily to prevent the victory of Communist parties in European elections, the NSC and its CIA first targeted Italy. Directive NSC 4-A ordered the CIA to undertake covert activities to prevent a victory by the Communists in the 1948 elections. After these operations succeeded, directive NSC 10/2 created the Office of Policy Coordination, which was authorized to carry out covert operations in all countries in the world. Such operations were to include "propaganda; economic warfare; preventive direct action, including sabotage [and] demolition . . . ; subversion against hostile states, including assistance to underground resistance movements, guerrillas . . . and anti-Communist elements."[24]

With the creation in 1949 of the North Atlantic Treaty Organization (NATO), these operations came to be coordinated by a secret unit within NATO called the Clandestine Planning Committee (CPC), which was guided primarily by the CIA and the Pentagon. (U.S. control was guaranteed by the fact that NATO's supreme commander would always be an American general.) When NATO was expelled from France in 1966 by French President Charles de Gaulle, it moved to Brussels, Belgium. But the real headquarters—of NATO in general and the CPC in particular—remained in the Pentagon.[25]

These operations involved the creation of secret armies, composed of members of the extreme right. (In Germany, for example, they included former members of Hitler's SS.[26]) They were officially called "stay-behind armies," since their official function was, in the case of a Soviet invasion of Western Europe, to stay behind enemy lines, thereby being in position to mobilize a resistance movement against the occupiers. These secret armies never played this role, of course, since no such invasion ever occurred. They only engaged in terrorism and other forms of subversion, which, insofar as they have been officially admitted, have been portrayed as secondary operations. It is not clear, however, that the United States ever believed that there would be a Soviet invasion. All of the so-called stay-behind armies may have—from the first, as some critics have charged—been created entirely to do battle against domestic Communist parties, with the stay-behind function serving simply as a cover story.[27]

Although these right-wing armies engaged in many kinds of operations, including coups, I focus here entirely on false-flag operations, giving examples from four countries.

Italy

The Italian secret army, which came to be called Gladio, and other right-wing extremists, with whom Gladio linked up, had together been waging a secret war since the end of World War II. But from 1969 to 1974, during the presidency of Richard Nixon, Operation Gladio became much more violent, engaging in many false-flag attacks.

On December 12, 1969, four bombs exploded in Rome and in Milan's Piazza Fontana, killing sixteen people and injuring another eighty. This attack, known as the Piazza Fontana massacre, was blamed on the left by the military secret service, which destroyed evidence (a bomb that had failed to go off), then planted bomb parts in a leftist editor's villa.

In 1972, some members of Italy's paramilitary police were set up to be killed by a car bomb near Peteano. An anonymous caller implicated a Communist group called the Red Brigades, after which some two hundred Communists were arrested.[28]

In 1978, after the Communist Party had won an unprecedented number of seats in parliament, former Prime Minister Aldo Moro decided, against the strongly stated wishes of Washington, to propose that Communists be included in the government. Before he could do so, Moro was kidnapped and murdered. The Red Brigades were again blamed.[29]

The deadliest attack in Italy occurred in 1980, when a massive explosion at the Bologna railway station killed eighty-five people and wounded another two hundred.[30]

For over a decade, the Italian public believed that Communists and other leftists had committed these atrocities.[31] However, Italian authorities, beginning in 1984 with an investigation of the Peteano incident, discovered that these crimes were actually orchestrated by right-wing forces. Judge Felice Casson, who spearheaded the investigation, later said: "The Peteano attack is part of what has been called 'the strategy of tension' . . . to create tension within the country to promote conservative, reactionary social and political tendencies."[32] This interpretation was later confirmed by a member of the extreme right-wing organization Ordine Nuovo, who confessed to having planted the Peteano bomb, adding: "You had to attack civilians, the people, women, children, innocent people. . . . The reason was . . . to force these people, the Italian public, to turn to the State to ask for greater security. This is the political logic that lies behind all the massacres and the bombings."[33]

In 1990, Judge Casson discovered documents revealing the existence of Gladio and its connection to NATO and the United States. The truth of these discoveries was then confirmed by Prime Minister Giulio Andreotti, who emphasized the responsibility of the White House.[34]

In 2000, a parliamentary committee to study Operation Gladio concluded that "those massacres . . . had been organized or . . . supported by men . . . linked to the structures of United States intelligence." This conclusion was confirmed in 2001 by General Giandelio Maletti, former head of Italian counterintelligence, who said of the Piazza Fontana massacre: "The CIA, following the directives of its government, wanted to create an Italian nationalism capable of halting what it saw as a slide to the left." It seemed, he added, that to achieve this goal, "the Americans would do anything."[35]

One of the things the Pentagon evidently did was to have its own secret service, the Defense Intelligence Agency (DIA), prepare an instruction book, called Field Manual 30-31, for Gladio and NATO's other secret armies.[36] This manual came with two "supplements," entitled simply A and B. Supplement B, dated March 18, 1970, came to be known as the "Westmoreland Manual," because it contained the signature of General William Westmoreland, who, after commanding U.S. military operations in Vietnam, served as U.S. Army chief of staff from 1968 to 1972.

This Westmoreland Manual instructed these armies to carry out acts of violence, then blame them on Communists, and also to infiltrate left-wing organizations, then encourage them to use violence. Through these means, Supplement B says, "US army intelligence [will] have the means of launching special operations which will convince Host Country Governments and public opinion of the reality of the insurgent danger." However, the manual continues: "These special operations must remain strictly secret. . . . [T]he involvement of the US Army in the internal affairs of an allied country . . . shall not become known under any circumstances."[37]

The existence of FM 30-31 first became publicly known in 1973, when a Turkish newspaper announced that one of its journalists had come into possession of it. Although this journalist soon disappeared, never to be heard from again, the manual was translated into Turkish in 1975, after which it became known in Spain and Italy.

In 2006, after Ganser's book appeared, the U.S. Department of State claimed that Supplement B was a Soviet forgery. Its evidence for this claim, however, is extremely weak, consisting merely of the claim that "Field Manual 30-31B . . . was exposed as a 'total fabrication' in February 1980 hearings before the U.S. House of Representatives Permanent Select Committee on Intelligence."[38] The State Department does not reveal whether this was a conclusion reached by the committee as a whole or simply a statement of someone testifying at the hearings. It also does not mention the discovery of the document in Turkey and the disappearance of the journalist who discovered it. It does not mention that Ganser, rather than being oblivious to the claim that Supplement B was a forgery, pointed out that this claim had been made by Michael Ledeen (who has worked at the Pentagon, the National Security Council, and the Department of State; was involved in the Iran-Contra affair; and was earlier allegedly involved in Operation Gladio). And it does not mention that Ganser presents two strong pieces of evidence against that claim. First, when Ray Cline, former CIA deputy director of intelligence, was asked about FM 30-31B in a BBC-aired film about Gladio produced by investigative journalist Allan Francovich, Cline said: "I suspect it is an authentic document. I don't doubt it. I never saw it, but it's the kind of special forces military operations that are described." Second, when Licio Gelli, the leader of one of Italy's anti-Communist organizations, was asked in the same film how he came into possession of the document, he replied, "The CIA gave it to me."[39]

The State Department, in spite of providing such a weak defense of the claim that FM 30-31B was a Soviet forgery, then used that claim to support its more sweeping conclusion that the idea "that West European 'stay-behind' networks engaged in terrorism . . . at U.S. instigation" is "not true." That conclusion would not follow, however, even if the State Department had made a good case for its allegation that FM 30-31B was forged, because Ganser's conclusion rests on far more than this document, as we have already seen and will see further below.[40]

France

After World War II, the French Communist Party (PCF) was very popular, due to the leading role it had played in the resistance against the fascist Vichy regime, which had collaborated with the Nazis. These Vichy collaborators in military and business circles were frightened by the prospect that the PCF might come to power. The United States shared this fear.[41]

U.S. fears increased in 1946, when national elections showed the PCF to be the strongest party in France. As a result, Ganser says, "Washington and the US secret service were convinced that the PCF had to be attacked and defeated in a secret war."[42] The resulting strategy, known as "Plan Bleu," was "to escalate the already tense political climate in France by committing acts of terror, blame them on the left, and thus create suitable conditions for [a] coup d'état." There was reportedly even a plan to assassinate former Prime Minister Charles de Gaulle to increase public resentment.[43]

This secret plan was exposed in 1947 by the French Socialist party, then in power, before it could be carried out. But this exposure did not end the secret war. It was carried on by a new anti-Communist secret army, code named "Rose des Vents"—a reference to NATO's star-shaped symbol.[44]

Although France experienced its share of violence, it evidently did not suffer the kinds of false-flag attacks experienced by other countries from the late 1960s through the 1980s, perhaps because in 1966 de Gaulle expelled NATO and its covert agents from France.[45] France did, nevertheless, contribute to those attacks.

An especially important person in this respect was Yves Guerain Serac, a CIA recruit. In 1962, Serac went to Portugal, where he created the Aginter Press, a front for a secret CIA-sponsored army. Aginter Press set up training camps to teach bomb terrorism and other kinds of clandestine operations. Between 1967 and 1968, for example, some of its agents went to Rome to teach the use of explosives to members of Avanguardia Nazionale, one of the right-wing organizations behind the Piazza Fontana massacre in 1969.

Serac also became influential through his writings. Describing how to target a democratic state that is insufficiently anti-Communist, Serac wrote: "The destruction of the state must be carried out as much as possible under the cover of 'Communist activities.' . . . [W]e must . . . demonstrate the weakness of the present legal apparatus. . . . Popular opinion must be polarized in such a way that we are being presented as the only instrument capable of saving the nation."[46] Serac explicitly advocated, as this statement shows, false-flag operations to turn the public to the right.

The Pentagon's involvement in the French and Italian secret armies is revealed in a 1952 top-secret memorandum of the U.S. Joint Chiefs of Staff entitled "Operation Demagnetize." It laid out ways in which "political, paramilitary and psychological operations" are to be used "to reduce . . . the danger that Communism could gain strength in Italy and France and endanger the interests of the United States in the two countries." (Note that in this memo, intended to remain secret, there is nothing about protecting democracy or the freedom of the French and Italian peoples; the only concern is "the interests of the United States.") This memo added that "the limitation of the strength of the Communists in Italy and France is a top priority objective," which is "to be reached by the employment of all means"—a standard phrase to refer to the use of violence.

Turkey

In Turkey, the CIA and the Pentagon used a secret army that had been set up by Colonel Alparsan Türks, a Nazi collaborator. This army, known as Counter-Guerrilla, was composed largely of fascists.[47]

One of the most active periods for Counter-Guerrilla was "the terror of the 1970s," during which some 5,000 people were killed, most of whom were identified with the political left. The attacks suddenly came to an end in 1980 after a military coup, planned by the CIA, which gave the presidency to General Kenan Evren, the head of Counter-Guerrilla. The terror of the 1970s, a right-wing extremist on trial later said, had been a strategy to bring Evren and the military right to power.[48]

In the 1990s, the Turkish people learned that this secret army was funded by the CIA and run by NATO—which means, of course, by the Pentagon.[49] A book written by a former paramilitary commander who had battled the PKK—the organization fighting for an independent Kurdish state—revealed that Counter-Guerrilla had run false-flag operations. In order to turn Kurds against the PKK, he reported, Counter-Guerrilla troops would dress up as PKK fighters and attack Kurdish villages, then engage in rapes and random executions.[50]

Belgium

In the 1980s, Belgium suffered a terrifying series of terrorist attacks known as the Brabant massacres. (Brabant is the geographic area around Brussels, where NATO has been headquartered since 1966.) The attacks usually occurred at shopping areas, especially supermarkets. In November 1985, for example, hooded men stepped out of their car and started firing at shoppers with a pump-action shotgun. Eight people were killed. "A husband and wife and their fourteen-year-old daughter were finished off in cold blood. . . . Another father and his nine-year-old daughter were killed in their car trying to flee." Between 1982 and 1985, there were sixteen such attacks, which "reduced Belgium to a state of panic."[51]

Although the responsibility for the Brabant massacres remained a mystery for many years, evidence later surfaced that they were carried out by a neo-Nazi organization known as Westland New Post (WNP). Michel Libert, a former WNP member, confirmed in 1992 that from 1982 to 1985, it was his job to scout out supermarkets, seeing if they had any protection that could interfere with WNP's operations. Libert's orders came from WNP commander Paul Latinus, who was paid by the Pentagon's DIA. A Belgian journalist reports that when he asked Latinus who had asked him to set up the WNP, he said, "American military secret services."[52]

With regard to the motivation behind the massacres, a member of WNP later said that the plan was to "make the population believe that these terrorist attempts were done by the Left."[53] A report issued by the Belgian parliament in 1990 said that the Brabant killings were "part of a conspiracy to destabilize Belgium's democratic regime, possibly to prepare the ground for a right-wing coup."[54]

Following the exposure of Operation Gladio in Italy in 1990, the discovery that other NATO countries had similar clandestine units became a major scandal in Europe (although it was scarcely mentioned in the U.S. media). NATO has officially denied the whole story, but in 1990 Secretary General Manfred Wörner reportedly confirmed to the NATO ambassadors that "the military command of the allied forces—Supreme Headquarters Allied Powers Europe (SHAPE)—coordinated the activities of the 'Gladio Network.'"[55] One member of the European Parliament, speaking about this secret network, was especially incensed by "the fact that it was set up by the CIA and NATO which, while purporting to defend democracy were actually undermining it and using it for their own nefarious purposes." Another member said, "I should like to protest most strongly against the fact that the American military, whether through SHAPE, NATO or the CIA, think they can interfere in what is our democratic right."[56]

As these revelations show, the assumption that U.S. military leaders would not order the killing of innocent civilians in allied countries for political purposes is false. Some Americans, however, might grant this and still assume that our military leaders would not run false-flag operations that would kill fellow Americans. This assumption has, however, been disproved by the discovery of Operation Northwoods.

OPERATION NORTHWOODS

Early in 1962, the Joint Chiefs of Staff presented President John Kennedy with a plan, called Operation Northwoods, describing "pretexts which would provide justification for US military intervention in Cuba." Exemplifying the "strategy of tension" that was being used by the Pentagon in Europe, this document advocated "a period of heightened US-Cuban tensions which place the United States in the position of suffering justifiable grievances." This plan would make the world ready for U.S. intervention "by developing the international image of the Cuban government as rash and irresponsible, and as an alarming and unpredictable threat to the peace of the Western Hemisphere."[57]

The document then suggests several possible actions that would help create this image, such as a "Communist Cuban terror campaign in the Miami area . . . and even in Washington." One of the possibilities was what the Joint Chiefs called a "Remember the *Maine*" incident: "We could blow up a U.S. ship in Guantánamo Bay and blame Cuba." Accordingly, this false-flag operation, devised by the Pentagon's military leaders, would have involved killing American citizens. President Kennedy did not approve this plan, but who can say that some other person in the Oval Office, such as Richard Nixon, would not have done so?

9/11 AS A FALSE-FLAG OPERATION

The facts discussed thus far undermine the main *a priori* reason for not examining the evidence that 9/11 was an inside job—namely, the assumption that American political and military leaders simply would not orchestrate murderous false-flag operations. When the official story and the relevant evidence are examined apart from that assumption, they provide many signs that 9/11 was such an operation. I give a few examples.

The Alleged Hijackers

Central members of the Bush administration, including Dick Cheney and Donald Rumsfeld, came into office intent on attacking Iraq, an Arab Muslim nation.[58] The Bush administration had also been planning an attack on Afghanistan, a Muslim nation, for several months prior to 9/11.[59] The official story, by crediting the attacks to an Arab Muslim organization headquartered in Afghanistan, provided a basis for both wars—not a legal basis, to be sure, but an emotional basis sufficient to marshal support from a majority of the American people and their representatives in Congress. There are, however, many problems with this official story.

Not Devout Muslims. The alleged hijackers are portrayed in the official story as devout Muslims, ready to meet their maker. Mohamed Atta, called the ringleader, is said by *The 9/11 Commission Report* to have become very religious, even "fanatically so."[60] Some journalists, however, found that he loved cocaine, alcohol, gambling, pork, and lap dances. According to an editorial in the *Wall Street Journal*, moreover, not only Atta but several of the other men indulged such tastes in Las Vegas.[61] But the 9/11 Commission, ignoring these reports, professed to have no idea why these men met in Las Vegas several times.[62] This is only one of over a hundred issues on which the Commission distorted or simply omitted evidence contradicting the official story.[63]

Names Not on Flight Manifests. Another problem is that, although we are told that four or five of the alleged hijackers were on each of the four flights, the flight manifests that have been released have no Arab names on them.[64] *The 9/11 Commission Report* simply omits any mention of this problem.

Not Even Dead? Another serious problem is that several of the nineteen men, according to stories published by the BBC and British newspapers, are still alive. For example, *The 9/11 Commission Report* named Waleed al-Shehri as one of the hijackers and reproduced the FBI's photograph of him. It even suggested that al-Shehri, stabbed one of the flight attendants shortly before Flight 11 crashed into the north tower.[65] But as BBC News had reported eleven days after 9/11, al-Shehri, having seen his photograph in newspapers and TV programs, notified authorities and journalists in Morocco, where he works as a pilot, that he was still alive.[66]

Planted Evidence? Just as evidence was sometimes planted in the European operations to convince the public that the attacks were carried out by Communists, it appears that evidence was planted to convince the public that the 9/11 attacks were carried out by the supposed hijackers. One such example involves the alleged discovery of two of Mohamed Atta's bags, which supposedly did not get loaded onto Flight 11 because his commuter flight from Portland, Maine, was late. These bags contained flight simulation manuals for Boeing airplanes, a copy of the Koran, a religious cassette tape, a note to other hijackers about mental preparation, and Atta's passport and will.[67]

But this story is riddled with problems. First, there was, as even the 9/11 Commission points out, a full hour between the arrival of Atta's commuter flight and the departure of Flight 11,[68] so there is no explanation as to why his bags would have been left behind. Second, Atta, after already being in Boston on September 10, drove up to Portland and stayed overnight, hence making the early-morning commuter flight necessary. Since that commuter flight *might* have been delayed, why would he have taken the risk of missing Flight 11? The 9/11 Commission admits that it has no answer.[69] Third, if Atta was planning to fly into the World Trade Center, why would he have taken his will? The whole episode appears to have been set up by someone so that Atta's luggage with the incriminating contents would be "found."[70]

The Legend of Osama bin Laden

Part and parcel of the official story about the Arab Muslim hijackers is that they, as members of al-Qaeda, were under the influence of Osama bin Laden (OBL), who had become America's archenemy. There are also many problems in this part of the story.

First, in June 2001, when OBL was already America's "most wanted" criminal, he reportedly spent two weeks in the American Hospital in Dubai, where he was visited by the local CIA agent.[71]

Second, it is claimed that Osama had become a "black sheep," estranged from the rest of the bin Laden family (some members of which had been closely involved with the Bush family). There are reports, however, that family members visited him at the hospital in Dubai and also came to Afghanistan to attend his son's wedding.[72]

Third, after 9/11, when America was reportedly trying to get OBL "dead or alive," the U.S. military evidently allowed him to escape on at least four occasions, the last one being the "battle of Tora Bora," which the London *Telegraph* labeled "a grand charade."[73]

Fourth, the Bush administration promised to provide a white paper with proof that the attacks had been planned by OBL, but this paper was never produced. Also, although the Taliban said that it would hand OBL over if the United States presented evidence of his involvement in 9/11, Bush refused to provide any evidence.[74]

Fifth, two weeks after 9/11, OBL denied any involvement in the attacks. The Bush administration, however, claims that bin Laden did admit responsibility in a video allegedly found in Afghanistan two months later. But the man in this video has much darker skin, fuller cheeks, and a broader nose than the OBL of all the other videos, including one broadcast on al Jazeera only six weeks later.[75] We again seem to have planted evidence.

President Bush and His Secret Service

On the morning of 9/11, President George W. Bush reportedly believed, upon hearing that a plane had struck one of the Twin Towers, that it was an accident. It was not terribly strange, therefore, that he decided to go ahead with the photo-op at the school in Sarasota, Florida. Word of the second strike, however, should have indicated to him and his Secret Service agents—assuming the truth of the official story, according to which these strikes were unexpected—that the country was undergoing an unprecedented terrorist attack. Yet the Secret Service allowed him to remain at the school for another half-hour.

This behavior was very strange. The president's location had been highly publicized. If the attacks were indeed unexpected, the Secret Service would have had no idea how many planes had been hijacked. They would have had to assume that the president himself might be one of the targets: what could be more satisfying to foreign terrorists attacking high-value targets in the United States than to kill the president? For all the Secret Service would have known, a hijacked airliner might have been bearing down on the school at that very minute, ready to crash into it, killing the president and everyone else there—including the Secret Service agents themselves.

It is, in any case, standard procedure for the Secret Service to rush the president to a safe location whenever there is any sign that he may be in danger. Yet these agents, besides allowing the president to remain in the classroom another ten minutes, permitted him to speak on television, thereby announcing to the world that he was still at the school.

Would not this behavior be explainable only if the head of the Secret Service detail knew that the planned attacks did not include an attack on the president? And how could this have been known for certain unless the attacks were being carried out by people within our own government?

The 9/11 Commission, far from asking these questions, was content to report that "[t]he Secret Service told us they . . . did not think it imperative for [the president] to run out the door."[76] The commissioners give the impression, in other words, of simply accepting the implied suggestion that maintaining presidential decorum was more important than protecting the president's life. There is no indication that any of the commissioners raised the obvious point that the options available to the Secret Service agents were not limited to running the president out the door or leaving him at the school for another half-hour. They could have, for example, simply *walked* him out of the room.

This episode provides additional reason to believe, therefore, that the attacks were a false-flag operation, carried out by our own military forces.

The Strike on the Pentagon

This same conclusion is suggested by an examination of the strike on the Pentagon. According to the official account, the Pentagon was hit by American Airlines Flight 77, under the control of al-Qaeda hijacker Hani Hanjour. But this part of the official story is challenged by many facts.

First, Flight 77 allegedly, after making a U-turn in the Midwest, flew back to Washington undetected for forty minutes, even though the U.S. military, which by then clearly knew that hijacked airliners were being used as weapons, has the best radar systems in the world, one of which, it brags, "does not miss anything occurring in North American airspace."[77]

Second, the aircraft, in order to hit the west wing of the Pentagon, reportedly executed a 270-degree downward spiral, which according to some pilots would have been impossible for a Boeing 757 even with an expert pilot. Hanjour, moreover, was known as "a terrible pilot," who could not even fly a small airplane.[78]

Third, terrorists brilliant enough to get through the U.S. military's defense system would not have struck the Pentagon's west wing, for many reasons: It had been reinforced, so the damage was less severe than a strike anywhere else would have been; it was still being renovated, so relatively few people were there; and the secretary of defense and all the top brass, whom terrorists would presumably have wanted to kill, were in the east wing.

Fourth, there is considerable evidence that the aircraft that struck the Pentagon was not even a Boeing 757. For one thing, unlike the strikes on the Twin Towers, the strike on the Pentagon did not create a detectable seismic signal.[79] Also, the kind of damage and debris that would have been produced by the impact of a Boeing 757 were not produced by the strike on the Pentagon, according to both eyewitnesses[80] and photographs.[81] Former pilot Ralph Omholt, discussing the photographic evidence, writes: "[T]here is no doubt that a [large] plane did not hit the Pentagon. There is no hole big enough to swallow a 757. . . . There was no tail, no wings; no damage consistent with a B-757 'crash.'"[82]

Evidence was again destroyed. Shortly after the strike, government agents picked up debris from the Pentagon in front of the impact site and carried it off.[83] Shortly thereafter the entire lawn was covered with dirt and gravel, so that any remaining forensic evidence was literally covered up.[84] Finally, the videos from security cameras on nearby buildings, which would show what really hit the Pentagon, were immediately confiscated by FBI agents.[85] The Department of Justice has refused to release these videos, and the 9/11 Commission did not use its subpoena power to force it to do so.[86]

Evidence again appears to have been planted. One example: a video frame, allegedly taken by a surveillance camera at Dulles Airport in Washington, D.C., supposedly shows alleged hijacker Khalid al-Mihdhar going through a checkpoint shortly before Flight 77 took off. But whereas a typical security video indicates the time, the location, and the camera, there are no such indications on this video frame. A second example: proof that Flight 77 was hijacked and heading back toward Washington was allegedly provided in a phone call from passenger Barbara Olson to her husband, attorney Ted Olson. But except for the claim of Ted Olson, who works for the Bush-Cheney administration, no evidence has been provided for the occurrence of this call (from, for example, telephone records).

Here we have looked at only a few of the signs that 9/11 was a false-flag operation. In the following chapters, we examine several more such signs.

Chapter 2

Explosive Testimony

Revelations about the Twin Towers in the 9/11 Oral Histories

> *"[T]here was just an explosion [in the south tower]. It seemed like on television [when] they blow up these buildings. It seemed like it was going all the way around like a belt, all these explosions."*
> —Firefighter Richard Banaciski

> *"I saw a flash flash flash [at] the lower level of the building. You know like when they demolish a building?"*
> —Assistant Fire Commissioner Stephen Gregory

> *"[I]t was [like a] professional demolition where they set the charges on certain floors and then you hear 'Pop, pop, pop, pop, pop.'"*
> —Paramedic Daniel Rivera

The above quotations come from a collection of 9/11 oral histories that, although recorded by the Fire Department of New York (FDNY) at the end of 2001, were publicly released only on August 12, 2005. Prior to that date, very few Americans knew the content of these accounts or even the fact that they existed.

Why have we not known about them until recently? Part of the answer is that the City of New York would not release them until it was forced to do so. Early in 2002, the *New York Times* requested copies under the Freedom of Information Act, but Mayor Michael Bloomberg's administration refused. So the *Times*, joined by several families of 9/11 victims, filed suit. After a long process, the City was finally ordered by the New York Court of Appeals to release the records (with some exceptions and redactions allowed). Included were oral histories, in interview form, provided by 503 firefighters and medical workers.[1]

21

(Emergency Medical Services had become a division within the Fire Department.[2]) The *Times* then made these oral histories publicly available.[3]

Once the content of these testimonies is examined, it is easy to see why persons concerned to protect the official story about 9/11 would try to keep them hidden. By suggesting that explosions were occurring in the World Trade Center's Twin Towers, they pose a challenge to the official account of 9/11, according to which the towers were caused to collapse solely by the impact of the airplanes and the resulting fires.

In any case, now that the oral histories have finally been released, it is time for Americans and the world in general to see what these brave men and women reported about that fateful day. If this information forces a reevaluation of the official story about 9/11, better now than later.

That said, it must be added that although these oral histories are of great significance, they do not contain the first reports of explosions in the Twin Towers. Such reports—from firefighters, reporters, and people who had worked in the towers—started becoming available right after 9/11.

These reports, however, were not widely publicized by the mainstream press and, as a result, have for the most part been known only within the 9/11 truth movement, which has focused on evidence that seems inconsistent with the official story.

I begin by summarizing some of those previously available reports. Readers will then be able to see that although in some respects the newly released oral histories simply add reinforcement, they also are revelatory documents: Some of the testimonies are quite stunning, even to people familiar with the earlier reports; and there are now *so many* testimonies that even the most skeptical reader is likely to find the cumulative effect impressive.

PREVIOUSLY AVAILABLE TESTIMONY SUGGESTIVE OF EXPLOSIONS IN THE TWIN TOWERS

The day after 9/11, a story in the *Los Angeles Times*, referring to the south tower, said: "There were reports of an explosion right before the tower fell, then a strange sucking sound, and finally the sound of floors collapsing." Referring to the north tower, it said: "The top of the building exploded with smoke and dust. There were no flames, just an explosion of debris."[4]

A story in the *Guardian* said that "police and fire officials were carrying out the first wave of evacuations when the first of the World Trade Centre towers collapsed. Some eyewitnesses reported hearing another explosion just before the structure crumbled. Police said that it looked almost like a 'planned implosion.'"[5]

To speak of a "planned implosion" is to speak of a "controlled demolition," in which explosives are placed at crucial places throughout a building so that, when set off in the proper order, they will cause the building to come down in the desired way. When it is close to other buildings, the desired way will be straight down into, or at least close to, the building's footprint, so that it does not damage the surrounding buildings. This type of controlled demolition is called an "implosion." To induce an implosion in steel-frame buildings, the explosives must be set so as to break the steel columns. Each of the Twin Towers had 47 massive steel columns in its core and 236 steel columns around the periphery.

To return now to early testimonies about explosions: There were many reports about an explosion in the basement of the north tower. For example, janitor William Rodriguez reported that he and others felt an explosion below the first sublevel office at 9 a.m., after which coworker Felipe David, who had been in front of a nearby freight elevator, came into the office with severe burns on his face and arms yelling, "Explosion! explosion! explosion!"[6]

Rodriguez's account has been corroborated by José Sanchez, who was in the workshop on the fourth sublevel. Sanchez said that he and a coworker heard a big blast that "sounded like a bomb," after which "a huge ball of fire went through the freight elevator."[7]

Engineer Mike Pecoraro, who was working in the sixth subbasement of the north tower, said that after an explosion he and a coworker went up to the C level, where there was a small machine shop. "There was nothing there but rubble," said Pecoraro. "We're talking about a 50 ton hydraulic press—gone!" They then went to the parking garage, but found that it was also gone. Then on the B level, they found that a steel-and-concrete fire door, which weighed about 300 pounds, was wrinkled up "like a piece of aluminum foil." Having seen similar things after the terrorist attack in 1993, Pecoraro was convinced that a bomb had gone off.[8]

Given these testimonies to explosions in the basement levels of the towers, it is interesting that Mark Loizeaux, head of Controlled Demolition, Inc., has been quoted as saying, "If I were to bring the towers down, I would put explosives in the basement to get the weight of the building to help collapse the structure."[9]

Multiple Explosions

Some of the testimonies suggested that more than one explosion occurred in one tower or the other. FDNY Captain Dennis Tardio, speaking of the south tower, said: "I hear an explosion and I look up. It is as if the building is being imploded, from the top floor down, one after another, *boom, boom, boom*."[10]

In June 2002, NBC television played segments from tapes recorded on 9/11. One segment contained the following exchange, which involved firefighters in the south tower:

Official: Battalion 3 to dispatch, we've just had another explosion.

Official: Battalion 3 to dispatch, we've had additional explosion.
Dispatcher: Received battalion command. Additional explosion.[11]

Firefighter Louie Cacchioli, after entering the north tower lobby and seeing elevator doors completely blown out and people being hit with debris,
asked himself, "How could this be happening so quickly if a plane hit way
above?" After he reached the twenty-fourth floor, he and another fireman
"heard this huge explosion that sounded like a bomb [and] knocked off the
lights and stalled the elevator." After they pried themselves out of the elevator,
"Another huge explosion like the first one hits. This one hits about two minutes later . . . [and] I'm thinking, 'Oh. My God, these bastards put bombs in
here like they did in 1993!' "[12]

Multiple explosions were also reported by Teresa Veliz, who worked for a
software development company in the north tower. She was on the forty-seventh
floor, she reported, when suddenly "the whole building shook. . . . [Shortly
thereafter] the building shook again, this time even more violently." Then,
while Veliz was making her way downstairs and outside: "There were explosions going off everywhere. I was convinced that there were bombs planted
all over the place and someone was sitting at a control panel pushing detona-
tor buttons. . . . There was another explosion. And another. I didn't know where
to run."[13]

Steve Evans, a New York–based correspondent for the BBC, said: "I was at
the base of the second tower . . . that was hit. . . . There was an explosion. . . .
The base of the building shook. . . . [T]hen there was a series of explosions."[14]

Sue Keane, an officer in the New Jersey Police Department who was previously a sergeant in the U.S. Army, said in her account of the onset of the collapse of the south tower: "[I]t sounded like bombs going off. That's when the
explosions happened. . . . I knew something was going to happen. . . . It started
to get dark, then all of a sudden there was this massive explosion." Then, discussing her experiences during the collapse of the north tower, she said:
"[There was] another explosion. That sent me and the two firefighters down
the stairs. . . . I can't tell you how many times I got banged around. Each one
of those explosions picked me up and threw me. . . . There was another explosion, and I got thrown with two firefighters out onto the street."[15]

Wall Street Journal reporter John Bussey, describing his observation of the
collapse of the south tower from the ninth floor of the WSJ office building, said:
"I . . . looked up out of the office window to see what seemed like perfectly synchronized explosions coming from each floor. . . . One after the other, from top
to bottom, with a fraction of a second between, the floors blew to pieces."[16]

Another *Wall Street Journal* reporter said that after seeing what appeared to
be "individual floors, one after the other exploding outward," he thought: " 'My
God, they're going to bring the building down.' And they, whoever they are,
HAD SET CHARGES. . . . I saw the explosions."[17]

A similar perception was reported by Beth Fertig of WNYC Radio, who said: "It just descended like a timed explosion—like when they are deliberately bringing a building down. . . . It was coming down so perfectly that in one part of my brain I was thinking, 'They got everyone out, and they're bringing the building down because they have to.'"[18]

A more graphic testimony to this perception was provided on the film made by the Naudet brothers. In a clip from that film, one can watch two firemen describing their experiences to other firemen.

> *Fireman 1*: We made it outside, we made it about a block. . . .
> *Fireman 2*: We made it at least two blocks and we started running. (*He makes explosive sounds and then uses a chopping hand motion to emphasize his next point.*) Floor by floor it started popping out. . . ."
> *Fireman 1*: It was as if they had detonated—as if they were planning to take down a building, boom boom boom boom boom. . . .
> *Fireman 2*: All the way down. I was watching it and running. And then you just saw this cloud of shit chasing you down.[19]

As shown by these illustrations, along with testimony that can now be viewed on the Internet,[20] quite impressive testimony to the occurrence of explosions in the Twin Towers existed even prior to the release of the oral histories. As we will see, however, these oral histories have made the testimony much more impressive, qualitatively as well as quantitatively. The cumulative testimony now points even more clearly than before not simply to explosions but to controlled demolition.

TESTIMONIES IN THE ORAL HISTORIES SUGGESTIVE OF CONTROLLED DEMOLITION

Several FDNY members reported that they heard an explosion just before the south tower collapsed. For example, Battalion Chief John Sudnik said that while he and others were working at the command post, "We heard a loud explosion or what sounded like a loud explosion and looked up and I saw tower two start coming down."[21]

Firefighter Timothy Julian said: "First I thought it was an explosion. I thought maybe there was a bomb on the plane, but delayed type of thing, you know secondary device. . . . I just heard like an explosion and then a cracking type of noise, and then it sounded like a freight train, rumbling and picking up speed, and I remember I looked up, and I saw it coming down."[22]

Emergency medical technician Michael Ober said: "We heard a rumble, some twisting metal, we looked up in the air, and . . . it looked to me just like an explosion. It didn't look like the building was coming down, it looked like just one floor had blown completely outside of it. . . . I didn't think they were coming down. I just froze and stood there looking at it."[23] Ober's testimony suggests that he heard and saw the explosion before he saw any sign that the building was coming down.

This point is made even more clearly by Chief Frank Cruthers, who said: "There was what appeared to be at first an explosion. It appeared at the very top, simultaneously from all four sides, materials shot out horizontally. And then there seemed to be a momentary delay before you could see the beginning of the collapse."[24]

These statements by Ober and Cruthers, indicating that there was a delay between the explosion and the beginning of the collapse, suggest that the sounds and the horizontal ejection of materials could not be attributed simply to the onset of the collapse.

Shaking Ground before the Collapse

As we saw earlier, some people in the towers reported powerful explosions in the basements. Such explosions would likely have caused the ground to shake.

Such shaking was reported by medical technician Lonnie Penn, who said that just before the collapse of the south tower: "I felt the ground shake, I turned around and ran for my life. I made it as far as the Financial Center when the collapse happened."[25]

According to the official account, the vibrations that people felt were produced by material from the collapsing towers hitting the ground. Penn's account, however, indicates that the shaking must have occurred several seconds before the collapse.

Shaking prior to the collapse of the north tower was described by fire patrolman Paul Curran. He was standing near it, he said, when "All of a sudden the ground just started shaking. It felt like a train was running under my feet. . . . The next thing we know, we look up and the tower is collapsing."[26]

Lieutenant Bradley Mann of the fire department, one of the people to witness both collapses, described shaking prior to each of them. "Shortly before the first tower came down," he said, "I remember feeling the ground shaking. I heard a terrible noise, and then debris just started flying everywhere. People started running." Then, after they had returned to the area, he said, "We basically had the same thing: The ground shook again, and we heard another terrible noise and the next thing we knew the second tower was coming down."[27]

Multiple Explosions

The oral histories contain numerous testimonies with reports of more than one explosion. Paramedic Kevin Darnowski, for example, said: "I started walking back up towards Vesey Street. I heard three explosions, and then we heard like groaning and grinding, and tower two started to come down."[28]

Gregg Brady, an emergency medical technician, reported the same thing about the north tower, saying: "I heard three loud explosions. I look up and the north tower is coming down now."[29]

Somewhat more explosions were reported by firefighter Thomas Turilli, who said, referring to the south tower, that "it almost sounded like bombs going off, like boom, boom, boom, like seven or eight."[30]

Even more explosions were reported by Craig Carlsen, who said that while he and other firefighters were looking up at the towers, they "heard explosions coming from building two, the south tower. It seemed like it took forever, but there were about ten explosions. . . . We then realized the building started to come down."[31]

"Pops"

As before, "pops" were reported by some witnesses. "As we are looking up at the [south tower]," said firefighter Joseph Meola, "it looked like the building was blowing out on all four sides. We actually heard the pops. Didn't realize it was the falling—you know, you heard the pops of the building. You thought it was just blowing out."[32]

"Pops" were also reported by paramedic Daniel Rivera in the following exchange:

> Q. How did you know that it [the south tower] was coming down?
> A. That noise. It was noise.
> Q. What did you hear? What did you see?
> A. It was a frigging noise. At first I thought it was—do you ever see professional demolition where they set the charges on certain floors and then you hear "Pop, pop, pop, pop, pop"? That's exactly what—because I thought it was that. When I heard that frigging noise, that's when I saw the building coming down.[33]

Collapse Beginning below the Strike Zone and Fire

According to the official account, the "pancaking" of the floors began when the floors above the strike zone, where the supports were weakened by the impact of the airplanes and the resulting fires, fell on the floors below. Some witnesses reported, however, that the collapse of the south tower began *lower* than the floors that were struck by the airliner and hence lower than the fires.

Timothy Burke reported that while he was watching flames coming out of the south tower, "The building popped, lower than the fire." He later heard a rumor that "the aviation fuel fell into the pit, and whatever floor it fell on heated up really bad, and that's why it popped at that floor." At the time, however, he said, "I was going oh, my god, there is a secondary device because the way the building popped. I thought it was an explosion."[34]

This same twofold observation was made by firefighter Edward Cachia, who said: "As my officer and I were looking at the south tower, it just gave. It actually gave at a lower floor, not the floor where the plane hit. . . . [W]e originally had thought there was like an internal detonation, explosives, because it went in succession, boom, boom, boom, boom, and then the tower came down."[35]

Other Indications of Controlled Demolition

Some witnesses reported other phenomena, beyond explosions, suggestive of controlled demolition.

The Appearance of Implosion. When a building close to other buildings is brought down by controlled demolition, as mentioned earlier, it typically implodes and hence comes straight down into, or at least close to, its own footprint, so that it does not fall over on surrounding structures.

As we saw above in the accounts that were previously available, both police and fire officials were quoted as saying that the towers seemed to implode. This perception was also stated in the oral history of Lieutenant James Walsh, who said: "The [north tower] didn't fall the way you would think tall buildings would fall. Pretty much it looked like it imploded on itself."[36]

Flashes. Another common feature of controlled demolitions is that people who are properly situated may see flashes when the explosives go off. Assistant Commissioner Stephen Gregory said: "I thought . . . before . . . No. 2 came down, that I saw low-level flashes. . . . Lieutenant Evangelista . . . asked me if I saw low-level flashes in front of the building, and I agreed with him because I . . . saw a flash flash flash . . . [at] the lower level of the building. You know like when they demolish a building, how when they blow up a building, when it falls down? That's what I thought I saw."[37]

Flashes were reported in the north tower by Captain Karin Deshore, who said: "Somewhere around the middle of the World Trade Center, there was this orange and red flash coming out. Initially it was just one flash."[38]

Demolition Rings. At this point, Deshore's account moved to another standard phenomenon seen by those who watch controlled demolitions: explosion rings, in which a series of explosions runs rapidly around a building. Deshore's next words were: "Then this flash just kept popping all the way around the building and that building had started to explode. The popping sound, and with each popping sound it was initially an orange and then a red flash came out of the building and then it would just go all around the building on both sides as far as I could see. These popping sounds and the explosions were getting bigger, going both up and down and then all around the building."[39]

An explosion ring (or belt) was also described by firefighter Richard Banaciski. Speaking of the south tower, he said: "[T]here was just an explosion. It seemed like on television [when] they blow up these buildings. It seemed like it was going all the way around like a belt, all these explosions."[40]

A description of what appeared to be a ring of explosions was also given by Deputy Commissioner Thomas Fitzpatrick, who said: "We looked up at the [south tower]. . . . All we saw was a puff of smoke coming from about two-thirds of the way up. . . . It looked like sparkling around one specific layer of the building. . . . My initial reaction was that this was exactly the way it looks when they show you those implosions on TV."[41]

Horizontal Ejections. Another feature of controlled demolition, at least when quite powerful explosives are used, is that things are ejected horizontally from the floors on which the explosions occur. Such ejections were mentioned in the testimony of Chief Frank Cruthers above. Similarly, Captain Jay Swithers said, "I took a quick glance at the building and while I didn't see it falling, I saw a large section of it blasting out, which led me to believe it was just an explosion."[42]

Firefighter James Curran said: "When I got underneath the north bridge I looked back and . . . I heard like every floor went chu-chu-chu. Looked back and from the pressure everything was getting blown out of the floors before it actually collapsed."[43]

Battalion Chief Brian Dixon said: "I was . . . hearing a noise and looking up. . . . The lowest floor of fire in the south tower actually looked like someone had planted explosives around it because . . . everything blew out on the one floor. I thought, geez, this looks like an explosion up there, it blew out."[44]

These reports by Curran and Dixon conform to what can be seen by looking at photographs and videos of the collapses, which show that various materials, including sections of steel and aluminum, were blown out hundreds of feet.[45] Such powerful ejections of materials are exactly what would be expected from explosions powerful enough to cause such huge buildings to collapse.

Dust Clouds. The most visible material ejected horizontally from buildings during controlled demolition, especially buildings with lots of concrete, is dust, which forms more or less expansive dust clouds. Some of the testimonies about the collapse of the south tower mention that it produced an enormous amount of dust, which formed clouds so big and thick that they blocked out all light.

Firefighter Stephen Viola said: "You heard like loud booms . . . and then we got covered with rubble and dust, and I thought we'd actually fallen through the floor . . . because it was so dark you couldn't see anything."[46]

Firefighter Angel Rivera said: "That's when hell came down. It was like a huge, enormous explosion. . . . The wind rushed . . . , all the dust . . . and everything went dark."[47]

Lieutenant William Wall said: "We heard an explosion. We looked up and the building was coming down right on top of us. . . . We ran a little bit and then we were overtaken by the cloud."[48]

Paramedic Louis Cook said that after the debris started falling, "everything went black" and "you couldn't breathe because [of] all the dust. There was just an incredible amount of dust and smoke." He then found that there was, "without exaggerating, a foot and a half of dust on [his] car."[49]

The kind of dust clouds typically produced during a controlled demolition can be seen on videos of the demolition of Seattle's Kingdome and the Reading Grain Facility.[50] If these videos are then compared with photos and videos of the collapses of the Twin Towers,[51] it can be seen that the dust clouds in the latter are even bigger.[52]

Timed or Synchronized Explosions. Some people said that the collapses had the appearance of timed, synchronized demolitions. Battalion Chief Dominick DeRubbio, speaking of the collapse of the south tower, said: "It was weird how it started to come down. It looked like it was a timed explosion."[53]

Firefighter Kenneth Rogers said: "There was an explosion in the south tower. . . . I kept watching. Floor after floor after floor. One floor under another after another and when it hit about the fifth floor, I figured it was a bomb, because it looked like a synchronized deliberate kind of thing. I was there in '93."[54]

Debates about Controlled Demolition

Given so many signs that the buildings had been brought down by controlled demolition, we might expect that debates about this issue would have taken place. And they did.

Firefighter Christopher Fenyo, after describing events that occurred after the first collapse, said: "At that point, a debate began to rage because . . . many people had felt that possibly explosives had taken out 2 World Trade, and officers were gathering companies together and the officers were debating whether or not to go immediately back in or to see what was going to happen with 1 World Trade at that point. The debate ended pretty quickly because 1 World Trade came down."[55]

Firefighter William Reynolds reported on a conversation he had with a battalion chief: "I said, 'Chief, they're evacuating the other building; right?' He said, 'No.' . . . I said, 'Why not? They blew up the other one.' I thought they blew it up with a bomb. I said, 'If they blew up the one, you know they're gonna blow up the other one.' He said, 'No, they're not.' I said, 'Well, you gotta tell them to evacuate it, because it's gonna fall down and you gotta get the guys out.' . . . He said, 'I'm just the Battalion Chief. I can't order that.' . . . I said, 'You got a fucking radio and you got a fucking mouth. Use the fucking things. Empty this fucking building.' Again he said, 'I'm just a Battalion Chief. I can't do that.' . . . Eventually this other chief came back and said, 'They are evacuating this tower.' . . . And sometime after that . . . I watched the north tower fall."[56]

As both accounts suggest, the perception that the south tower had been brought down by explosives may have resulted in fewer lives being lost in the north tower collapse than would otherwise have been the case.

WHY TESTIMONY ABOUT EXPLOSIONS HAS NOT BECOME PUBLIC KNOWLEDGE

If so many witnesses reported effects that seemed to be produced by explosives, with some of them explicitly saying that the collapses appeared to be cases of controlled demolition, why is this testimony not public knowledge? Part of the answer, as I mentioned at the outset, is that the City of New York refused to release it until forced to do so by the highest court of the State of New York.

But why did we have to wait for this court-ordered release to learn about these testimonies? Should not they have been discussed in *The 9/11 Commission Report*, which was issued over a year earlier? This report, we are told in the preface, sought "to provide the fullest possible account of the events surrounding 9/11." Why does it not include any of the testimony in the 9/11 oral histories suggestive of controlled demolition?

The answer cannot be that the Commission did not know about these oral histories. Although "the city also initially refused access to the records to investigators from . . . the 9/11 Commission," Jim Dwyer of the *New York Times* tells us, it "relented when legal action was threatened."[57] So the Commission could have discussed the testimonies about explosions in the oral histories. It also, in order to help educate the public, could have called some of the firefighters and medical workers to repeat their testimony during one of the Commission's public hearings, but it did not.

Why, we may wonder, have the firefighters and medical workers not been speaking out? At least part of the reason may be suggested by a statement made by Auxiliary Lieutenant Fireman Paul Isaac. Having said that "there were definitely bombs in those buildings," Isaac added that "many other firemen know there were bombs in the buildings, but they're afraid for their jobs to admit it because the 'higher-ups' forbid discussion of this fact."[58]

Would we not expect, however, that a few courageous members of the fire department would have contacted the 9/11 Commission to tell their story? Indeed. But telling their story to the Commission was no guarantee that it would find its way into the final report—as indicated by the account of one fireman who made the effort.

Firefighter Louie Cacchioli, who was quoted earlier, testified in 2004 to members of the Commission's staff. But, he reported, they were so unreceptive that he ended up walking out in anger. "I felt like I was being put on trial in a court room," said Cacchioli. "They were trying to twist my words and make the story fit only what they wanted to hear. All I wanted to do was tell the truth and when they wouldn't let me do that, I walked out."[59]

That Cacchioli's experience was not atypical is suggested by janitor William Rodriguez, whose testimony was also quoted earlier. Although Rodriguez was invited to the White House as a national hero for his rescue efforts on 9/11, he was, he said, treated quite differently by the Commission: "I met with the 9/11 Commission behind closed doors and they essentially discounted everything I said regarding the use of explosives to bring down the north tower."[60]

When reading *The 9/11 Commission Report*, one will not find the name of Cacchioli, Rodriguez, or anyone else reporting explosions in the towers. It would appear that the Commission deliberately withheld this information, as it apparently did with regard to Able Danger[61] and many other things that should have been included in "the fullest possible account of the events surrounding 9/11."[62]

The definitive report about the collapse of the towers was to have been provided by the National Institute of Standards and Technology (NIST). According to Rodriguez, however, this investigative body was equally uninterested in his testimony: "I contacted NIST . . . four times without a response. Finally, [at a public hearing] I asked them before they came up with their conclusion . . . if they ever considered my statements or the statements of any of the other survivors who heard the explosions. They just stared at me with blank faces."[63]

In light of this report of NIST's response, it is not surprising to find that its final report, which in the course of supporting the official story about the collapses ignores many vital issues,[64] makes no mention of reports of explosions and other phenomena suggestive of controlled demolition.

CONCLUSION

It is sometimes said that the mandate of an official commission is, by definition, to support the official story. Insofar as that is true, it is not surprising that neither NIST nor the 9/11 Commission saw fit to discuss testimony suggestive of explosions in the Twin Towers, since this testimony is in strong tension with the official story.

At least most of those who offered this testimony did not, to be sure, mean to challenge the most important element in the official story about 9/11, which is that the attacks were entirely the work of foreign terrorists. For example, firefighter Timothy Julian, after saying that he "thought it was an explosion," added, "I thought maybe there was a bomb on the plane, but delayed type of thing, you know secondary device."[65] Assistant Commissioner James Drury said, "I thought the terrorists planted explosives somewhere in the building."[66]

The problem, however, is that a bomb delivered by a plane, or even a few explosives planted "somewhere in the building," would not explain the many phenomena suggestive of controlled demolition, such as explosion rings and other features indicating that the explosions were "synchronized" and otherwise "timed." As Mark Loizeaux, the head of Controlled Demolition, Inc., has explained, "To bring [a building] down as we want, so no one or no other structure is harmed," the demolition must be "completely planned." One needs "the right explosive [and] the right pattern of laying the charges."[67]

The 9/11 oral histories, therefore, create a difficult question for those who defend the official story: how could al-Qaeda terrorists have gotten access to the Twin Towers for all the hours required to place all the explosives needed to bring down buildings of that size? It is primarily because they force this question that the testimony about explosions in the towers is itself explosive.[68]

Chapter 3

The Destruction of the World Trade Center

Why the Official Account Cannot Be True

The previous chapter provided testimonial evidence suggesting that the Twin Towers were brought down by explosives in the procedure known as controlled demolition. This testimony thereby provides some limited evidence that the official account—that the collapses of the towers were caused entirely by the impacts of the airliners plus the ensuing fires—is false. The present chapter provides much more extensive evidence that this official account of the collapse of the Twin Towers is false. This chapter also deals with the collapse of Building 7 of the World Trade Center.

This aspect of the official story about 9/11—the collapses of these three buildings—can be most clearly shown to be false. This aspect provides, therefore, one of the best signs that 9/11 was a false-flag operation. I begin with the question of whether the airplane attacks and the ensuing fires could possibly explain the collapses of the Twin Towers. I then ask why Building 7, which was not even hit by a plane, also collapsed.

THE COLLAPSE OF THE TWIN TOWERS

Shortly after 9/11, President Bush advised people not to tolerate "outrageous conspiracy theories about the attacks of 11 September."[1] Philip Zelikow, who directed the work of the 9/11 Commission, has likewise warned against "outrageous conspiracy theories."[2] What do these men mean by this expression? They cannot mean that we should reject *all* conspiracy theories about 9/11, because the government's own account is a conspiracy theory, with the conspirators all being members of al-Qaeda. They mean only that we should reject *outrageous* theories.

But what distinguishes an outrageous theory from a nonoutrageous one? This is one of the central questions in the philosophy of science. When confronted by rival theories, such as Neo-Darwinian Evolution and Intelligent Design, scientists and philosophers of science ask which theory is better and why. The mark of a good theory is that it can explain, in a coherent way, all or at least most of the relevant facts and is not contradicted by any of them. A bad theory is one that is contradicted by some of the relevant facts. An outrageous theory would be one that is contradicted by virtually *all* the relevant facts.

With this definition in mind, let us look at the official theory about the Twin Towers, which says that they collapsed because of the combined effect of the impact of the airplanes and the resulting fires. The report put out by FEMA explained, "The structural damage sustained by each tower from the impact, combined with the ensuing fires, resulted in the total collapse of each building."[3] This theory clearly belongs in the category of outrageous theories, because it is contradicted by virtually all the relevant facts. Although this statement may seem extreme, I will explain why it is not.

No Prior Collapse Induced by Fire

The official theory is rendered implausible by two major problems. The first is the simple fact that fire has never—prior to or after 9/11—caused steel-frame high-rise buildings to collapse. Defenders of the official story seldom if ever mention this simple fact. Indeed, the supposedly definitive report put out by the National Institute for Standards and Technology, abbreviated NIST,[4] even implies that fire-induced collapses of large steel-frame buildings are normal events.[5] Far from being normal, however, such collapses have never occurred, except for the alleged cases of 9/11.

Defenders of the official theory, of course, say that the collapses were caused not simply by the fire but the fire combined with the damage inflicted by the airliners. The towers, however, were designed to withstand the impact of airliners about the same size as Boeing 767s. John Skilling, who was responsible for the structural design of the Twin Towers, said in 1993, after the bombing of the World Trade Center, that his analysis showed that if one of these buildings were to suffer a strike by a jet plane loaded with jet fuel, "there would be a horrendous fire" and "a lot of people would be killed" but "the building structure would still be there." Leslie Robertson, who was a member of Skilling's firm (Worthington, Skilling, Helle and Jackson) when the Twin Towers were built, has said that they were designed to withstand the impact of a Boeing 707, which at that time (1966) was the largest airliner.[6] Hyman Brown, the construction manager of the Twin Towers, said: "They were over-designed to withstand almost anything, including hurricanes, . . . bombings and an airplane hitting [them]."[7] Even experts who have contributed to the official account agree. Thomas Eagar, an MIT professor of materials engineering who developed an influential "pancake" theory of the collapses, says that the impact of the airplanes would not have been significant, because "the number of columns lost on the initial impact was not large and the loads were shifted to remaining columns in this highly redundant structure."[8] Likewise, the NIST Report, in discussing how the impact of the planes contributed to the collapse, focuses primarily on the claim that the planes dislodged a lot of the fireproofing from the steel.[9]

The official theory of the collapse, therefore, is essentially a fire theory, so it cannot be emphasized too much that fire has never caused large steel-frame buildings to collapse—never, whether *before* 9/11, or *after* 9/11, or anywhere in the world *on* 9/11 except allegedly New York City—*never*.

One might say, of course, that there is a first time for everything, and that a truly extraordinary fire might induce a collapse. Let us examine this idea. What would count as an extraordinary fire? Given the properties of steel, a fire would need to be very hot, very big, and very long-lasting. But the fires in the towers did not have even one of these characteristics, let alone all three.

There have been claims, to be sure, that the fires were very hot. Some television specials claimed that the towers collapsed because the fire was hot enough to melt the steel. For example, an early BBC News special quoted Hyman Brown as saying, "Steel melts, and 24,000 gallons of aviation fluid melted the steel." Another man, presented as a structural engineer, said: "It was the fire that killed the buildings. There's nothing on earth that could survive those temperatures with that amount of fuel burning. . . . The columns would have melted."[10]

These claims, however, are absurd. Steel does not even begin to melt until it reaches almost 2800° Fahrenheit.[11] And yet open fires fueled by hydrocarbons, such as kerosene—which is what jet fuel is—can at most rise to 1700°F, which is 1100 degrees below the melting point of steel.[12] We can, accordingly, dismiss the claim that the towers collapsed because their steel columns melted.[13]

Most defenders of the official theory, in fact, do not make this absurd claim. They say merely that the fire heated the steel up to the point where it lost so much of its strength that it buckled.[14] For example, Thomas Eagar, saying that steel loses 80 percent of its strength when it is heated to 1300°F, argues that this is what happened. But for even this claim to be plausible, the fires would have still had to be very hot.

But they were not. Claims have been made, as we have seen, about the jet fuel. But much of it burned up very quickly in the enormous fireballs produced when the planes hit the buildings, and the rest was gone within ten minutes,[15] after which the flames died down. Photographs of the towers fifteen minutes after they were struck show few flames and lots of black smoke, a sign that the fires were oxygen-starved. Eagar, recognizing this fact, says that the fires were "probably only about 1,200 or 1,300°F."[16]

There are reasons to believe, moreover, that the fires were not even that hot. As photographs show, the fires did not break windows or even spread much beyond their points of origin.[17] This photographic evidence is supported by scientific studies carried out by NIST, which found that of the sixteen perimeter columns examined, "only three columns had evidence that the steel reached temperatures above 250°C [482°F]," and no evidence that any of the core columns had reached even those temperatures.[18]

NIST says that it "did not generalize these results, since the examined columns represented only 3 percent of the perimeter columns and 1 percent of the core columns from the fire floors."[19] That only such a tiny percentage of the columns was available was due, of course, to the fact that government officials had most of the steel immediately sold and shipped off. In any case, NIST's findings on the basis of this tiny percentage of the columns are not irrelevant: they mean that any speculations that some of the core columns reached much higher temperatures would be just that—pure speculation not backed up by any empirical evidence.

Moreover, even if the fire had reached 1300°F, as Eagar supposes, that does not mean that any of the steel would have reached that temperature. Steel is an excellent conductor of heat. Put a fire to one part of a long bar of steel, and the heat will quickly diffuse to the other parts and to any other pieces of steel to which that bar is connected.[20]

For fires to have heated up some of the steel columns to anywhere close to their own temperature, they would have needed to be very big, relative to the size of the buildings and the amount of steel in them. The towers, of course, were huge and had an enormous amount of steel. A small, localized fire of 1300°F would never have heated any of the steel columns even close to that temperature, because the heat would have been quickly dispersed throughout the building.

Some defenders of the official story have claimed that the fires were indeed very big, turning the buildings into "towering infernos." But all the evidence counts against this claim, especially with regard to the south tower, which collapsed first. This tower was struck between floors 78 and 84, so that region is where the fire would have been the biggest. And yet Brian Clark, a survivor, said that when he got down to the eightieth floor: "You could see through the wall and the cracks and see flames . . . just licking up, not a roaring inferno, just quiet flames licking up and smoke sort of eking through the wall."[21] Likewise, one of the fire chiefs who had reached the seventy-eighth floor found only "two isolated pockets of fire."[22]

The north tower, to be sure, did have fires that were big enough and hot enough to cause many people to jump to their deaths. But as anyone with a fireplace grate or a potbellied stove knows, fire that will not harm steel or even iron will burn human flesh. In many cases, moreover, it may have been more the smoke than the heat that led people to jump.

In any case, the fires, to weaken the steel columns, would have needed to be not only very big and very hot but also very long-lasting.[23] The public was told that the towers had such fires, with CNN saying that "very intense" fires "burned for a long time."[24] But they did not. The north tower collapsed an hour and forty-two minutes after it was struck; the south tower collapsed after only fifty-six minutes.

To see how ludicrous is the claim that the short-lived fires in the towers could have induced structural collapse, we can compare them with some other fires. In 1988, a fire in the First Interstate Bank Building in Los Angeles raged for three-and-a-half hours and gutted five of this building's sixty-two floors, but there was no significant structural damage.[25] In 1991, a huge fire in Philadelphia's One Meridian Plaza lasted for eighteen hours and gutted eight of the building's thirty-eight floors, but, said the FEMA report, although "beams and girders sagged and twisted . . . under severe fire exposures . . . , the columns continued to support their loads without obvious damage."[26] In Caracas in 2004, a fire in a fifty-story building raged for seventeen hours, completely gutting the building's top twenty floors, and yet it did not collapse.[27] We are supposed to believe, nevertheless, that a fifty-six-minute fire caused the south tower to collapse.

Unlike the fires in the towers, moreover, the fires in Los Angeles, Philadelphia, and Caracas were hot enough to break windows.

Another important comparison is afforded by a series of experiments run in Great Britain in the mid-1990s to see what kind of damage could be done to steel-frame buildings by subjecting them to extremely hot, all-consuming fires that lasted for many hours. FEMA, having reviewed those experiments, said: "Despite the temperature of the steel beams reaching 800–900°C (1,500–1,700°F) in three of the tests . . . , no collapse was observed in any of the six experiments."[28]

These comparisons bring out the absurdity of NIST's claim that the towers collapsed because the planes knocked the fireproofing off the steel columns. Fireproofing provides protection for only a few hours, so the steel in the buildings in Philadelphia and Caracas would have been directly exposed to raging fires for fourteen or more hours, and yet this steel did not buckle. NIST claims, nevertheless, that the steel in the south tower buckled because it was directly exposed to flames for fifty-six minutes.[29]

A claim made by some defenders of the official theory is to speculate that there was something about the Twin Towers that made them uniquely vulnerable to fire, but no evidence available supports these speculations. And, as Norman Glover has pointed out: "Almost all large buildings will be the location for a major fire in their useful life. No major high-rise building has ever collapsed from fire. The WTC was the location for such a fire in 1975; however, the building survived with minor damage and was repaired and returned to service."[30]

Multiple Evidence of Controlled Demolition

There is a reverse truth to the fact that, aside from the alleged cases of 9/11, fire has never caused large steel-frame buildings to collapse. This reverse truth is that every previous total collapse has been caused by the procedure known as "controlled demolition," in which explosives capable of cutting steel have been placed in crucial places throughout the building and then set off in a particular order. Just from knowing that the towers collapsed, therefore, the natural assumption would be that they were brought down by explosives.

This *a priori* assumption is, moreover, supported by an empirical examination of the particular nature of the collapses. Here we come to the second major problem with the official theory—namely, that the collapses had at least eleven features that would be expected if, and only if, explosives were used. I will briefly describe these eleven features.

Sudden Onset

In controlled demolition, the onset of the collapse is sudden. One moment, the building is perfectly motionless; the next moment, it suddenly begins to collapse. But steel, when heated, does not suddenly buckle or break. So in fire-induced collapses—if we had any examples of such—the onset would be gradual. Horizontal beams and trusses would begin to sag; vertical columns, if subjected to strong forces, would begin to bend. But as videos of the towers show,[31] there were no signs of bending or sagging, even on the floors just above the damage caused by the impact of the planes. The buildings were perfectly motionless up to the moment they began their collapse.

Straight Down

The most important thing in a controlled demolition of a tall building close to other buildings is that it come straight down into, or at least close to, its own footprint, so that it does not harm the other buildings. This result is achieved by the type of controlled demolition known as "implosion." The whole art or science of controlled implosion is oriented primarily around this goal. As Mark Loizeaux, the president of Controlled Demolition, Inc., has explained, "to bring [a building] down as we want, so . . . no other structure is harmed," the demolition must be "completely planned," using "the right explosive [and] the right pattern of laying the charges."[32] If the 110-story Twin Towers had fallen over, they would have caused an enormous amount of damage to buildings covering many city blocks. But the towers came straight down. Accordingly, the official theory, by implying that fire produced collapses that perfectly mimicked the collapses that have otherwise been produced only by precisely placed explosives, requires a miracle. The miraculous nature of a straight-down collapse (if explosives were not used) is indicated by the reaction of structural engineer Joseph Burns, a partner in the Chicago firm of Thornton-Thomasetti Engineers. Saying that he was "in absolute shock over the whole thing," he exclaimed: "It just came straight down. I've seen buildings collapse like that, but they are buildings set for demolition."[33]

Almost Free-Fall Speed

Buildings brought down by controlled implosion collapse at almost free-fall speed. This effect occurs because the supports for the lower floors are destroyed, so that when the upper floors come down, they encounter no resistance. The fact that the collapses of the towers mimicked this feature of controlled demolition was mentioned indirectly by *The 9/11 Commission Report*, which said that the "South Tower collapsed in 10 seconds."[34] The authors of the report evidently thought that the rapidity of this collapse did not conflict with the official theory at the time, known as the "pancake" theory. According to this theory, the floors above the floors that were weakened by the impact of the airliner fell on the floor below, which started a chain reaction, so that the floors "pancaked" all the way down.

But if that is what happened, the lower floors, with all their steel and concrete, would have provided resistance. The upper floors could not have fallen through them at the same speed as they would fall through air. However, the videos of the collapses show that the rubble falling inside the building's profile falls at the same speed as the rubble outside.[35] As Dave Heller, a building engineer with degrees in physics and architecture, explains:

> The floors could not have been pancaking. The buildings fell too quickly. The floors must all have been falling simultaneously to reach the ground in such a short amount of time. But how? . . . In [the method known as controlled implosion], each floor of a building is destroyed at just the moment the floor above is about to strike it. Thus, the floors fall simultaneously, and in virtual freefall.[36]

Total Collapse

The official theory is even more decisively ruled out by the fact that the collapses were total. These 110-story buildings collapsed into piles of rubble only a few stories high. How was that possible? The core of each tower contained forty-seven massive steel box columns.[37] According to the pancake theory, the horizontal steel supports broke free from the vertical columns. But if that is what had happened, the forty-seven core columns would have still been standing. The 9/11 Commission came up with a bold solution to this problem. It simply denied the existence of the forty-seven core columns, saying, "The interior core of the buildings was a hollow steel shaft, in which elevators and stairwells were grouped."[38] Voila! With no forty-seven core columns, the main problem is removed.

The NIST Report handled this most difficult problem by claiming that when the floors collapsed, they pulled on the columns, causing the perimeter columns to become unstable. This instability then increased the gravity load on the core columns, which had been weakened by tremendously hot fires in the core, which, NIST claims, reached 1832°F, and this combination of factors somehow produced "global collapse."[39]

This theory faces two problems. First, NIST's claim about tremendously hot fires in the core is completely unsupported by evidence. As we saw earlier, its own studies found no evidence that any of the core columns had reached temperatures of even 482°F (250°C), so its theory involves a purely speculative temperature.[40] Second, even if this sequence of events had occurred, NIST provides no explanation as to why it would have produced global—that is, total—collapse. The NIST Report asserts that "column failure" occurred in the core as well as the perimeter columns, but this remains a bare assertion. There is no plausible explanation of why the core columns would have broken or even buckled, so as to produce global collapse at virtually free-fall speed, even if they had reached such temperatures.[41]

Sliced Steel

In controlled demolitions of steel-frame buildings, explosives are used to slice the steel columns into pieces. A consultant for Controlled Demolition, Inc., has said of RDX, one of the commonly used high explosives, that it slices steel like a "razor blade through a tomato." The steel is, moreover, not merely sliced; it is generally sliced into manageable lengths. As Controlled Demolition, Inc., says in its publicity: "Our DREXS™ systems . . . segment steel components into pieces matching the lifting capacity of the available equipment."[42]

The collapses of the Twin Towers, it seems, somehow managed to mimic this feature of controlled implosions as well. Jim Hoffman, after studying various photos of the collapse site, said that much of the steel seemed to be "chopped up into . . . sections that could be easily loaded onto the equipment that was cleaning up Ground Zero."[43]

Pulverization of Concrete and Other Materials

Another feature of controlled demolition is the production of a lot of dust, because explosives powerful enough to slice steel will pulverize concrete and most other nonmetallic substances into tiny particles. And, Hoffman reports, "Nearly all of the non-metallic constituents of the towers were pulverized into fine powder."[44] That observation was also made by Colonel John O'Dowd of the U.S. Army Corps of Engineers. "At the World Trade Center sites," he told the History Channel, "it seemed like everything was pulverized."[45]

This fact creates a problem for the official theory, according to which the only

energy available was the gravitational energy. This energy would have been sufficient to break most of the concrete into fairly small pieces. But it would not have
been anywhere close to the amount of energy needed to turn the concrete and
virtually all the nonmetallic contents of the buildings into tiny particles of dust.

Dust Clouds

Yet another common feature of controlled demolitions is the production of dust
clouds, which result when explosions eject the dust from the building with great
energy. And, as one can see by comparing videos on the Web, the collapses of
the towers produced clouds that are very similar to those produced by controlled demolitions of other structures, such as Seattle's Kingdome and the
Reading Grain Facility. The only difference is that the clouds produced during
the collapses of the towers were proportionally much bigger.[46]

The question of the source of the needed energy again arises. Hoffman,
focusing on the expansion of the north tower's dust cloud, calculates that the
energy required simply for this expansion—ignoring the energy needed to slice
the steel and pulverize the concrete and other materials—exceeded by at least
ten times the gravitational energy available.[47]

The official account, therefore, involves a huge violation of the laws of
physics—a violation that becomes even more enormous once we factor in the
energy required to pulverize the concrete and break the steel.

Besides the sheer quantity of energy needed, another problem with the official theory is that gravitational energy is wholly unsuited to explain the production of these dust clouds. This is most obviously the case in the first few seconds.
In Hoffman's words: "You can see thick clouds of pulverized concrete being
ejected within the first two seconds. That's when the relative motion of the top
of the tower to the intact portion was only a few feet per second."[48] Jeff King,
in the same vein, says, "[A great amount of] very fine concrete dust is ejected
from the top of the building very early in the collapse . . . [when] concrete slabs
[would have been] bumping into each other at [only] 20 or 30 mph."[49]

The importance of King's point can be appreciated by juxtaposing it with
the claim by Shyam Sunder, NIST's lead investigator, that although the clouds
of dust created during the collapses of the Twin Towers may create the impression of a controlled demolition, "It is the floor pancaking that leads to that
perception."[50] The pancaking, according to the official theory being defended
by Sunder, began at the floor beneath the holes created by the impact of the
airliners. As King points out, this theory cannot handle the facts as revealed by
the photographs and videos, that dust clouds were created far above the points
of impact.

Horizontal Ejections

Another common feature of controlled demolition is the horizontal ejection of
other materials, besides dust, from those areas of the building in which explo-

sives are set off. In the case of the Twin Towers, photos and videos reveal that "heavy pieces of steel were ejected in all directions for distances up to 500 feet, while aluminum cladding was blown up to 700 feet away from the towers."[51] But gravitational energy is, of course, vertical, so it cannot even begin to explain these horizontal ejections.

Demolition Rings

Still another common feature of collapses induced by explosions are demolition rings, in which series of small explosions run rapidly around a building. This feature, as chapter 2 showed, was also manifested by the collapses of the towers.[52]

Molten Steel

A tenth feature that would be expected only if explosives were used to slice the steel columns would be molten steel, and its existence at the WTC site was indeed reported by several witnesses, including the two main figures involved in the cleanup, Peter Tully, president of Tully Construction, and Mark Loizeaux, president of Controlled Demolition, Inc. Tully said that he saw pools of "literally molten steel" at the site. Loizeaux said that several weeks after 9/11, when the rubble was being removed, "hot spots of molten steel" were found "at the bottoms of the elevator shafts of the main towers, down seven [basement] levels."[53]

The witnesses also include Leslie Robertson, a member of the engineering firm that designed the Twin Towers, who said: "As of 21 days after the attack, the fires were still burning and molten steel was still running."[54] Some observers even reported that molten steel was dripping from pieces of steel. Joe O'Toole, a Bronx firefighter who worked for many months on the rescue and cleanup efforts, said about a beam that was lifted from deep below the surface: "It was dripping from the molten steel."[55] Greg Fuchek, vice president of a company that supplied some of the computer equipment used to identify human remains, reported that "sometimes when a worker would pull a steel beam from the wreckage, the end of the beam would be dripping molten steel."[56] And still more witnesses spoke of molten steel.[57]

This testimony is of great significance, since it would be hard to imagine what, other than high explosives, could have caused some of the steel to melt.

Sounds Produced by Explosions

The use of explosives to induce collapses produces, of course, sounds caused by the explosions. As we saw in the previous chapter, there is abundant testimony to the occurrence of explosive sounds, along with other phenomena suggestive of controlled demolition.

The importance of the nature of the collapses, as summarized in these eleven features, is shown by the fact that attempts to defend the official theory typically ignore most of them. For example, an article in *Popular*

Mechanics, seeking to debunk what it calls some of the most prevalent myths about 9/11 fabricated by "conspiracy theorists," completely ignores the suddenness, verticality, rapidity, and totality of the collapses as well as failing to mention the testimonies about molten steel, demolition rings, and the sounds of explosions.[58]

FIVE MORE RELEVANT FACTS

The official theory about the collapse of the towers, I have suggested, is rendered extremely implausible by two main facts. First, aside from the alleged exception of 9/11, steel-frame high-rise buildings have never been caused to collapse by fire; all such collapses have been produced by carefully placed explosives. Second, the collapses of the Twin Towers manifested at least eleven typical features of controlled demolitions. The probability that any of these features would occur in the absence of explosives is extremely low. The probability that all eleven of them would occur is essentially zero.[59]

We can say, therefore, that the official theory about the towers is disproved about as thoroughly as such a theory could possibly be, whereas all the evidence can be explained by the alternative theory, according to which the towers were brought down by explosives. The official theory is, accordingly, an outrageous theory, whereas the alternative theory is, from a scientific point of view, the only reasonable theory available.

There are, moreover, five more facts pointing to the conclusion that the towers were brought down by explosives.

Removal of the Steel

In false-flag operations, as we have seen, it is standard procedure for authorities to remove evidence that would point to the true perpetrators. It would appear that the operation in New York involved the greatest destruction of evidence ever. Over 100 tons of steel from the buildings were removed before it could be properly examined,[60] with virtually all of it being sold to scrap dealers, who put most of it on ships to Asia.[61] Only a few pieces were available for study. Generally, removing any evidence from the scene of a crime is a federal offense. But in this case, federal officials facilitated the removal.[62]

This removal evoked protest. On Christmas day, 2001, the *New York Times* said: "The decision to rapidly recycle the steel columns, beams and trusses from the WTC in the days immediately after 9/11 means definitive answers may never be known."[63] The next week, writers in *Fire Engineering* magazine exclaimed: "We are literally treating the steel removed from the site like garbage, not like crucial fire scene evidence."[64] The editor added: "The destruction and removal of evidence must stop immediately."[65]

However, Mayor Bloomberg, defending the decision to dispose of the steel, said: "If you want to take a look at the construction methods and the design, that's in this day and age what computers do.[66] Just looking at a piece of metal generally doesn't tell you anything."[67] But that is not true. An examination of the steel could have revealed whether it had been sliced by explosives.

This removal of an unprecedented amount of material from a crime scene suggests that an unprecedented crime was being covered up.[68] That this was the motive is more obvious when Building 7 is brought into the discussion. The semiofficial explanation for why the steel needed to be removed quickly was that some of the victims might still be alive in the rubble, so the steel needed to be removed to aid this search-and-rescue mission. In the case of Building 7, however, everyone was evacuated hours before it collapsed (as discussed below). And yet the removal of the steel from the site of Building 7 proceeded just as quickly as the removal from the sites of the Twin Towers.

Evidence that the cover-up was continued by NIST is provided by its treatment of a provocative finding mentioned by FEMA. Some of the specimens of steel, FEMA reported, were "rapidly corroded by sulfidation."[69] This report is significant, because sulfidation is an effect of explosives. FEMA appropriately called for further investigation of this finding, which the *New York Times* called "perhaps the deepest mystery uncovered in the investigation."[70] A closely related problem, expressed shortly after 9/11 by Dr. Jonathan Barnett, professor of fire protection engineering at Worcester Polytechnic Institute, is that "fire and the structural damage . . . would *not* explain steel members in the debris pile that appear to have been partly evaporated."[71] But the NIST Report, in its section headed "Learning from the Recovered Steel," fails even to mention either evaporation or sulfidation.[72] Why would the NIST scientists apparently share Mayor Bloomberg's disdain for empirical studies of recovered steel?

North Tower Antenna Drop

Another problem noted by FEMA is that videos show that, in the words of the FEMA Report, "The transmission tower on top of the [north tower] began to move downward and laterally slightly before movement was evident at the exterior wall. This suggests that collapse began with one or more failures in the central core area of the building."[73] This drop was also mentioned in a *New York Times* story by James Glanz and Eric Lipton, which said: "Videos of the north tower's collapse appear to show that its television antenna began to drop a fraction of a second before the rest of the building. The observations suggest that the building's steel core somehow gave way first."[74] In the supposedly definitive NIST Report, however, we find no mention of this fact. This is another convenient omission, since the most plausible, and probably only possible, explanation would be that the core columns were cut by explosives—an explanation that would fit with the testimony of some of the witnesses.

South Tower Tipping and Disintegration

If the north tower's antenna drop was anomalous (from the perspective of the official theory), the south tower's collapse contained an even stranger anomaly. The uppermost floors—above the level struck by the airplane—began tipping toward the corner most damaged by the impact. According to conservation-of-momentum laws, this block of approximately thirty-four floors should have fallen to the ground far outside the building's footprint. "However," observe Don Paul and Jim Hoffman, "as the top then began to fall, the rotation decelerated. Then it reversed direction [even though the] law of conservation of angular momentum states that a solid object in rotation will continue to rotate at the same speed unless acted on by a torque."[75]

And then, in the words of Steven Jones, a physics professor at BYU, "This block turned mostly to powder *in mid-air!*" This disintegration stopped the tipping and allowed the uppermost floors to fall straight down into, or at least close to, the building's footprint. As Jones notes, this extremely strange behavior was one of many things that NIST was able to ignore by virtue of the fact that its analysis, in its own words, "does not actually include the structural behavior of the tower after the conditions for collapse initiation were reached." This is convenient because it means that NIST did not have to answer Jones's question: "How can we understand this strange behavior, without explosives?"[76]

This behavior is, however, not strange to experts in controlled demolition. Mark Loizeaux, the head of Controlled Demolition, Inc., has said, "By differentially controlling the velocity of failure in different parts of the structure, you can make it walk, you can make it spin, you can make it dance. . . . We'll have structures start facing north and end up going to the north-west."[77] Once again, something that is inexplicable in terms of the official theory becomes a matter of course if the theory of controlled demolition is adopted.

WTC Security

The suggestion that explosives might have been used raises the question of how anyone wanting to place explosives in the towers could have gotten through the security checks. This question brings us to a possibly relevant fact about a company—now called Stratesec but then called Securacom—that was in charge of security for the World Trade Center. From 1993 to 2000, during which Securacom installed a new security system, Marvin Bush, the president's brother, was one of the company's directors. And from 1999 until January 2002, their cousin Wirt Walker III was the CEO.[78] One would think these facts should have made the evening news—or at least *The 9/11 Commission Report.*

These facts, in any case, may be relevant to some testimony given by people who had worked in the World Trade Center. Some of them reportedly said that although in the weeks before 9/11 there had been a security alert that mandated the use of bomb-sniffing dogs, that alert was lifted five days before 9/11.[79]

Also, a man named Scott Forbes, who worked for Fiduciary Trust—the company for which the husband of Kristen Breitweiser (probably the best-known of the family members of the 9/11 victims) worked—has written:

> On the weekend of [September 8–9, 2001], there was a "power down" condition in . . . the south tower. This power down condition meant there was no electrical supply for approximately 36 hours from floor 50 up. . . . The reason given by the WTC for the power down was that cabling in the tower was being upgraded. . . . Of course without power there were no security cameras, no security locks on doors [while] many, many "engineers" [were] coming in and out of the tower.[80]

Also, a man named Ben Fountain, who was a financial analyst with Fireman's Fund in the south tower, was quoted in *People* magazine as saying that during the weeks before 9/11, the towers were evacuated "a number of times."[81]

Foreknowledge of the Collapse of the South Tower

One more possibly relevant fact is that then-Mayor Rudy Giuliani, talking on ABC News about his temporary emergency command center at 75 Barkley Street, said, "We were operating out of there when we were told that the World Trade Center was gonna collapse, and it did collapse before we could get out of the building."[82] This is an amazing statement. Prior to 9/11, fire had never brought down a steel-frame high-rise. The firemen who reached the seventy-eighth floor of the south tower certainly did not believe it was going to collapse. Even the 9/11 Commission has said that to its knowledge, "None of the [fire] chiefs present believed that a total collapse of either tower was possible."[83] So why in the world would anyone have told Giuliani that at least one of the towers was about to collapse?

The most reasonable answer, especially in light of the new evidence provided by the release of the 9/11 oral histories,[84] is that someone knew that explosives had been set in the south tower and were about to be discharged. It is even possible that the explosives were going to be discharged earlier than originally planned because the fires in the south tower were dying down more quickly than expected, due to the fact that so much of the plane's jet fuel had burned up in the fireball outside the building.[85] This could explain why although the south tower was struck second, suffered less structural damage, and had smaller fires, it collapsed first—after only fifty-six minutes. That is, if the official story was going to be that the fire caused the collapse, the building had to be brought down before the fire went completely out.[86]

We now learn from the oral histories, moreover, that Giuliani is not the only one who was told that a collapse was coming. At least four of the testimonies in the 9/11 oral histories indicate that shortly before the collapse of the south tower, the Office of Emergency Management (OEM) had predicted the collapse of at least one tower.[87] The director of OEM reported directly to Giuliani.[88] So although Giuliani said that he and others "were told" that the towers were going to collapse, it was his own people who were doing the telling.

As *New York Times* reporter Jim Dwyer has pointed out, the 9/11 Commission had access to the oral histories.[89] It should have discussed these facts, but it did not.

The neglect of most of the relevant facts about the collapses, manifested by *The 9/11 Commission Report*, was continued by the NIST Report, which said, amazingly:

> The focus of the Investigation was on the sequence of events from the instant of aircraft impact to the initiation of collapse for each tower. For brevity in this report, this sequence is referred to as the "probable collapse sequence," although it does not actually include the structural behavior of the tower after the conditions for collapse initiation were reached.... [Our simulation treats only] the structural deterioration of each tower from the time of aircraft impact to the time at which the building . . . was poised for collapse.[90]

Steven Jones comments, appropriately:

> What about the subsequent complete, rapid and symmetrical collapse of the buildings? . . . What about the antenna dropping first in the North Tower? What about the molten metal observed in the basement areas . . . ? Never mind all that: NIST did not discuss at all any data after the buildings were "poised for collapse." Well, some of us want to look at *all* the data, without computer simulations that are "adjusted" to make them fit the desired outcome.[91]

Summary

When we add these five additional suspicious facts to the eleven features that the collapses of the Twin Towers had in common with controlled demolitions, we have a total of sixteen facts about the collapses of these buildings that, while being inexplicable in terms of the official theory, are fully understandable on the theory that the destruction of the towers was an inside job. Another indication that this was a false-flag operation is the fact that evidence was apparently planted: We were told that the passport of one of the alleged Flight 11 hijackers, Satam al-Sugami, was found in the rubble, which would mean that it survived both the fire and whatever caused everything except the steel to be pulverized into tiny particles.[92]

THE COLLAPSE OF BUILDING 7

As we have seen, the 9/11 Commission simply ignored the facts discussed above. Still another matter not discussed by the Commission was the collapse of Building 7. And yet the official story about it is, if anything, even more problematic than the official story about the towers—as suggested by the title of a *New York Times* story, "Engineers Are Baffled over the Collapse of 7 WTC."[93]

Even More Difficult to Explain

The collapse of Building 7 is even more difficult to explain than the collapse of the towers, in part because it was not struck by an airliner; none of the theories about how the impacts of the airliners contributed to the collapses of the towers can be employed in relation to it.

Also, all the photographic evidence suggests that the fires in this building were small, not very hot, and limited to a few floors. Photographs of the north side of the building show fires only on two or three floors of this forty-seven-story building. So if the south side, which faced the towers, had fires on many other floors, as defenders of the official account claim, they were not big enough to be seen from the other side of the building.[94]

It would not be surprising, of course, if the fires in this building were even smaller than those in the towers, because there was no jet fuel to start a big fire. Some defenders of the official story have claimed, to be sure, that the diesel fuel stored in this building somehow caught fire and created a towering inferno. But if Building 7 had become engulfed in flames, why did none of the many photographers and TV camera crews on the scene capture this sight?

The extreme difficulty of explaining the collapse of Building 7—assuming that it is not permissible to mention controlled demolition—has been recognized by the official bodies. The report prepared under FEMA's supervision came up with a scenario employing the diesel fuel, then admitted that this scenario had "only a low probability of occurrence."[95] Even that statement is generous, because the probability that some version of the official story of Building 7 is true is the same as it is for the towers, essentially zero, because it would violate several laws of physics. In any case, the 9/11 Commission, perhaps because of this admission by FEMA, avoided the problem by simply not even mentioning the fact that this building collapsed.

This was one of the Commission's most amazing omissions. According to the official theory, Building 7 demonstrated, contrary to the universal conviction prior to 9/11, that large steel-frame buildings *could* collapse from fire alone, even without having been hit by an airplane. This demonstration should have meant that building codes and insurance premiums for all steel-frame buildings in the world needed to be changed. And yet the 9/11 Commission, in preparing its 571-page report, did not devote a single sentence to this historic event.

Even More Similar to Standard Controlled Implosions

Yet another reason that the collapse of Building 7 is especially problematic is that it was even more like the best-known type of controlled demolition—namely, an implosion, which begins at the bottom (whereas the collapse of each tower originated high up, near the region struck by the plane). As Eric Hufschmid has written, "Building 7 collapsed at its bottom. . . . [T]he interior fell first. . . . The result was a very tiny pile of rubble, with the outside of the building collapsing on top of the pile."[96]

Implosionworld.com, a Web site about the demolition industry, states that an implosion is "by far the trickiest type of explosive project, and there are only a handful of blasting companies in the world that possess enough experience . . . to perform these true building implosions."[97] Can anyone really believe that fire would have just happened to produce the kind of collapse that can be reliably produced by only a few demolition companies in the world? The building had twenty-four core columns and fifty-seven perimeter columns. To hold that fire caused this building to collapse straight down would mean believing that the fire caused all eighty-one columns to fail at exactly the same time. To accept the official story is, in other words, to accept a miracle. Physicist Steven Jones agrees, saying, "The likelihood of near-symmetrical collapse of WTC 7 due to random fires (the 'official' theory)—requiring as it does near-simultaneous failure of many support columns—is infinitesimal. I conclude that the evidence for the 9/11 use of pre-positioned explosives in WTC 7 (also in Towers 1 and 2) is truly compelling."[98]

Much More Extensive Foreknowledge

Another reason that the collapse of Building 7 creates special problems involves foreknowledge of its collapse. We know of only a few people with advance knowledge that the Twin Towers were going to collapse, and the information we have would be consistent with the supposition that this knowledge was acquired only a few minutes before the south tower collapsed. People can imagine, therefore, that someone saw something suggesting that the building was going to collapse. But the foreknowledge of Building 7's collapse was more widespread and of longer duration. This has been known for a long time, at least by people who read firefighters' magazines.[99] But now the oral histories have provided a fuller picture.

Widespread Notification. At least twenty-five of the firefighters and medical workers reported that, at some time that day, they learned that Building 7 was going to collapse. Firefighters who had been fighting the fires in the building said they were ordered to leave the building, after which a collapse zone was established. As medical worker Decosta Wright put it, "They measured out how far the building was going to come, so we knew exactly where we could stand," which was "5 blocks away."[100]

Early Warning. As to exactly when the expectation of the collapse began circulating, the testimonies differ. But most of the evidence suggests that the expectation of collapse was communicated four or five hours in advance.[101]

The Alleged Reason for the Expectation. But why would this expectation have arisen? The fires in Building 7 were, according to all the photographic evidence, few and small. So why would the decision makers in the department have decided to pull firefighters out of Building 7 and have them simply stand around waiting for it to collapse?

The chiefs gave a twofold explanation: damage plus fire. Chief Frank Fellini said: "When [the north tower] fell, it ripped steel out from between the third and sixth floors across the facade on Vesey Street. We were concerned that the fires on several floors and the missing steel would result in the building collapsing."[102]

There are two problems with each part of this explanation. One problem with the accounts of the structural damage is that they vary greatly. According to Fellini's testimony, there was a four-floor hole between the third and sixth floors. In the telling of Captain Chris Boyle, however, the hole was "20 stories tall."[103] It would appear that Shyam Sunder, the lead investigator for NIST, settled on a compromise between these two views, telling *Popular Mechanics*, "On about a third of the face to the center and to the bottom—approximately 10 stories—about 25 percent of the depth of the building was scooped out."[104]

The different accounts of the problem on the building's south side are not, moreover, limited to the issue of the size of the hole. According to Deputy Chief Peter Hayden, the problem was not a hole at all but a "bulge," and it was "between floors 10 and 13."[105]

The second problem with these accounts of the damage is if there was a hole that was ten or twenty floors high, or even a hole—or a bulge—that was four floors high, why was this fact not captured on film by any of the photographers or videographers in the area that day?

There are also two problems with the claims about the fire. One problem is that the accounts again vary greatly. Chief Daniel Nigro spoke of "very heavy fire on many floors."[106] According to Harry Meyers, an assistant chief, "When the building came down it was completely involved in fire, all forty-seven stories."[107] That obvious exaggeration was also stated by firefighter Tiernach Cassidy, who said: "[Building 7] was fully engulfed. . . . [Y]ou could see the flames going straight through from one side of the building to the other."[108]

Several of the testimonies, however, did not support the official line. For example, medical technician Decosta Wright said: "I think the fourth floor was on fire. . . . [W]e were like, are you guys going to put that fire out?"[109] Chief Thomas McCarthy said: "[T]hey were waiting for 7 World Trade to come down. . . . They had . . . fire on three separate floors . . . , just burning merrily. It was pretty amazing, you know, it's the afternoon in lower Manhattan, a major high-rise is burning, and they said 'we know.'"[110]

The second problem with the official claims about the fire is that if there was "very heavy fire on many floors," why is this fact not captured on any film? A photograph of the north side of the building taken by Terry Schmidt about two hours before the building collapsed supports Chief McCarthy's view that there was fire on three floors.[111] Even if there were fires on additional floors on the south side of the building, there is no photographic support for Cassidy's claim that "the flames [on these additional floors went] straight through from one side of the building to the other." In Schmidt's photograph, fires were visible on the north side on only three floors.

Moreover, even if the department's official story about the collapse of Building 7 were not contradicted by physical evidence and some of the oral histories, it would not explain why the building collapsed, because no amount of fire and structural damage, unless caused by explosives, had ever caused the total collapse of a large steel-frame building.[112] And it certainly would not explain the particular nature of the collapse—that the building imploded and fell straight down rather than falling over in some direction, as purportedly expected by those who gave the order to create a large collapse zone. Battalion Chief John Norman, for example, said, "We expected it to fall to the south."[113] Nor would the damage-plus-fire theory explain this building's collapse at virtually free-fall speed or the creation of an enormous amount of dust—additional features of the collapses that are typically ignored by defenders of the official account.

The great difficulty presented to the official theory about the WTC by the collapse of Building 7 is illustrated by a book titled *102 Minutes: The Untold Story of the Fight to Survive inside the Twin Towers*, one of the authors of which is *New York Times* reporter Jim Dwyer, who wrote stories in the *Times* about the release of the 9/11 oral histories.[114] With regard to the Twin Towers, Dwyer and his coauthor, Kevin Flynn, support the theory put out by NIST, according to which the towers collapsed because the airplanes knocked the fireproofing off the steel columns, making them vulnerable to the "intense heat" of the ensuing fires.[115] When they come to Building 7, however, Dwyer and Flynn do not ask why it collapsed, given the fact that it was *not* hit by a plane. They simply say: "The firefighters had decided to let the fire there burn itself out."[116] But that, of course, is not what happened. Rather, shortly after 5:20 that day, Building 7 suddenly collapsed, in essentially the same way as did the Twin Towers.

Should this fact not have led Dwyer and Flynn to question NIST's theory that the towers collapsed because their fireproofing had been knocked loose? I would especially think that Dwyer, who reported on the release of the 9/11 oral histories, should reassess NIST's theory in light of the abundant evidence of explosions in the towers provided in those testimonies (some of which was summarized in the previous chapter).[117]

Another Explanation. There is, in any case, only one theory that explains both the nature and the expectation of the collapse of Building 7: explosives had been set, and someone who knew this spread the word to the fire chiefs.

Amazingly enough, a version of this theory was publicly stated by an insider, Larry Silverstein, who owned Building 7. In a PBS documentary aired in September of 2002, Silverstein, discussing Building 7, said, "I remember getting a call from the, er, fire department commander, telling me that they were not sure they were gonna be able to contain the fire, and I said, 'We've had such terrible loss of life, maybe the smartest thing to do is pull it.'[118] And they made that decision to pull and we watched the building collapse."[119]

It is very puzzling, to be sure, that Silverstein—who was ready to receive billions of dollars in insurance payments for Building 7 and the rest of the World Trade Center complex, on the assumption that they had been destroyed by acts of terrorism—would have made such a statement in public, especially with TV cameras running. But his assertion that Building 7 was brought down by explosives, whatever the motive behind it, explains why and how it collapsed.

We still, however, have the question of why the fire department came to expect the building to collapse. It would be interesting, of course, if that information came from the same agency, the Office of Emergency Management, that had earlier informed the department that one of the towers was going to collapse. And, in fact, we have it on good authority that it did. Captain Michael Currid, the president of the Uniformed Fire Officers Association, said that some time after the collapse of the Twin Towers, "Someone from the city's Office of Emergency Management" told him that Building 7 was "basically a lost cause and we should not lose anyone else trying to save it," after which the firefighters in the building were told to get out.[120]

But that answer, assuming it to be correct, leaves us with more questions, beginning with: Who in the Office of Emergency Management knew in advance that the Twin Towers and Building 7 were going to collapse? How did they know this? And so on. These questions could be answered only by a real investigation, which has yet to begin.

CONCLUSION

It is, in any case, already possible to know, beyond a reasonable doubt, one very important thing: the official account of the destruction of the World Trade Center is false. The evidence suggests very strongly that it was a false-flag operation, orchestrated by domestic terrorists. Foreign terrorists could not have secured access to the buildings to plant the explosives. And they probably would not have had the courtesy to make sure that the buildings collapsed straight down, rather than falling over onto surrounding buildings. Federal officials, however, could have obtained access and would have had the means and the motivation to bring the buildings straight down. They would also have had the ability to orchestrate a cover-up, from the quick disposal of the steel and the planting of evidence to the FEMA Report to *The 9/11 Commission Report* and to the NIST Report.

The evidence that 9/11 was orchestrated by forces within our own government has thus far been largely ignored by the mainstream press, perhaps under the guise of obeying President Bush's advice not to tolerate "outrageous conspiracy theories." We have seen, however, that it is the Bush administration's conspiracy theory that is the outrageous one, because it is violently contradicted by numerous facts, including some basic laws of physics.

There is, of course, another reason that the mainstream press has not pointed out these contradictions. As a recent letter to the *Los Angeles Times* said: "The number of contradictions in the official version of . . . 9/11 is so overwhelming that . . . it simply cannot be believed. Yet . . . the official version cannot be abandoned because the implication of rejecting it is far too disturbing: that we are subject to a government conspiracy of 'X-Files' proportions and insidiousness."[121]

The implications are indeed disturbing. Many people who know or at least suspect the truth about 9/11 probably believe that revealing it would be so disturbing to the American psyche, the American form of government, and global stability that it is better to pretend to believe the official version. I would suggest, however, that any merit this argument may have had earlier has been overcome by more recent events and realizations. Far more devastating to the American psyche, the American form of government, and the world as a whole will be the continued rule of those who brought us 9/11, because the values reflected in that horrendous event have been reflected in the Bush administration's lies to justify the attack on Iraq, its disregard for environmental science and the Bill of Rights, its criminal negligence both before and after Katrina, and now its apparent plan not only to weaponize space but also to authorize the use of nuclear weapons in a preemptive strike.

In light of this situation and the facts discussed in these chapters I call on the *New York Times* to take the lead in finally exposing to the American people and the world the truth about 9/11. Taking the lead on such a story will, of course, involve enormous risks. But if any news organization has the power, the prestige, and the credibility to break this story, it is the *Times*. It performed yeoman service in getting the 9/11 oral histories released. But now the welfare of our republic and perhaps even the survival of our civilization depend on getting the truth about 9/11 exposed. I am calling on the *Times* to rise to the occasion.

EPILOGUE: THE VAN ROMERO EPISODE

If the collapses of the World Trade Center buildings were indeed instances of controlled demolition, we would expect that immediately after the collapses, before the official account had been made clear to everyone, some expert on controlled demolition would have said that the buildings appeared to have been brought down by explosives. And, in fact, this was reportedly stated, at least with regard to the Twin Towers, by Van Romero, vice president for research at the New Mexico Institute of Mining and Technology, who had previously been the director of this institute's center for studying the effects of explosions on buildings. According to an article in the *Albuquerque Journal* by Olivier Uyttebrouck, Romero said on 9/11 itself, after viewing the collapses on videotapes, that they not only resembled those produced by controlled implosions but must, in fact, have been caused by "some explosive devices inside the buildings," because they were "too methodical" to have been chance results of the airplane strikes.[122]

Romero, however, changed his public stance ten days later, according to an article in the same journal by John Fleck.[123] But this article fails to supply any plausible reason for a real change of mind (as distinct from merely a public change of stance). "Subsequent conversations with structural engineers and more detailed looks at the tape," claimed Fleck, led Romero to conclude that "intense heat of the jet fuel fires weakened the skyscrapers' steel structural beams to the point that they gave way under the weight of the floors above." But there is no indication of what these alleged structural engineers said, or what Romero saw in his "more detailed looks at the tape," that led him to change his earlier view that the collapses were "too methodical" to have been produced by anything except explosives. There is also no suggestion as to how "weakened beams" could have led to a collapse that began suddenly, occurred at virtually free-fall speed, and was total, leaving no steel columns standing.[124]

A clue to the real reason for this change in Romero's public stance may be provided by another statement in the original article, which said that when the Pentagon was struck, "[Romero] and Denny Peterson, vice president for administration and finance [at New Mexico Tech], were en route to an office building near the Pentagon to discuss defense-funded research programs at Tech." Indeed, as a later story points out, *Influence* magazine named Romero one of "six lobbyists who made an impact in 2003," adding that "[a] major chunk of [Romero's] job involves lobbying for federal government funding, and if the 2003 fiscal year was any indication, Romero was a superstar," having obtained about $56 million for New Mexico Tech in that year alone.[125]

In light of the fact that Romero gave no scientific reasons for his change of stance, it does not seem unreasonable to infer that the real reason was his realization, perhaps forced upon him by government officials, that unless he publicly retracted his initial statements, his effectiveness in lobbying the federal government for funds would be greatly reduced. Romero, to be sure, denies this, saying: "Conspiracy theorists came out saying that the government got to me. That is the farthest thing from the truth."[126] But that, of course, is what Romero would be expected to say in either case. He could have avoided this charge only by providing a persuasive account of how the buildings could have come down, in the manner they did, without explosives.

I have related this episode not only because Romero's initial statement, before there was time for pressure to be brought to bear on him, provided expert testimony that the buildings must have been brought down by explosives, but also because this episode may illustrate one of the ways in which a government, after orchestrating a false-flag operation, is able to induce experts to keep silent or, if they have already spoken out, to change their public stance.

Chapter 4

Flights of Fancy

The 9/11 Commission's Incredible Tales of Flights 11, 175, 77, and 93

In the second half of *The 9/11 Commission Report: Omissions and Distortions*,[1] I provided a critique of the Commission's explanation as to why the U.S. military was unable to intercept any of the hijacked airplanes. This explanation had been given in the first chapter of the official *9/11 Commission Report*. Although that chapter is only forty-five pages long, the issues involved are so complex that my analysis of it filled six chapters.

The complexity of my analysis, however, has made that part of my book the most difficult for readers. It has been especially difficult, I have learned, for readers to grasp the central points: Too many trees make it difficult to see the forest. In this chapter, accordingly, I provide an abbreviated analysis of the Commission's first chapter, intended to make the most essential problems in it stand out.

One of the reasons that this issue is so complex is that the 9/11 Commission's account is the third official explanation we have been given as to why the military could not intercept the hijacked airliners. Why have three versions of this explanation been deemed necessary? To approach this question, we need to review the standard operating procedures that are supposed to prevent hijacked airliners from causing the kinds of damage that occurred on 9/11.

Standard operating procedures dictate that if an FAA flight controller notices anything that suggests a possible hijacking—if radio contact is lost, if the plane's transponder goes off, or if the plane deviates from its flight plan—the controller is to contact a superior. If the problem cannot be fixed quickly—within about a minute—the superior is to ask NORAD (the North American Aerospace Defense Command) to scramble jet fighters to find out what is going on. NORAD then issues a scramble order to the nearest air force base with fighters on alert. On 9/11, all the hijacked airliners occurred in NORAD's Northeast Air Defense Sector, known as NEADS. So all the scramble orders would have come from NEADS.

The jet fighters at the disposal of NEADS could respond very quickly. According to the U.S. Air Force Web site, F-15s can go from "scramble order" to 29,000 feet in only 2.5 minutes, after which they can then fly over 1800 miles per hour (140). (All page numbers given parenthetically in the text of this chapter are to my aforementioned book, *The 9/11 Commission Report: Omissions and Distortions*.) Therefore—according to General Ralph Eberhart, the head of NORAD—after the FAA senses that something is wrong, "It takes about one minute" for it to contact NORAD, after which, according to a spokesperson, NORAD can scramble fighter jets "within a matter of minutes to anywhere in the United States" (140). These statements were, to be sure, made after 9/11, so we might suspect that they reflect a post-9/11 speedup in procedures. But an Air Traffic Control document put out in 1998 warned pilots that any airplanes persisting in unusual behavior "will likely find two [jet fighters] on their tail within 10 or so minutes" (141).

The First Version of the Official Story. On 9/11, however, that did not happen. Why not? Where was the military? The military's first answer was given immediately after 9/11 by General Richard Myers, then the acting chair of the Joint Chiefs of Staff, and Mike Snyder, a spokesperson for NORAD. They both said, independently, that no military jets were sent up until after the strike on the Pentagon. That strike occurred at 9:38, and yet American Airlines Flight 11 had shown two of the standard signs of hijacking, losing both the radio and the transponder signal, at 8:15. Thus, procedures that usually result in an interception within "10 or so minutes" had not been carried out in 80 or so minutes.

That enormous delay suggested that a stand-down order, canceling standard procedures, must have been given. Some people started raising this possibility.

The Second Version of the Official Story. Very quickly, a new story appeared. On Friday, September 14, CBS News said: "Contrary to early reports, U.S. Air Force jets did get into the air on Tuesday while the attacks were under way," although they arrived too late to prevent the attacks (141–42). This second story was then made official on September 18, when NORAD produced a timeline stating the times that it was notified about the hijackings followed by the

times at which fighters were scrambled (143). The implicit message of the timeline was that the failure was due entirely to the FAA, because in each case it notified the military so late that interceptions were impossible.

Not quite everyone, however, accepted that conclusion. Some early members of the 9/11 truth movement, doing the math, showed that NORAD's new
timeline did not get it off the hook.[2] With regard to the first flight, even if we
accept NORAD's claim that NEADS was not notified about Flight 11 until
8:40 (which would mean that the FAA had waited twenty-five minutes after it
saw danger signs before it made the call), NORAD's implicit claim that it could
not have prevented the first attack on the WTC is problematic. If fighters had
immediately been scrambled from McGuire Air Force Base in New Jersey, they
could easily have intercepted Flight 11 before 8:47, which is when the north
tower of the WTC was struck.

NORAD, to be sure, had a built-in answer to that question. It claimed that
McGuire had no fighters on alert, so that NEADS had to give the scramble
order to Otis Air Force Base in Cape Cod. Critics argued that this claim is probably false, for reasons to be discussed later. They also pointed out that the F-
15s, even if they had to come from Otis, might have made it to Manhattan in
time to intercept Flight 11, if the scramble order had been given immediately,
at 8:40, and then the fighters had taken off immediately. NORAD said, however, that the scramble order was not given until 8:46 and that the F-15s did
not get airborne until 8:52 (144–45). It looked to critics, therefore, like the failure was not entirely the FAA's.

Even less plausible, the critics said, was NORAD's claim that NEADS did
not have time to prevent the second attack. According to NORAD's timeline,
NEADS had been notified about United Airlines Flight 175 at 8:43, twenty
minutes before the south tower was struck. The F-15s originally ordered to go
after Flight 11 were now to go after Flight 175. According to NORAD, as we
saw earlier, the scramble order to Otis was given at 8:46. In light of the military's
own statement that F-15s can go from scramble order to 29,000 feet in 2.5 minutes, the F-15s would have been streaking toward Manhattan by 8:49. So they
could easily have gotten there before 9:03, when the south tower was struck.
NORAD said, however, that it took the fighters six minutes just to get airborne.[3]
Critics said that it looked as if at least a slowdown order had been issued.

Critics also pointed out that even if the F-15s did not take off, as NORAD
said, until 8:52, they still could have reached Manhattan in time to prevent
the second attack, assuming that they were going full speed. And, according
to one of the pilots, they were. Lieutenant Colonel Timothy Duffy said they
went "full-blower all the way." And yet, according to NORAD's timeline,
when the south tower was hit at 9:03, the F-15s were still seventy-one miles
away. Doing the math showed that the fighters could not have been going even
half-blower (146). It still looked like a stand-down order, or at least a slowdown order, had been issued.

The same problem existed with respect to NORAD's explanation of its failure to protect the Pentagon. NORAD again blamed the FAA, saying that although the FAA knew about the hijacking of American Airlines Flight 77 before 9:00, it did not notify NEADS until 9:24, too late for NEADS to respond.

Again, doing the math showed that this explanation did not work. NORAD claimed that it issued the scramble order immediately, at 9:24. The attack on the Pentagon did not occur until fourteen minutes later, at 9:38. That would have been more than enough time for fighters to get there from Andrews Air Force Base, which is only a few miles away. Why, then, did NORAD not prevent the attack?

Part of NORAD's answer was that no fighters were on alert at Andrews, so that NEADS had to give the scramble order to Langley Air Force Base, which is about 130 miles away. Also, it again took the pilots six minutes to get airborne, so they did not get away until 9:30.

However, even if those explanations are accepted, the scrambled F-16s, critics pointed out, could go 1500 miles per hour, so they could have reached Washington a couple of minutes before the Pentagon was struck. According to NORAD, however, they were still 105 miles away. That would mean that the F-16s were going less than 200 miles per hour, which would not even be one-quarter blower (147-48).

In all three cases, therefore, NORAD's attempt to put all the blame on the FAA failed. Critics were able to show, especially with regard to the second and third flights, that NORAD's new story still implied that a stand-down order must have been issued. It is perhaps not surprising, therefore, that the 9/11 Commission came up with a third story, which is not subject to the same objections.

The main question, however, is still the same: Is it true? One reason to suspect that it is *not* true is the very fact that it is the third story we have been given. When suspects in a criminal case keep changing their story, we assume that they must be trying to conceal the truth. But an even more serious problem with the Commission's new story is that many of its elements are contradicted by credible evidence or are otherwise implausible. I will show this by examining the Commission's treatment of each flight, beginning with Flight 11.

THE COMMISSION'S TREATMENT OF AMERICAN AIRLINES FLIGHT 11

A Picture of FAA Incompetence

As we saw, flight controllers are supposed to react quickly if they see any one of the three standard signs of a hijacking. But Flight 11 hit the trifecta, showing all three signs, and yet no one at the Boston FAA Center, we are told, took any action for some time. Eventually, Boston, having heard hijackers giving orders, called the FAA Command Center in Herndon. Herndon then called FAA head-quarters in Washington, but no one there, we are told, called the military. Finally, the FAA center in Boston called NEADS directly at 8:38 (the Commission here revised NORAD's timeline, which had said 8:40) (158).

To accept this story, we would have to believe that although the FAA should have notified the military about Flight 11 within a minute of seeing the danger signals at 8:15, the FAA personnel at Boston, Herndon, and Washington were all so incompetent that twenty-three minutes passed before the military was notified. We would then need to reconcile this picture of top-to-bottom dereliction of duty, which contributed to thousands of deaths, with the fact that no FAA personnel were fired.

An Eight-Minute Phone Call

The next implausible element in the story involves Colonel Robert Marr, the commander at NEADS. As we saw earlier, if he had had planes scrambled immediately, even from Otis, they might have prevented the first attack on the World Trade Center. And yet, we are told, he called down to Florida to General Larry Arnold, the head of NORAD's U.S. Continental Region, to get authorization to have planes scrambled, and this phone call took eight minutes (165).[4]

Besides the fact that this would be an extraordinarily long phone call in an emergency situation, this call was not even necessary. The Commission, to be sure, would have us believe that Marr had to get approval from superiors. But the very document from the Department of Defense cited by the Commission indicates that anyone in the military chain of command, upon receiving "verbal requests from civil authorities for support in an . . . emergency may . . . immediately respond" (166).[5] Colonel Marr, therefore, could have responded on his own.

Evidence of Earlier Notification

But this tale of an eight-minute phone call is probably not the biggest lie in the Commission's story about Flight 11. That award seems to belong to the claim that although the FAA saw signs of a hijacking at 8:15, the military was not notified until 8:38. Laura Brown, the FAA's deputy in public affairs, reportedly said that the National Military Command Center in the Pentagon had set up an air threat teleconference that morning at about 8:20 (187).[6] If she is correct, it would seem that the military knew about Flight 11's erratic behavior shortly after 8:15, which suggests that the FAA *had* followed standard procedures.

THE COMMISSION'S TREATMENT OF UNITED AIRLINES FLIGHT 175

More FAA Incompetence

The Commission claims that NORAD did not intercept this flight because the FAA never reported its hijacking until after it crashed. According to the Commission, the FAA flight controller did not even notify a manager until 8:55. This manager then called the FAA Command Center at Herndon, saying: "[The situation is] escalating . . . big time. We need to get the military involved." But no one at Herndon, we are told, called the military or even FAA headquarters. As a result, NORAD did not learn about the hijacking of Flight 175 until 9:03, when it was crashing into the WTC's south tower (175).

Contradicting Earlier Reports

One problem with this story is that such incompetence by FAA officials is not believable. An even more serious problem is that this story is contradicted by many prior reports.

One of these reports is NORAD's own previous timeline. As we saw earlier, NORAD had maintained since September 18, 2001, that it had been notified about Flight 175 at 8:43. If that was *not* true, as the Commission now claims, NORAD must have been either lying or confused when it put out its timeline one week after 9/11. And it is hard to believe that it could have been confused so soon after the event. So it must have been lying. But that would suggest that it had an ugly truth to conceal. The Commission, being unable to embrace either of the possible explanations, simply tells us that NORAD's previous statement was incorrect, but without giving us any explanation as to how this could be.

The Commission's claim that the military did not know about Flight 175 until it crashed is also contradicted by a report involving Captain Michael Jellinek, a Canadian who on 9/11 was overseeing NORAD's headquarters in Colorado. According to a story in the *Toronto Star*, Jellinek was on the phone with NEADS as he watched Flight 175 crash into the south tower. He then asked NEADS: "Was that the hijacked aircraft you were dealing with?"—to which NEADS said "yes" (176).

Two Problematic Teleconferences

Still another problem with the Commission's new story is that there appear to have been two teleconferences during which FAA officials would have talked to the military about Flight 175. I have already mentioned the teleconference initiated by the National Military Command Center in the Pentagon. The 9/11

Commission claims, to be sure, that this teleconference did not begin until 9:29 (186–88), long after Flight 175 had crashed into the south tower. But this late starting time is contradicted by Richard Clarke (188). It is also contradicted by Laura Brown of the FAA, who said that it started at about 8:20. Although Brown later, perhaps under pressure from superiors, changed the starting time to 8:45 (187), this was still early enough for discussions of Flight 175 to have occurred.

There was also a teleconference initiated by the FAA. According to the 9/11 Commission, this teleconference was set up at 9:20 (205). On May 22, 2003, however, Laura Brown sent to the Commission a memo headed: "FAA Communications with NORAD on September 11, 2001."[7] The memo, which used the term "phone bridges" instead of "teleconference," began: "Within minutes after the first aircraft hit the World Trade Center, the FAA immediately established several phone bridges." Since the attack on the north tower was at 8:47, "within minutes" would mean that this teleconference began about 8:50, a full half-hour earlier than the Commission claims. The memo made clear, moreover, that the teleconference included both NORAD and the National Military Command Center in the Pentagon. During this teleconference, Brown's memo said, "The FAA shared real-time information . . . about the . . . loss of communication with aircraft, loss of transponder signals, unauthorized changes in course, and other actions being taken by all the flights of interest" (253). And by 8:50, everyone agrees, Flight 175 was a "flight of interest"—everyone except, of course, the 9/11 Commission, which claims that FAA headquarters had not yet learned about it. Laura Brown's memo, in any case, was read into the Commission's record on May 23, 2003.[8] But when the Commission published its final report, it simply pretended that this memo did not exist. Only through this pretense could the Commission claim that the FAA's teleconferences did not begin until 9:20.

For several reasons, therefore, it appears that the Commission's claim that the military was not notified about Flight 175 until after it struck the south tower is a lie from beginning to end.

THE COMMISSION'S TREATMENT OF AMERICAN AIR-LINES FLIGHT 77 AND THE ATTACK ON THE PENTAGON

As we saw earlier, if the FAA told NORAD about Flight 77 at 9:24, as NORAD's timeline of September 18 said, NEADS should have had fighter jets over Washington well before 9:38, when the Pentagon was struck. The 9/11 Commission's solution to this problem was to tell another new tale, according to which the FAA *never* told NORAD about Flight 77.

One inconvenient fact was that General Larry Arnold, the head of NORAD's U.S. Continental region, had, in open testimony to the Commission in 2003, repeated NORAD's statement that it had been notified about this hijacking at 9:24. Other NORAD officials, moreover, had testified that fighters at Langley had been scrambled in response to this notification. The Commission handled this problem by simply saying that these statements by Arnold and the other NORAD officials were "incorrect" (192). The Commission again did not explain why NORAD officials had made incorrect statements. But it said that those statements were "unfortunate" because they "made it appear that the military was notified in time to respond" (192). The Commission's task was to convince us that this was not true.

More FAA Incompetence

Basic to the Commission's new story about Flight 77 is another tale of incredible incompetence by FAA officials. This tale goes like this: At 8:54, the FAA controller in Indianapolis, after seeing Flight 77 go off course, lost its transponder signal and even its radar track. Rather than reporting the flight as possibly hijacked, however, he assumed that it had crashed. Evidently it did not occur to him that a possible crash should be reported. In any case, he later, after hearing about the other hijackings, came to suspect that Flight 77 may also have been hijacked. He then shared this suspicion with Herndon, which in turn shared it with FAA headquarters. But no one, we are told, called the military. The result, the Commission says, is that "NEADS never received notice that American 77 was hijacked" (192).

Explaining the Langley Scramble: Phantom Flight 11

But even if we could believe this implausible tale, there is still the problem of why F-16s at Langley Air Force Base were airborne at 9:30. FAA incompetence again comes to the rescue. At 9:21—thirty-four minutes after Flight 11 had crashed into the World Trade Center—some technician at NEADS, we are told, heard from some FAA controller in Boston that Flight 11 was still in the air and was heading toward Washington. This NEADS technician then notified the NEADS mission crew commander, who issued a scramble order to Langley. So, the Commission claims, the Langley jets were scrambled in response to "a phantom aircraft," not to "an actual hijacked aircraft" (193). This new story, however, is riddled with problems.

One problem is simply that phantom Flight 11 had never before been mentioned. As the Commission itself says, this story about phantom Flight 11 "was not recounted in a single public timeline or statement issued by the FAA or Department of Defense" (196). It was, for example, not in NORAD'S official report, *Air War over America*, the foreword for which was written by General Larry Arnold.[9]

General Arnold's ignorance of phantom Flight 11 was, in fact, an occasion for public humiliation. The 9/11 Commission, at a hearing in June 2004, berated him for not remembering that the Langley jets had really been scrambled in response to phantom Flight 11, not in response to a warning about Flight 77. Commissioner Richard Ben-Veniste began a lengthy grilling by asking: "General Arnold. Why did no one mention the false report received from the FAA that Flight 11 was heading south during your initial appearance before the 9/11 Commission back in May of last year?" After an embarrassing exchange, Ben-Veniste stuck the knife in even further, asking:

> General, is it not a fact that the failure to call our attention to the . . . notion of a phantom Flight 11 continuing from New York City south . . . skewed the official Air Force report, . . . which does not contain any information about the fact that . . . you had not received notification that Flight 77 had been hijacked? . . . Surely by May of last year, when you testified before this commission, you knew those facts. (197)

In *Alice in Wonderland*, the White Queen says, "It's a poor sort of memory that only works backwards." One must wonder if General Arnold felt that he was being criticized for not remembering the future—that is, for not "remembering" a story that had been invented only after he had given his testimony. Arnold, in any case, simply replied that he "didn't recall those facts in May of last year."

But if those alleged facts were real facts, that reply would be beyond belief. According to the Commission's new story, NORAD, under Arnold's command, failed to scramble fighter jets in response to Flights 11, 175, 77, and 93. The one time it scrambled fighters, it did so in response to a false report. Surely that would have been the biggest embarrassment of Arnold's professional life. And yet twenty months later, he "didn't recall those facts."

A second problem is that there is no way for this story about phantom Flight 11 to be verified. The Commission says that the truth of this story "is clear . . . from taped conversations at FAA centers; contemporaneous logs compiled at NEADS, Continental Region headquarters, and NORAD; and other records" (193–94). But when we look in the notes at the back of *The 9/11 Commission Report*, we find no references for any of these records; we simply have to take the Commission's word. The sole reference is to a NEADS audiofile, on which someone at the FAA's Boston Center allegedly tells someone at NEADS: "I just had a report that American 11 is still in the air, and it's . . . heading towards Washington" (194). The Commission claims to have *discovered* this audiofile. Again, however, we simply have to take the Commission's word. We cannot obtain this audiofile. And there is no mention of any tests, carried out by an independent agency, to verify that this audiofile, if it exists, really dates from 9/11, rather than having been created later, after someone decided that the story about phantom Flight 11 was needed.

But could not reporters interview the people at NEADS and the FAA who had this conversation? No, because the Commission says, nonchalantly: "We have been unable to identify the source of this mistaken FAA information" (194). This disclaimer is difficult to believe. It is now very easy to identify people from recordings of their voices. And yet the Commission was supposedly not able to discover the identity of either the individual at Boston who made the mistake or the NEADS technician who received and passed on this misinformation.

Another implausible element is the very idea that someone at Boston would have concluded that Flight 11 was still airborne. According to stories immediately after 9/11, flight controllers at Boston said that they never lost sight of Flight 11. Flight controller Mark Hodgkins later said: "I watched the target of American 11 the whole way down" (194). If so, everyone at the Boston Center would have known this. How could anything on a radar screen have convinced anyone at the Boston Center, thirty-four minutes later, that Flight 11 was still aloft?

Still another implausible element in the story is the idea that the mission commander at NEADS, having received this implausible report from a technician, would have been so confident of its truth that he would have immediately ordered Langley to scramble F-16s.[10]

This entire story about phantom Flight 11 is the Commission's attempt to explain why, if the U.S. military had *not* been notified about Flight 77, a scramble order was issued to Langley at 9:24, which resulted in F-16s taking off at 9:30. As we have seen, every element in this story is implausible.

Why Were the Langley F-16s So Far from Washington?

Equally implausible is the Commission's explanation as to why, if the F-16s were airborne at 9:30, they were not close enough to Washington to protect the Pentagon at 9:38. To answer this question, the Commission once again calls on FAA incompetence.

The F-16s, we are told, were supposed to go to Baltimore, to intercept (phantom) Flight 11 before it reached Washington. But the FAA controller, along with the lead pilot, thought the orders were for the F-16s to go "east over the ocean," so at 9:38, when the Pentagon was struck, "The Langley fighters were about 150 miles away" (201). Has there ever been, since the days of the Marx Brothers and the Three Stooges, such a comedy of errors? This explanation, in any case, is not believable. By the time of the scramble order, it was clear that the threat was from hijacked airliners, not from abroad. My seven-year-old grandson would have known to double-check the order before sending the fighters out to sea.

The Military's Alleged Ignorance about Flight 77

Even more problematic is the Commission's claim that Pentagon officials were in the dark about the hijacking of Flight 77.

That claim is flatly contradicted by Laura Brown's memo. Having said that the FAA had established its teleconference with military officials "within minutes" of the first strike, she said that the FAA shared "real-time information" about "all the flights of interest, including Flight 77." Moreover, explicitly taking issue with NORAD's claim that it knew nothing about Flight 77 until 9:24, she said: "NORAD logs indicate that the FAA made formal notification about American Flight 77 at 9:24 a.m., but information about the flight was conveyed continuously during the phone bridges before the formal notification" (204).[11]

This statement about *informal* notification was known by the Commission. Richard Ben-Veniste, after reading Laura Brown's memo into the record, said, "So now we have in question whether there was an informal real-time communication of the situation, including Flight 77's situation, to personnel at NORAD."[12] But when the Commission wrote up its final report, with its claim that the FAA had not notified the military about Flight 77 (whether formally or informally), it wrote as if this discussion had never occurred.[13]

The Pentagon's Alleged Ignorance of an Aircraft Headed Its Way

The Commission also claims that people in the Pentagon had no idea that an aircraft was heading in their direction until shortly before the Pentagon was struck. But this claim was contradicted by Secretary of Transportation Norman Mineta, in open testimony given to the Commission itself. Mineta testified that at 9:20 that morning, he went down to the shelter conference room (technically the Presidential Emergency Operations Center) under the White House, where Vice President Cheney was in charge. Mineta then said:

> During the time that the airplane was coming in to the Pentagon, there was a young man who would come in and say to the Vice President, "The plane is 50 miles out." "The plane is 30 miles out." And when it got down to "the plane is 10 miles out," the young man also said to the Vice President, "Do the orders still stand?" And the Vice President turned and whipped his neck around and said, "Of course the orders still stand. Have you heard anything to the contrary?" (220)[14]

When Mineta was asked by Commissioner Timothy Roemer how long this conversation occurred after he arrived, Mineta said, "Probably about five or six minutes," which, as Roemer pointed out, would mean "about 9:25 or 9:26."

According to the 9/11 Commission, no one in our government knew that an aircraft was approaching the Pentagon until 9:36,[15] so there was no time to shoot it down. But the Commission had been told by Mineta that the vice president knew at least ten minutes earlier, at 9:26. The 9/11 Commission dealt with Mineta's testimony in the same way it dealt with almost everything else that threatened its story—by simply ignoring it in the final report.[16]

This testimony by Mineta was a big threat not only because it indicated that there was knowledge of the approaching aircraft at least twelve minutes before the Pentagon was struck, but also because it implied that Cheney had issued stand-down orders. Mineta himself did not make this allegation, to be sure. He assumed, he said, that "the orders" mentioned by the young man were orders to have the plane shot down. Mineta's interpretation, however, does not fit with what actually happened: the aircraft was *not* shot down. That interpretation, moreover, would make the story unintelligible. If the orders had been to shoot down the aircraft if it got close to the Pentagon, the young man would have had no reason to ask if the orders still stood. His question makes sense only if the orders were to do something unexpected—*not* to shoot down the aircraft. The implication of Mineta's story is, therefore, that the attack on the Pentagon was desired.

Why Did the Scramble Order Go to Langley?

The same implication follows from another problem. Every part of the story about the fighters from Langley, we saw, is implausible. But an even more basic implausibility is the very claim that the order had to go to Langley because Andrews had no fighters on alert (158–59).

One reason to doubt that claim is simply that it is, in a word, preposterous. Andrews has primary responsibility for protecting the nation's capital (160). Can anyone seriously believe that Andrews, given the task of protecting the Pentagon, Air Force One, the White House, the houses of Congress, the Supreme Court, the U.S. Treasury Building, and so on, would not have fighters on alert at all times?

In addition to this *a priori* consideration, there is the empirical fact that the U.S. military's own Web site said at the time—although it was modified after 9/11 (163–64)—that several fighter jets were kept on alert at all times. The 121st Fighter Squadron of the 113th Fighter Wing was said to provide "capable and ready response forces for the District of Columbia in the event of natural disaster or civil emergency." The Marine Fighter Attack Squadron 321 was said to be supported by a reserve squadron providing "maintenance and supply functions necessary to maintain a force in readiness." And the District of Columbia Air National Guard was said "to provide combat units in the highest possible state of readiness" (163).

The assumption that Andrews did have fighters on alert on which NORAD could have called is supported, moreover, by a report given by Kyle Hence of 9/11 Citizens Watch about a telephone conversation he had with Donald Arias, the chief of public affairs for NORAD's Continental Region. After Arias had told Hence that "Andrews was not part of NORAD," Hence asked him "whether or not there were assets at Andrews that, though not technically part of NORAD, could have been tasked." Rather than answer, Arias hung up (161).

There are many reasons to conclude, therefore, that the claim that there were no fighters on alert at Andrews is a lie.

Some Implications

The realization that Andrews must have had fighters on alert has many implications. For one thing, if Andrews had fighters on alert, then it would seem likely that McGuire did too, so that fighters to protect New York City did not have to be scrambled from Otis Air Force Base on Cape Cod. National security expert (and former ABC producer) James Bamford says, moreover, that NEADS was also able to call on "alert fighter pilots at National Guard units at Burlington, Vermont; Atlantic City, New Jersey; . . . and Duluth, Minnesota" (258). If so, then there were at least seven bases from which NEADS could have scrambled fighters, not merely two, as the official story has it (158–59). And if that part of the official story is a lie, then it seems likely that that story as a whole is a lie. This conclusion will be reinforced by our examination of the Commission's treatment of United Airlines Flight 93.

THE COMMISSION'S TREATMENT OF UNITED AIRLINES FLIGHT 93

Flight 93 presented the 9/11 Commission with a different task. In relation to the previous flights, the Commission's task was to explain why the U.S. military did not intercept and shoot them down. With regard to Flight 93, the Commission had to convince us that the military did *not* shoot it down. It sought to do this not by refuting the evidence, which is considerable, that the airliner *was* shot down, but by simply constructing a new story intended to show that the U.S. military *could not* have shot down Flight 93.

The Military's Ignorance of the Hijacking

The Commission makes two major claims about Flight 93. The first one is that "By the time the military learned about the flight, it had crashed" (229). The centrality of this claim is shown by the fact that it is repeated, almost mantra-like, throughout the Commission's chapter.[17]

Incredible FAA Incompetence

The main support for this claim is provided by yet another tale of amazing incompetence by FAA officials. At 9:28, we are told, the traffic controller in Cleveland heard "sounds of possible screaming" and noticed that Flight 93 had descended 700 feet, but he did nothing. Four minutes later, at 9:32, he heard a voice saying, "We have a bomb on board." This controller, not being completely brain dead, finally notified his supervisor, who in turn notified FAA headquarters. However, four minutes later, at 9:36, Cleveland asked Herndon whether the military had been called and, the Commission claims, Herndon "told Cleveland that FAA personnel well above them in the chain of command had to make the decision to seek military assistance and were working on the issue" (227). To accept this account, we must believe that, on a day on which there had already been attacks by hijacked airliners, officials at FAA headquarters had to debate whether a hijacked airliner with a bomb on board was important enough to disturb the military. And we must believe that they were still debating this question thirteen minutes later, when, we are told, the following conversation between Herndon and FAA headquarters occurred:

> *Command Center*: Uh, do we want to think, uh, about scrambling aircraft?
> *FAA Headquarters*: Oh, God, I don't know.
> *Command Center*: Uh, that's a decision somebody's gonna have to make probably in the next ten minutes. (228)

But obviously the decision was that the military should *not* be disturbed, because another fourteen minutes later, at 10:03, when Flight 93 crashed in Pennsylvania, we are told, "No one from FAA headquarters [had yet] requested military assistance regarding United 93" (229). We are expected to believe, in other words, that FAA officials acted like complete idiots.

Worthless Teleconferences

In any case, besides arguing, by means of this tale of incredible incompetence, that the FAA never formally notified the military about Flight 93, the Commission argued that there was also no *informal* notification during any teleconference. In this case, not being able to argue that the teleconferences began too late, the Commission argued that they were worthless. Its summary statement said: "The FAA, the White House, and the Defense Department each initiated a multiagency teleconference before 9:30. [But] none of these teleconferences . . . included the right officials from both the FAA and the Defense Department" (211).

Let us begin with the teleconference initiated by the National Military Command Center. Why was it worthless for transmitting information from the FAA to the military? Because, we are told, Pentagon operators were unable to get the FAA on the line. This is a very implausible claim, especially since, we are told, the operators were able to reach everyone else (230–31). Also, as we saw earlier, Laura Brown of the FAA seemed to have independent knowledge about when this teleconference started—which suggests that the FAA *was* reached.

Why was the FAA-initiated teleconference equally worthless? The problem here, the Commission claimed, was that the officer at the NMCC said that "the information was of little value" so he did not pay attention (234).

However, even if we could believe that no one at the Pentagon was monitoring the call, Laura Brown's memo had said that in addition to the phone bridge set up by the FAA with the Pentagon, the "Air Force liaison to the FAA . . . established contact with NORAD on a separate line." So even if no one at the Pentagon was paying attention, the military still would have received the information. Her memo said, moreover, that "The FAA shared real-time information . . . about . . . all the flights of interest" (183), and the Commission itself agrees that by 9:34, FAA headquarters knew about the hijacking of Flight 93, so it was a "flight of interest." The Commission's claim is, therefore, flatly contradicted by this memo, which was read into the Commission's record.

What about the White House videoconference, which was run by Richard Clarke? The Commissioners say: "We do not know who from Defense participated" (210). But this claim is completely unbelievable. One problem is that it contradicts the Commission's assurance that "the right people" were not involved in this conference: How could they know this if they did not know who was involved? The main problem, however, is simply that the claim is absurd. Surely any number of people at the Pentagon could have told the Commissioners who participated in Clarke's videoconference. Simpler yet, they could have looked at Clarke's book, *Against All Enemies*, which became a national best seller during the Commission's hearings. It clearly states that the participants from the Pentagon were Secretary of Defense Donald Rumsfeld and General Richard Myers, acting chair of the Joint Chiefs of Staff (210–12).[18] It also reports that the FAA was represented by its top official, Jane Garvey. And if these were not "the right people," who would have been?

The Commission's attempt to prove that the military could not have learned about Flight 93 from this videoconference is even more explicitly contradicted by Clarke, who reports that at about 9:35, Jane Garvey reported on a number of "potential hijacks," which included "United 93 over Pennsylvania" (232). Therefore, more than twenty-five minutes before Flight 93 crashed, according to Clarke, both Myers and Rumsfeld heard from the head of the FAA that Flight 93 was considered a potential hijack.

The Commission's tales about FAA incompetence and worthless teleconferences are, therefore, directly contradicted by Laura Brown's memo and Richard Clarke's book. Their combined testimony implies that the Commission's main claim—that "[b]y the time the military learned about the flight, it had crashed"—is a bald-faced lie.

Cheney's Arrival at the Shelter Conference Room

To recall where we are: The Commission's first major claim is that the U.S. military could not have shot down Flight 93 because it did not know about the hijacking of this flight until after it crashed at 10:03. The Commission's second main point, to which we now turn, is that the authorization to shoot planes down was not issued until several minutes *after* 10:03.

In support of this point, the Commission claims that Vice President Cheney, who was known to have issued the shoot-down authorization from the shelter conference room under the White House, did not get down there until about almost 10:00, "perhaps at 9:58" (241). This claim, however, is doubly problematic.

One problem is that this claim is not supported by any documentation. The Commission says that the Secret Service ordered Cheney to go downstairs "just before 9:36"; that Cheney entered the underground corridor at 9:37; that he then, instead of going straight to the shelter conference room at the other end of the corridor, spent some twenty minutes calling the president and watching television coverage of the aftermath of the strike on the Pentagon (241). This timeline is said to be based on Secret Service alarm data showing that the Vice President entered the underground corridor at 9:37. However, *The 9/11 Commission Report* then says that this "alarm data . . . is no longer retrievable" (244). We must, therefore, simply take the Commission's claim on faith.

And this is very difficult, since the Commission's claim is contradicted by every prior report. A White House photographer, who was an eyewitness, and various newspapers, including the *New York Times*, said that Cheney went below shortly after 9:00. Richard Clarke's account suggests that Cheney went below before 9:15 (242). Even Cheney himself, speaking on *Meet the Press* five days after 9/11, indicated that he was taken downstairs at about that time (243). The Commission, showing its usual disdain for evidence that contradicts its story, makes no mention of any of these reports.

The most dramatic contradiction of the Commission's timeline was provided by Norman Mineta. In open testimony to the Commission itself, he said, as we saw earlier, that when he got to the underground shelter at 9:20, Cheney was already there and fully in charge. The Commission, insisting that Cheney did not get there until almost 10:00, simply omitted any mention of this testimony in its Final Report. But Mineta's testimony is still available for anyone to read.[19]

We can say with a very high level of confidence, therefore, that the Commission's account is a lie.

The Time of the Shoot-Down Authorization

The same is true of the Commission's claim that the shoot-down authorization was not issued until after 10:10.

In making this claim, the Commission tells a tale of yet another incredible error made by the FAA. Flight 93, according to the Commission, crashed at 10:03 (249–50). And yet sometime between 10:10 and 10:15, the Commission claims, the FAA told the military that Flight 93 was still headed toward Washington and was, in fact, only eighty miles out. Once again, FAA headquarters managed to call the military only when it had false information. In any case, we are told, the military requested permission to engage an aircraft, and Cheney immediately gave the authorization (237). The implication is that the military could not possibly have shot down Flight 93, since it had crashed about ten minutes earlier.

However, the Commission's new timeline is again contradicted by several previous reports.

First, although the Commission says that Richard Clarke did not receive the shoot-down authorization until 10:25, Clarke himself says that he received it some thirty-five or forty minutes earlier, at 9:45 or 9:50 (240).

Second, the story of Cheney's giving permission to engage an aircraft that was eighty miles out originally appeared in stories published shortly after 9/11. In these stories, the permission was given earlier, when Flight 93 truly was still aloft, after which an F-16 was sent in pursuit (239).

That original account is supported, moreover, by several reports stating that prior to crashing, Flight 93 was being tailed by U.S. military fighters. One such report came from CBS; another came from a flight controller who had ignored an order not to talk to the media; and one such report even came from Deputy Secretary of Defense Paul Wolfowitz (238–39). Evidently the Commission felt that if it could ignore statements from the secretary of transportation and even the vice president, it could also ignore a statement by the deputy secretary of defense.

In any case, the Commission's timeline, besides being contradicted by all those reports, is also contradicted by James Bamford's account, which is based on a transcript from ABC News. According to this account, Cheney's authorization was transmitted to Colonel Marr at NEADS, who then "sent out word to air traffic controllers to instruct fighter pilots to destroy the United jetliner." Marr reportedly said, "United Airlines Flight 93 will not be allowed to reach Washington, D.C." (238). But the Commission simply tells its new tale as if this report had never been broadcast.

The Commission's account is contradicted, finally, by reports that the shoot-down actually occurred. Major Daniel Nash, one of the two F-15 pilots sent to New York City from Otis, later reported that after he returned to base, he was told that a military F-16 had shot down an airliner in Pennsylvania (239).

That rumor was so widespread that during General Myers's interview with the Senate Armed Services Committee on September 13, 2001, chairman Carl Levin said that "there have been statements that the aircraft that crashed in Pennsylvania was shot down," adding: "Those stories continue to exist" (151).

Besides ignoring all these reports, the Commission also ignored reports from people who lived near the spot where the airliner came down. These reports spoke of missilelike noises, sightings of a small military airplane, debris falling from the airliner miles from its crash site, and the discovery of part of an engine far from the site (151).

There is, in sum, an enormous amount of evidence suggesting that the FAA did notify the military about Flight 93; that Cheney went down to the underground shelter about forty-five minutes earlier than the Commission claims; that he gave the shoot-down authorization about twenty-five minutes earlier than the Commission claims; and that military jets went after and shot down Flight 93. It would appear that if some committee had set out to construct a fable about Flight 93, every part of which could be easily falsified, it could not have improved on the Commission's tale. And yet our mainstream media have not reported any of these obvious falsehoods.

SUMMARY AND CONCLUSION: THE PORTRAIT OF FAA INCOMPETENCE

The Commission, as we have seen, has attempted to exonerate the military for its failure to prevent the attacks of 9/11. According to the Commission, accounts suggesting that the military was notified in time to respond "overstated the FAA's ability to provide the military with timely and useful information that morning" (255). In its effort to correct that alleged overstatement, the Commission gave us a picture of incredible incompetence at every level of the FAA. We read of flight controllers who, instead of following instructions to treat every possible emergency as an actual one, would not respond after seeing two or even all three of the standard signs of a hijacking. We read of controllers who told the military that airplanes that had already crashed were still aloft and headed toward Washington. We read of officials at FAA headquarters who consistently refused to call the military—unless, of course, the airplane to be reported was merely a phantom.

This portrait of rampant incompetence by FAA officials is contradicted by several facts. One such fact is NORAD's timeline of September 18, 2001, which indicates that the FAA responded slowly but not nearly as slowly as the Commission now claims. A second fact is Laura Brown's memo of 2003, which says that the FAA was on the telephone with the military from about 8:50 on, talking about all flights of interest.

A third fact is that the FAA was called on to carry out an unprecedented operation that day: grounding all the aircraft in the country. And yet, the Commission itself says, the FAA "execut[ed] that unprecedented order flawlessly" (272–73). Is it plausible that FAA personnel, on the same day that they carried out an unprecedented task so flawlessly, would have failed so miserably with a task—asking the military to intercept problematic flights—that they had been carrying out about 100 times a year (140)?[20]

It would seem, therefore, that the first chapter of *The 9/11 Commission Report* is one long lie. As I have shown elsewhere, moreover, that is true of the report as a whole.[21] In chapter 5, I will discuss several more lies of omission and distortion. Then, in chapter 6, I will also explain why it is not surprising that the 9/11 Commission consciously participated in a cover-up of the fact that 9/11 was a false-flag operation.

Chapter 5

Bush Administration Responsibility for 9/11

From a Prima Facie *to a Conclusive Case*

After the attacks of 9/11, I accepted the blowback thesis, according to which the attacks were payback for U.S. foreign policy. As I explained in the preface, however, I eventually learned of Paul Thompson's 9/11 timeline, which contains an enormous number of reports, all from mainstream sources, that contradict the official account. This started a process that led me to publish *The New Pearl Harbor*, which summarized much of the evidence that had been discovered by previous researchers—evidence, I concluded, that provided a "strong *prima facie* case for official complicity."[1]

In a criminal trial, once the prosecution has presented its initial case, the defense asks the judge for a dismissal on the grounds that a *prima facie* case for guilt has not been presented. However, if the judge declares that such a case *has* been made, then the defense must rebut the various elements in the prosecution's case. The defense cannot simply offer another theory while ignoring the prosecution's case. If the defense fails to offer a convincing rebuttal, the *prima facie* case is presumed to be *conclusive*.

The Bush administration responded to the charges against it as a defense attorney would, declaring them too outrageous to be taken seriously. President

Bush himself advised people, perhaps especially reporters, not to tolerate "outrageous conspiracy theories."[2] What the president really meant is that people should not tolerate any outrageous conspiracy theories except his own, according to which nineteen Arab Muslims defeated the most powerful and sophisticated defense system in history and also defeated the laws of physics, bringing down three steel-frame buildings in a way that perfectly mimicked controlled demolition.

In any case, what was needed at that stage was someone to play the role of the judge, determining, from an impartial perspective, whether a *prima facie* case for the guilt of the Bush-Cheney administration had been made. This role should have been played by the press. But the mainstream press instead offered itself as a mouthpiece for the administration's conspiracy theory.

The fact that the president was finally forced to appoint a commission to investigate 9/11 gave many people hope that it would play the role of impartial judge. Indeed, this is how the 9/11 Commission presented itself. The Commission sought, according to its Chairman Thomas Kean and its Vice Chairman Lee Hamilton in their preface, "to be independent, impartial, thorough, and nonpartisan." Many readers of *The 9/11 Commission Report* have assumed that it indeed played the role of an impartial jury, simply evaluating the evidence for the competing conspiracy theories and deciding which one was more strongly supported.

In reality, however, the Commission took the role of the prosecution. Simply assuming the truth of the Bush administration's account of 9/11, the Commission devoted much of the report to Osama bin Laden, al-Qaeda, and the nineteen alleged hijackers, as if their responsibility for the attacks were unquestionable. In so doing, the Commission, far from examining evidence for the theory that 9/11 was an inside job, did not even mention this possibility.

The fact that the Commission was so one-sided in its approach is not surprising in light of its personnel. The Commission consisted of the ten commissioners, whom we saw on television during their public hearings; a seventy-five-person staff, which carried out most of the work; and an executive director, who guided the work of the staff.

The Commission's lack of impartiality can be partly explained by the fact that Chairman Kean, most of the other commissioners, and at least half of the members of the staff had potential conflicts of interest.[3]

The most serious problem, however, is that the executive director, Philip Zelikow, was essentially a member of the Bush-Cheney administration. This characterization of Zelikow is supported by many facts. He had worked with Condoleezza Rice on the National Security Council in the administration of George H. W. Bush. Then, when the Republicans were out of office during the Clinton administration, Zelikow and Rice coauthored a book. Rice then, as national security advisor for President George W. Bush, had Zelikow help make the transition to the new National Security Council. After that,

Zelikow was appointed to the President's Foreign Intelligence Advisory Board. And, most significantly, Rice brought him on to be the principal drafter of the Bush administration's 2002 version of the *National Security Strategy of the United States of America* (*NSS 2002*).[4] This document is discussed in the following chapter. For now, suffice it to say that it was in *NSS 2002* that the Bush-Cheney administration's post-9/11 imperialism first became the official policy of the U.S. government. Zelikow was, therefore, the White House's man inside the 9/11 Commission. As executive director, however, Zelikow directed the staff, which did virtually all the work of the Commission.[5] Zelikow was in position, therefore, to decide which topics would be investigated and which ones not. The staff was divided into eight investigative teams and, one disgruntled member reportedly said at the time, seven of these eight teams were "completely controlled by Zelikow." More generally, this staff member said, "Zelikow is calling the shots. He's skewing the investigation and running it his own way."[6]

So the 9/11 Commission was, it can be said without much exaggeration, the White House investigating itself. With Zelikow "calling the shots," the 9/11 Commission was not going to ask whether this administration had orchestrated 9/11 precisely for the sake of creating a national mood in which its post-9/11 imperialistic policy could be enacted. More about this in the next chapter.

For now the main point is that, in taking the role of the prosecution for the Bush administration's brief against al-Qaeda, the Commission, under Zelikow's leadership, implicitly took the role of the defense for the Bush administration. A good defense, as mentioned earlier, would involve a rebuttal of the various charges constitutive of the *prima facie* case against the Bush-Cheney administration—a case that I had summarized in *The New Pearl Harbor*. Accordingly, an important question to ask about *The 9/11 Commission Report* is: How effectively did it rebut this case?

In my second book, *The 9/11 Commission Report: Omissions and Distortions*, I showed that the Commission did *not* rebut this *prima facie* case. Rather, it distorted some of the relevant evidence constituting this case and simply ignored the rest. I have elsewhere summarized 115 omissions and distortions that I discussed in this book.[7] I discuss here a few distortions and then, referring back to points made in previous chapters, mention a number of omissions.

DISTORTIONS

The distinction between omissions and distortions is important. When the Commission distorted evidence, it did so to remove grounds for concluding that 9/11 was an inside job. The fact that the Commission sometimes engaged in this tactic shows that it was not averse to trying to rebut such evidence. I will give three examples of such distortion.

The Core of the Twin Towers

One of the main problems with the official theory of the collapses of the Twin Towers, as we saw in chapter 3, is that it cannot explain why the collapse of each building was a *total* collapse, leaving a pile of rubble only a few stories high. The chief problem resulted from the fact that the core of each tower contained forty-seven massive steel columns. According to the theory that was dominant at the time *The 9/11 Commission Report* was written, the floors above the point of impact fell on the floors below, after which each building "pancaked" all the way down. But if that had been what occurred, the core columns would still have been sticking up hundreds of feet in the air. The 9/11 Commission provided an implicit solution to this problem, as we saw, by saying that "[t]he interior core of the buildings was a hollow steel shaft, in which elevators and stairwells were grouped."[8] The distortion was quite extreme, denying the existence of the massive core columns.

Cheney's Timeline

The behavior of Vice President Cheney was suspect with regard to both the strike on the Pentagon and the crash of Flight 93. Secretary of Transportation Norman Mineta had, in testimony to the Commission, reported on an episode that could be interpreted to mean that Cheney, while in charge in the Presidential Emergency Operations Center under the White House, had given a stand-down order so as to allow the Pentagon to be struck. And there was strong evidence that after Cheney gave the shoot-down authorization, Flight 93 was shot down by a U.S. military plane.

The 9/11 Commission, as we saw in chapter 4, implicitly sought to rebut both suspicions by providing a new timeline for Cheney's actions. The Commission claimed that he did not enter the shelter conference room until almost 10:00 that morning, although all previous testimony, including Norman Mineta's, had him in there about forty-five minutes earlier. The Commission then claimed that Cheney did not give the shoot-down authorization until after 10:10, hence after the crash of Flight 93, even though all previous evidence, including Richard Clarke's testimony, had the order being received considerably before 10:00. The implicit twofold message of the Commission's new timeline is that Cheney could not have given either a stand-down order in relation to the Pentagon or a shoot-down order in relation to Flight 93.

Unusual Purchases of Put Options

A third example, not discussed earlier, involves an extraordinarily high volume of "put options" purchased in the three days before 9/11. To buy put options for a particular company is to bet that its stock price will go down.

These purchases included two, and only two, airlines—United and American—the two airlines used in the attacks. The unusual purchases also included Morgan Stanley Dean Witter, which occupied twenty-two stories of the World Trade Center. The price of these shares did, of course, plummet after 9/11, resulting in profits of tens of millions of dollars for the purchasers of the put options. As the *San Francisco Chronicle* said, these unusual purchases raise "suspicions that the investors . . . had advance knowledge of the strikes."[9] These purchases raised such suspicions because they suggested that those who made the purchases knew that United and American airliners were going to be used in attacks on the World Trade Center.

The 9/11 Commission tried to show that these suspicions were unfounded. Its most important claim was that the purchases of put options for United Airlines do not show that anyone other than al-Qaeda had foreknowledge of the attacks, because 95 percent of these options were purchased by "[a] single U.S.-based institutional investor with no conceivable ties to al Qaeda."[10] But the Commission, making this argument, simply assumed the truth of the official theory, according to which al-Qaeda, and only al-Qaeda, planned and knew about the attacks. Accordingly, runs the Commission's logic, if the investors who purchased the United Airlines put options had no ties with al-Qaeda, they could not possibly have had insider knowledge. They were simply lucky.

The Commission thereby distorted the issue at issue—namely, whether people other than al-Qaeda knew about the attacks in advance. It was only through this distortion that the Commission could pretend to have rebutted the claim that the unusual purchases of put options prior to 9/11 disproved the claim that no one other than members of al-Qaeda knew of attacks in advance.

The fact that *The 9/11 Commission Report* contains such distortions is important, I repeat, because they suggest that the Commission, when it thought it could make a persuasive case against some part of the evidence that conflicts with the official story, would do so. Seen in this light, the fact that the *Report* usually dealt with such evidence by simply omitting it is revealing, because each omission can be taken as an implicit admission by the authors of the *Report* that they could *not* offer a persuasive rebuttal to the evidence, even through the use of distortion. I next give several examples of such omissions.

OMISSIONS

The Alleged Hijackers and Osama bin Laden

The Commission did not deal with any of the points made in chapter 1 about the alleged hijackers, such as the fact that they did not appear to be devout Muslims; the fact that some of them are reportedly still alive; the fact that their names are not on the publicly released flight manifests; and the fact that the evidence allegedly found in Atta's luggage appears to have been planted. Nor did it discuss the various kinds of evidence suggesting that the Bush administration's relation to Osama bin Laden was other than it has been portrayed to be.

The Strike on the Pentagon

The Commission also failed to deal with any of the problems in the official account of the Pentagon, such as the fact that Hani Hanjour did not have the ability to perform the feats required, that foreign terrorists would not have chosen the west wing to strike, that neither the damage nor the debris appeared to be consistent with a strike by a Boeing 757, and that evidence was confiscated and covered up. The Commission also failed to subpoena, or even to mention the existence of, the FBI-confiscated videos, which could clear up the question of whether the aircraft that hit the Pentagon was a Boeing 757.

The President and His Secret Service

The Commission, as we saw, made no effort to rebut the charge that the behavior of President Bush and his Secret Service agents, while they were at the school in Florida that morning, implied foreknowledge that they would not be attacked. Within the framework of the official story—that the strikes on the World Trade Center were surprise attacks—the behavior of these Secret Service agents constituted a gross dereliction of duty. The failure of the 9/11 Commission to press this issue provides a striking piece of evidence that its mission was not to investigate what really happened, but to aid the cover-up.

The Destruction of the World Trade Center

The Commission failed to deal with a wide range of facts pointing to the conclusion that the destruction of the World Trade Center had to have been an inside job. These facts include the dozens of testimonies in the 9/11 oral histories indicating that the Twin Towers were brought down by explosives; the fact that the collapses of the Twin Towers and Building 7 had over ten characteristics of controlled demolitions; the fact that some officials evidently had foreknowledge of the collapses; and the fact that the steel was removed before it could be properly examined. The most remarkable omission was the failure even to mention the fact that Building 7 collapsed, which can be taken as the Commission's implicit concession that it, like FEMA, could not explain this collapse within the framework of the official theory.

The Failure to Intercept

Although the Commission implicitly attempted to rebut the claim that the military had sufficient time to intercept the hijacked airliners, this attempt is filled with problems. One problem is the failure to explain why, if NORAD's accounts of Flights 175 and 77 were false, as the Commission now says, these accounts were given and allowed to pass as the official story for almost three years. Another problem is that the Commission, to make its accounts of the strike on the Pentagon and the crash of Flight 93 seem plausible to the general reader, had to delete Laura Brown's memo and Norman Mineta's testimony.

CONCLUSION

The 9/11 Commission, under the direction of Bush administration insider Philip Zelikow, had the opportunity to rebut the *prima facie* case against the Bush administration. But as the above illustrations of both omissions and distortions show, it completely failed to do so. As a result, the *prima facie* case that the Bush administration orchestrated the attacks of 9/11 remained unrefuted. The publication of *The 9/11 Commission Report* should, accordingly, be recognized as a decisive event: the moment at which the *prima facie* case against the Bush administration became a *conclusive* case.

What is needed now is for the American people to be informed of this development, which is most important, given the fact that the official story about 9/11 has provided the pretext for most of the nefarious policies of the Bush-Cheney administration. Although the mainstream press should have provided this information, it has failed to do so. There is, however, another means through which this information could be conveyed—through the churches. In the second part of this book, I give reasons why Christians should take the lead in exposing the truth about 9/11.

PART TWO
A CHRISTIAN CRITIQUE OF 9/11 AND AMERICAN IMPERIALISM

Chapter 6

Imperial Motives for a "New Pearl Harbor"

This second part of the book begins with a dimension of the *prima facie* case against the Bush-Cheney administration that was not discussed in the first part. This is the fact that members of this administration had reasons to desire attacks of the sort that occurred on 9/11—attacks that could be portrayed as originating in the Arab-Muslim world. This point is important because in any criminal case, the prosecution must show that the accused party had the motive, means, and opportunity to commit the crime. The first part of the book provided reasons to believe that the Bush-Cheney administration, and only it, had both the means and the opportunity to bring about the attacks of 9/11. The present chapter shows that it also had sufficient motives.

This chapter is placed here, in the part of the book containing a Christian critique of 9/11 and American imperialism, because of the nature of these motives. By providing evidence that the motives behind the orchestration of 9/11 were *imperial* motives, this chapter begins this critique.

The effect of 9/11, in most general terms, was to allow the agenda developed in the 1990s by neoconservatives—often called simply "neocons"—to be implemented. There is wide agreement on this point. For example, Stefan Halper and

Jonathan Clarke, who are conservatives but not *neo*conservatives, say that 9/11 allowed the "preexisting ideological agenda" of the neoconservatives to be "taken off the shelf . . . and relabeled as *the* response to terror."[1] Stephen Sniegoski writes that "it was only the traumatic effects of the 9/11 terrorism that enabled the agenda of the neocons to become the policy of the United States of America."[2]

Can we infer from this effect that the hope to have this agenda fulfilled was the motive behind 9/11? Not necessarily. One of the basic principles of criminal investigations, however, is the question: who benefits? Those who most benefited from the crime are usually the most likely suspects. An answer to that question cannot, of course, by itself be used as proof of the suspects' guilt. The prosecution must also show that the suspects had the means and the opportunity to commit the crime. The prosecution must also present some evidence that the suspects actually committed the crime—at least *indirect* evidence, perhaps by showing that they were the only ones who *could* have done it.

Abundant evidence of this type has, however, already been presented. All that remained after the first part was the question of plausible motive. In this chapter, accordingly, I am simply, on the assumption that 9/11 was orchestrated by members of the Bush-Cheney administration, asking what their motive might have been. In most general terms, I suggest, this motive was to produce a context in which their radical agenda could be implemented.

What *is* this radical agenda? It is, in essence, that the United States should use its military supremacy to establish an empire that includes the whole world—a global *Pax Americana*. There are three major means to this end. One of these is to make U.S. military supremacy over other nations even greater, so that it is completely beyond challenge. This goal is to be achieved by increasing the money devoted to military purposes, then using this money to complete the "revolution in military affairs" made possible by the emergence of the information age. The second major way to achieve a global *Pax Americana* is to announce and implement a doctrine of preventive-preemptive war, usually for the sake of bringing about "regime change" in countries regarded as hostile to U.S. interests and values. The third means toward the goal of universal empire is to use this new doctrine to gain control of the world's oil, especially in the Middle East, most especially Iraq.

In discussing these ideas, I will include recognitions by some commentators that without 9/11, the various dimensions of this agenda could not have been implemented.

NEOCONSERVATIVES AND GLOBAL EMPIRE

The "neo" in the term "neoconservative" is a remnant of the fact that the first-generation neoconservatives, such as Irving Kristol and Norman Podhoretz, had moved to the right after having been members of the left. Kristol, often called "the godfather of neoconservatism," famously defined neoconservatives as liberals who had been "mugged by reality." No such change, however, has characterized most of the second-generation neocons, who came to dominate the movement in the 1990s. As Gary Dorrien says in *Imperial Designs: Neoconservatism and the New Pax Americana*, "The new neocons had never been progressives of any kind."[3] The term "neoconservatism" is, in any case, used here to refer strictly to an ideology, not to any biographical facts about those who hold this ideology.

I mean "biographical facts" to include ethnicity. Although many of the prominent neoconservatives have been Jewish, leading some people to think that Jewishness is a necessary condition for being a neoconservative, this is not so. As Dorrien points out, "A significant number of prominent neocons were not Jews."[4]

This discussion has its primary importance in relation to Dick Cheney and Donald Rumsfeld. If neoconservatism is understood to be entirely a matter of ideology, not also partly a matter of biography, then there is no reason not to consider Cheney and Rumsfeld neocons. As former neocon Michael Lind, says: "Neoconservatism is an ideology, like paleoconservatism and libertarianism, and Rumsfeld and Dick . . . Cheney are full-fledged neocons, . . . even though they are not Jewish and were never liberals or leftists."[5]

Neoconservatism in its early decades was a multifaceted phenomenon, but the focus here is on its foreign policy, which was originally oriented around opposition to Communism. This fact meant that the end of the Cold War produced a crisis for neocons. In 1991, after the fall of the Berlin Wall, Podhoretz said that he was not sure what "America's purpose should be now that the threat of Communism . . . had been decisively eliminated." Five years later, he even published a eulogy to the neoconservative movement, declaring it dead.[6]

Unipolarity

Other neocons, however, believed that they had a new cause to champion. Already in 1986, Irving Kristol argued that the United States needed to move toward a foreign policy of "global unilateralism." But that would be difficult, he pointed out, as long as America is "an imperial power with no imperial self-definition."[7] The new cause was to shape this new self-definition, thereby getting Americans ready to accept a policy of global unilateralism.

As soon as the Cold War ended, this cause was taken up by others. At the close of 1989, Charles Krauthammer, one of the best-known neocon columnists, published a piece entitled "Universal Dominion," in which he argued that America should work for "a qualitatively new outcome—a unipolar world."[8] In 1990, he argued that unipolarity has already arrived and that the United States, being the "unchallenged superpower," should act unilaterally. Saying that "the alternative to unipolarity is chaos," Krauthammer explained what unipolarity requires of the United States: "unashamedly laying down the rules of world order and being prepared to enforce them."[9] The following year, in an argument for a "robust interventionism," he said of this unipolar world: "We Americans should like it—and exploit it."[10]

The 1992 Defense Planning Guidance

The first effort to turn such thinking into official policy came in 1992, which was the last year of the presidency of George H. W. Bush and hence also the end of Dick Cheney's tenure as secretary of defense. Before leaving office, Cheney had Paul Wolfowitz, the undersecretary of defense for policy, prepare—with the help of his top assistant, Lewis "Scooter" Libby—a draft of the Pentagon's "Defense Planning Guidance" (DPG).[11] Stating that America's "first objective is to prevent the re-emergence of a new rival," this DPG draft was, in Andrew Bacevich's appraisal, "in effect a blueprint for permanent American global hegemony."[12]

This draft produced, after portions of a leaked copy were published in the *New York Times* and the *Washington Post*,[13] an outpouring of criticism. The ideas did get some support, especially from neoconservative publications such as the *Wall Street Journal*, which praised the draft's plan for a "Pax Americana."[14] But most of the reaction was critical. Senator Alan Cranston complained that the Bush administration was seeking to make the United States "the one, the only main honcho on the world block, the global Big Enchilada."[15] Senator Robert Byrd said that the document's stance seemed to be—in a statement that proved to be prescient—"We love being the sole remaining superpower in the world and we want so much to remain that way that we are willing to put at risk the basic health of our economy and well-being of our people to do so."[16]

Seeking to calm the waters, especially because it was an election year, the administration of George H. W. Bush distanced itself from this draft, depicting it, in Bacevich's words, "as the musings of an insignificant lower-tier appointee acting without official sanction."[17] Although Wolfowitz would refer to it as "my 1992 memorandum" many years later,[18] he claimed at the time that he had not seen it.[19] Cheney also claimed not to have seen it, even though one long section began by acknowledging "definitive guidance from the Secretary of Defense."

This latter fact has, incidentally, been pointed out by David Armstrong, who calls this draft an early version of Cheney's "Plan . . . to rule the world."[20] Although this draft came to be known as "the Wolfowitz plan," it is important to recognize that it was Cheney who, in Dorrien's words, "hatched the original unipolarist blueprint in 1992."[21] Indeed, as Nicholas Lemann has reported in the *New Yorker*, the DPG draft resulted from a secret team that Cheney had set up in the Pentagon "to think about American foreign policy after the Cold War."[22]

The recognition that this unipolarist blueprint was inspired by Cheney is important in light of the unprecedented power that he would exercise in the second Bush administration. As presidential historian Douglas Brinkley would say in 2002: "Cheney is unique in American history. . . . He is the vortex in the White House on foreign policymaking. Everything comes through him."[23]

In any case, Cheney, under pressure from the White House in 1992, had the document significantly rewritten by Libby, in language more acceptable at the time. For example, whereas the first draft spoke of *spurning* collective action through the United Nations, this new version spoke of *strengthening* the United Nations.[24] Cheney put an end to this brief public debate about the wisdom of a unipolarist foreign policy by having this softer version, which was later published,[25] leaked to the press.[26]

The 1990s and PNAC

This rewriting did not mean, however, that the ideas were dropped by Cheney and other neoconservatives. Indeed, after the election was over, Cheney, before leaving office, issued another revision, in which some of the neo-imperial language was restored.[27] Then Zalmay Khalilzad, who had joined Cheney's team in 1991, put out a book early in 1995 entitled *From Containment to Global Leadership? America and the World after the Cold War*, which expresses quite forthrightly the idea of preventing, by military force if necessary, the rise of any rival power.[28] In 1996, Robert Kagan, "who emerged in the 1990s as perhaps the most influential neocon foreign policy analyst,"[29] argued that the United States should use its military strength "actively to maintain a world order which both supports and rests upon American hegemony."[30] In 1998, Kagan and William Kristol, who in 1995 had founded the *Weekly Standard* (which quickly became the main organ of neocon thinking), wrote that unless America takes charge, we will have "world chaos, and a dangerous twenty-first century."[31] In January 2001, as the Bush-Cheney administration was ready to come to power, Kagan criticized "Clinton and his advisers" for "having the stomach only to be halfway imperialists."[32]

It is important to understand the development of this neoconservative ideology, given the fact that after 9/11, the neocon agenda became the agenda of the United States. As Halper and Clarke said in 2004, "if one wishes to understand the direction of American foreign policy today, one must read what neoconservatives were writing ten years or more ago."[33]

The most important development within the neocon movement in the 1990s was William Kristol's founding, in 1997, of a unipolarist think tank called the Project for the New American Century (PNAC).[34] Closely related to the American Enterprise Institute ideologically and even physically and financially, PNAC differs primarily in focusing entirely on foreign policy.[35] In its "Statement of Principles," PNAC called for "American global leadership," asking whether the

United States has "the resolve to shape a new century favorable to American principles and interests."[36]

In September 2000, just four months before the Bush-Cheney administration took office, PNAC published a seventy-six-page document entitled *Rebuilding America's Defenses* (*RAD*). Saying that "at present the United States faces no global rival," *RAD* declared that "America's grand strategy should aim to preserve and extend this advantageous position" and thereby "to preserve and enhance [the] 'American peace.'" To "enhance" the "American peace" means, of course, to increase the size of the American empire. Explicitly referring back to the Cheney-Wolfowitz Defense Planning Guidance draft of 1992, *RAD* said that "the basic tenets of the DPG, in our judgment, remain sound." The continuity between the two documents is no surprise, partly because Libby and Wolfowitz are listed as participants in the production of this 2000 document.[37]

What is said in PNAC's documents is highly important because many of PNAC's early members, including Elliott Abrams, John Bolton, Eliot Cohen, Paula Dobriansky, Zalmay Khalilzad, Richard Perle, Peter W. Rodman, James Woolsey, and—most significantly—Cheney, Libby, Rumsfeld, and Wolfowitz, became central members of the new Bush administration. PNAC neocons thereby took key positions in the vice president's office, the Pentagon, and the (only semi-independent) Defense Policy Board. They did so well primarily because of Cheney, who was put in charge of the transition team, and secondarily because of Rumsfeld, after Cheney chose him to head the Pentagon.[38]

I should perhaps explicitly add that it is probably only the neocons in office, and even only some of them, who should be suspected of involvement in the planning for 9/11. To say that 9/11 allowed the agenda of the neocons in general to be implemented does not imply that many or even any neocons outside the government were involved in the planning for, or even had advance knowledge of, the attacks of 9/11. About eight months after 9/11, for example, William Kristol and Robert Kagan wrote pieces urging the Bush-Cheney administration to undertake an investigation to see if the attacks might have been prevented. Dorrien reports that this call "earned a sharp rebuke from Cheney; the Bush administration had no intention of allowing an investigation on that subject."[39]

The neocons had during the 1990s provided an agenda for a more militarist, unipolarist, imperialist foreign policy and had helped shape a cultural-political context in which the implementation of this agenda would be easier than it otherwise would have been. The attacks of 9/11 allowed this agenda to be implemented. From these facts, however, we cannot legitimately infer that the various neocons whose writings are discussed here were in on the plans for 9/11. This inference can be made only about those who had become part of the new administration in 2001, and probably only some of them, especially Cheney and Rumsfeld.

9/11 and Empire Talk

In any case, with the new administration in place, neocon commentators such as Krauthammer became even more explicit and exuberant about the use of America's power for imperial ends. Mocking Clinton for being concerned to be "a good international citizen" and praising Bush for understanding that "the U.S. can reshape, indeed remake, reality on its own," Krauthammer said: "America is no mere international citizen. It is the dominant power in the world, more dominant than any since Rome. Accordingly, America is in a position to reshape norms . . . and create new realities. How? By unapologetic and implacable demonstrations of will."[40]

However, it was not until after 9/11, and especially after the devastating assault on Afghanistan, that the neocon effort to get Americans to accept an imperial self-definition started showing widespread success. Early in 2002, Krauthammer, having noticed the difference, said, "People are coming out of the closet on the word 'empire.'" Driving home his main message, Krauthammer added that Americans needed to face up to the responsibilities entailed by the fact that they are now "undisputed masters of the world."[41]

A year later, this unilateralist idea was voiced in the *Atlantic Monthly* by neocon Robert Kaplan, who argued that America should use its power unilaterally to "manage an unruly world," leaving behind "the so-called international community," especially the United Nations, with its "antiquated power arrangement."[42]

9/11 and the 9/11 wars—meaning those that have been justified by appeal to the attacks of 9/11[43]—have resulted in empire talk beyond the circles of neocons. Early in 2002, after the American assault on Afghanistan, Paul Kennedy, who had fifteen years earlier been predicting America's decline as a great power,[44] declared, "Nothing has ever existed like this disparity of power." Describing America's empire as the greatest of all time, he said: "Charlemagne's empire was merely Western European in reach. The Roman empire stretched farther afield, but there was another great empire in Persia, and a larger one in China. There is, therefore, no comparison."[45]

A very important development that same year was the publication of Andrew Bacevich's *American Empire*, which closes by saying that the question before Americans is "not whether the United States has become an imperial power" but only "what sort of empire they intend theirs to be."[46] Bacevich himself, while a conservative, strongly distances himself from the imperial agenda of the neocons.[47]

But it is their agenda, not Bacevich's cautionary critique, that has thus far determined the "sort of empire" that the United States has become in the twenty-first century. And it was 9/11 that allowed this agenda to be implemented. As Claes Ryn says, the neoconservatives "have taken full advantage of the nation's outrage over 9/11 to advance their already fully formed drive for empire."[48]

MILITARY OMNIPOTENCE

The tool for fulfilling this drive for empire, the neocons have always held, is military power. To a great extent, in fact, the neoconservative movement began in reaction to the widespread view after the Vietnam War that American military power should never again be used for imperialistic purposes. In the early 1980s, rejecting the left's conclusion that force had become "obsolete as an instrument of American political purposes," Norman Podhoretz argued that military power constitutes "the indispensable foundation of U.S. foreign policy," adding that "without it, nothing else we do will be effective."[49] The Cheney-Wolfowitz DPG of 1992, having said that "our first objective is to prevent the re-emergence of a new rival," added that "we must maintain the mechanisms for deterring potential competitors from even aspiring to a regional or global role." These "mechanisms" referred, of course, to various kinds of military power.

Space and Full Spectrum Dominance

The U.S. military in the 1990s developed concepts to attain the kind of military superiority envisaged in this document. One of these concepts was "Full Spectrum Dominance," which, says Bacevich, is the attempt "to achieve something approaching omnipotence."[50] He is here referring to a document entitled "Joint Vision 2010," which was first published by the U.S. Joint Chiefs of Staff in 1996. Defining "Full Spectrum Dominance" as "the capability to dominate an opponent across the range of military operations," this document says that it "will be the key characteristic we seek for our Armed Forces in the 21st century."[51] Given the fact that the U.S. military was already dominant on the land and the water and in the air, the new component needed was dominance in space.

Space dominance was described in a 1997 document entitled "Vision for 2020," published by the U.S. Space Command, which is presently a division of the air force. The unique mission of the Space Command is to "dominat[e] the space dimension of military operations." By merging this "space superiority with land, sea, and air superiority," the U.S. military will have Full Spectrum Dominance.[52]

This notion was further developed in the Pentagon's "Joint Vision 2020," which first appeared in 2000.[53] It speaks of full spectrum dominance as involving not just four but five dimensions: "space, sea, land, air, and information." In addition, this document says, "Given the global nature of our interests and obligations, the United States must maintain its overseas presence forces and the ability to rapidly project power worldwide in order to achieve full spectrum dominance." This statement gives support to Bacevich's observation that after the end of the Cold War, "the Department of Defense completed its transformation into a Department of Power Projection."[54]

PNAC's *Rebuilding America's Defenses* appeared in September of that same year. Written to influence the next administration, *RAD*'s main point was that "the next president of the United States . . . must increase military spending to preserve American geopolitical leadership."[55]

Besides arguing for increased spending across the board, *RAD* argued in particular for increased funding for the U.S. Space Command. Saying that "the ability to have access to, operate in, and dominate the aerospace environment has become the key to military success in modern, high-technology warfare," it advocated not only "missile defense" but also "placing . . . weapons in space." The weapons, moreover, are not simply for defensive purposes, but also for "the ability to conduct strikes from space," which will give the U.S. military a "global first-strike force."[56]

The Revolution in Military Affairs

This development of space-based weapons was presented as simply one part, albeit the most important part, of a more general transformation of the military that exploits the "revolution in military affairs" (RMA), which has been made possible by information technologies.[57] This RMA transformation of the military was said to be "sufficiently important to consider it a separate mission."[58]

In spite of this importance, however, the authors of *RAD*, ever mindful of budgetary constraints and widespread commitment to more traditional ways, warned that the needed transformation would not occur quickly, at least if the present climate continued. In a statement that has been widely quoted in the 9/11 truth movement, they wrote that "the process of transformation, even if it brings revolutionary change, is likely to be a long one, absent some catastrophic and catalyzing event—like a new Pearl Harbor."[59]

The emphasis in *RAD* on exploiting the RMA to transform the Pentagon's approach is no surprise, since one of the participants in the project to produce this document was Wolfowitz, who had long before fallen under the spell of Albert Wohlstetter (one of the models for "Dr. Strangelove"[60]). Wohlstetter had been the main early proponent of the ideas that came to be dubbed the "revolution in military affairs" by Andrew Marshall, who later became the main proponent.[61] Marshall, who at this writing was still serving as the RMA guru in the Pentagon, numbers Wolfowitz, Cheney, and Rumsfeld among his disciples.[62]

Rumsfeld, in fact, was at the same time heading up a special commission to make recommendations about the military use of space. This "Rumsfeld Commission," endorsing the idea of military transformation, including the weaponization of space, said that the United States should "employ space systems to help speed the transformation of the U.S. military into a modern force able to deter and defend against evolving threats directed at . . . [our] forward deployed forces."[63] (In other words, although the language of "defense" and "deterrence" is used, part of the purpose of the space weapons is to prevent attacks on America's *offensive* operations.) This report, interestingly, also used the Pearl Harbor analogy.

Warning against the tendency to consider an attack on U.S. space satellites as too improbable to worry about, the report of the Rumsfeld Commission said:

> History is replete with instances in which warning signs were ignored and change resisted until an external, "improbable" event forced resistant bureaucracies to take action. The question is whether the U.S. will be wise enough to act responsibly and soon enough to reduce U.S. space vulnerability. Or whether, as in the past, a disabling attack against the country and its people—a "Space Pearl Harbor"—will be the only event able to galvanize the nation and cause the U.S. Government to act.[64]

9/11 as the New Pearl Harbor

The attacks of 9/11 were widely referred to as a new Pearl Harbor. President Bush reportedly wrote in his diary on the night of 9/11: "The Pearl Harbor of the 21st century took place today."[65] Immediately after the attacks, many people, from Robert Kagan to Henry Kissinger to a writer for *Time* magazine, said that America should respond to the attacks of 9/11 in the same way it had responded to the attack on Pearl Harbor.[66]

Moreover, just as the attack on Pearl Harbor gave the United States the opportunity to enter World War II, which in turn allowed it to replace Great Britain as the leading imperial power, the attacks of 9/11 were widely regarded as an opportunity. Donald Rumsfeld stated that 9/11 created "the kind of opportunities that World War II offered, to refashion the world."[67] Condoleezza Rice reportedly told senior members of the National Security Council to "think about 'how do you capitalize on these opportunities' to fundamentally change American doctrine, and the shape of the world, in the wake of September 11th."[68] In a public address, she said, "If the collapse of the Soviet Union and 9/11 bookend a major shift in international politics, then this is a period not just of grave danger, but of enormous opportunity."[69] According to Bob Woodward, the president himself said that the attacks provided "a great opportunity."[70] Only two days after 9/11, in fact, Bush said in a telephone conversation with Mayor Rudy Giuliani and Governor George Pataki of New York, "Through the tears of sadness I see an opportunity." The next day, he reportedly used exactly the same words while talking to the press.[71]

Nicholas Lemann of the *New Yorker*, dealing with this response to 9/11 as an opportunity, reports that he was told by a senior official of the Bush administration (who insisted on anonymity) that, in Lemann's paraphrase, "The reason September 11th appears to have been 'a transformative moment' is not so much that it revealed the existence of a threat of which officials had previously been unaware as that it drastically reduced the American public's usual resistance to American military involvement overseas."[72] We will not, of course, hear that stated publicly by any member of the Bush-Cheney administration.

The attacks of 9/11 also reduced congressional resistance to providing increased funding for Pentagon programs. On the evening of 9/11 itself, Rumsfeld held a news briefing on the Pentagon attack. At this briefing, Senator Carl Levin, the chair of the Senate Armed Services Committee, was asked: "Senator Levin, you and other Democrats in Congress have voiced fear that you simply don't have enough money for the large increase in defense that the Pentagon is seeking, especially for missile defense. . . . Does this sort of thing convince you that an emergency exists in this country to increase defense spending?"[73] Congress immediately appropriated an additional $40 billion for the Pentagon and much more later, with few questions asked.

The attacks of 9/11, moreover, aided those who favored a transformation of the military along RMA lines. In the weeks before September 11, Bacevich reports, "Military transformation appeared to be dead in the water," because the military brass were "wedded to existing weapons systems, troop structure, and strategy."[74] But, Bacevich continues:

> President Bush's decision after September 11 to wage a global war against terror boosted the RMA's stock. After 9/11, the Pentagon shifted from the business of theorizing about war to the business of actually waging it. This created an opening for RMA advocates to make their case. War plans . . . became the means for demonstrating once for all the efficacy of the ideas advanced by Wohlstetter and Marshall and now supported by . . . Rumsfeld and his deputy Paul Wolfowitz.[75]

After the removal of Saddam Hussein, Richard Perle, who had long shared Wolfowitz's enthusiasm for Albert Wohlstetter's ideas, said, "This is the first war that's been fought in a way that would recognize Albert's vision of future wars."[76]

These ideas for achieving military omnipotence became official policy with the publication, one year after 9/11, of the Bush-Cheney administration's *National Security Strategy of the United States of America* (*NSS 2002*), which said, "We must build and maintain our defenses beyond challenge" so that we can "dissuade future military competition."[77]

The conviction that 9/11 provided an opportunity was also reflected in *NSS 2002*, which said, "The events of September 11, 2001, . . . opened vast, new opportunities."[78] One of the things for which it most clearly provided an opportunity was the doctrine of preemptive-preventive war.

PREEMPTIVE-PREVENTIVE WAR

This hyphenated term is used here for clarity. The doctrine in question, which involves attacking another country even though it poses no immediate threat, is technically called "preventive war." This doctrine, which violates international law as reflected in the charter of the United Nations, is to be distinguished from what is technically called "preemptive war," which occurs when Country A attacks Country B after learning that an attack from Country B is imminent—*too* imminent to allow time for the United Nations to intervene. These technical terms, however, are problematic, because although preventive war, being illegal, is worse than preemptive war, to most ears "preemption" sounds worse than "prevention." As a result, many people speak of "preemptive war" when they mean preventive war. The term "preemptive-preventive war," while somewhat cumbersome, solves this problem.[79]

Historical Emergence of the Doctrine

This doctrine of preemptive-preventive war had been advocated by neocons long before 9/11. It was contained already in the Cheney-Wolfowitz Defense Planning Guidance of 1992, which said that the United States should use force to "preempt" and "preclude threats."[80]

In 1996, Richard Perle and other neocons prepared a strategy paper entitled "A Clean Break" for Benjamin Netanyahu, who had recently been elected prime minister of Israel. This paper recommended that Israel, in making a clean break from previous strategies, establish "the principle of preemption."[81]

In 1997, PNAC's "Statement of Principles" argued that to exert "global leadership," America needs to "challenge regimes hostile to our interests and values."[82]

In 1998, a letter from PNAC, signed by Perle, Rumsfeld, Wolfowitz, and fifteen other members, urged President Clinton to "undertake military action" to eliminate "the possibility that Iraq will be able to use or threaten to use weapons of mass destruction."[83]

The Doctrine of Preemptive-Preventive War after 9/11

Although these neocons were anxious to have their doctrine of preemptive-preventive war accepted as national policy, this did not occur during the Clinton presidency or even during the first eight months of the Bush-Cheney administration. After 9/11, however, it did. "The events of 9/11," observes Bacevich, "provided the tailor-made opportunity to break free of the fetters restricting the exercise of American power."[84]

The idea of preemptive-preventive war, which came to be known as the "Bush doctrine," was first clearly expressed in the president's address at West Point in June 2002 (when the administration started preparing the American people psychologically for the attack on Iraq). Having stated that, in relation to the "new threats," deterrence "means nothing" and containment is "not possible," Bush even took aim at the traditional understanding of preemption, saying, "If we wait for threats to fully materialize, we will have waited too long." Then, using the language of preemption while really meaning preemptive-prevention, he said that America's security "will require all Americans . . . to be ready for preemptive action."[85]

NSS 2002

However, although the West Point speech provided a first statement of this new doctrine, it was in *NSS 2002*, published that September, that the new doctrine was laid out at some length. The covering letter, signed by the president, says that with regard to "our enemies' efforts to acquire dangerous technologies," America will, in self-defense, "act against such emerging threats before they are fully formed."[86] The document itself, saying that "our best defense is a good offense," also states:

> Given the goals of rogue states and terrorists, the United States can no longer rely on a reactive posture as we have in the past. The inability to deter a potential attacker, the immediacy of today's threats, and the magnitude of potential harm that could be caused by our adversaries' choice of weapons, do not permit that option. We cannot let our enemies strike first.[87]

To justify this doctrine, *NSS 2002* argues that the United States must "adapt" the traditional doctrine of preemption, long recognized as a right, to the new situation, thereby turning it into a right of anticipatory (preventive) preemption:

> For centuries, international law recognized that nations need not suffer an attack before they can lawfully take action to defend themselves against forces that present an imminent danger of attack. . . . We must adapt the concept of imminent threat to the capabilities and objectives of today's adversaries. . . . The United States has long maintained the option of preemptive actions to counter a sufficient threat to our national security. The greater the threat, . . . the more compelling the case for taking anticipatory action to defend ourselves, even if uncertainty remains as to the time and place of the enemy's attack. To forestall or prevent such hostile acts by our adversaries, the United States will, if necessary, act preemptively.[88]

With this argument, the authors of *NSS 2002* tried to suggest that, since this doctrine of anticipatory preemption simply involves adapting a traditionally recognized right to a new situation, it involves no great change. But it does. According to the traditional doctrine, one needed certain evidence that the other country was going to launch an immediate attack. According to the Bush doctrine, by contrast, the United States can attack another country "even if uncertainty remains" and even, more flagrantly, if the United States knows that the threat from the other country is not yet "fully formed."

The novelty here, to be sure, involves doctrine more than practice. The United States has in practice attacked several countries that presented no imminent military threat. But it always portrayed these attacks in such a way that they could appear to comport with international law. The attack on North

Vietnam after the alleged incident in the Tonkin Gulf provides an example. But "never before," point out Halper and Clarke, "had any president set out a formal national strategy *doctrine* that included [preventive] preemption."[89] This is a step of great significance, because it involves an explicit statement by the United States that the most basic principle of international law, as embodied in the United Nations, does not apply to its own behavior.

Zelikow as Primary Drafter of *NSS 2002*

Max Boot, a neocon who has become well known through his newspaper columns, has described *NSS 2002* as a "quintessentially neo-conservative document."[90] Now that the central ideas of this document have been laid out, we can see the accuracy of his observation.

Also, to return to a point begun in the previous chapter, we can see the importance of the astounding fact that Philip Zelikow, who later was selected as the executive director of the 9/11 Commission, was the primary drafter of *NSS 2002.* We can assume that in drafting this document, he was expressing ideas with which he agreed, since Condoleezza Rice brought him in to do the writing because she wanted "something bolder" than had been provided in a first draft, written by the State Department's director of policy planning, Richard Haass. Given the content and tone of the document, one might assume that Cheney, Rumsfeld, or Wolfowitz had been involved in the process of creating it. But, according to James Mann in *Rise of the Vulcans,* "The hawks in the Pentagon and in Vice President Cheney's office hadn't been closely involved, even though the document incorporated many of their key ideas. They had left the details and the drafting in the hands of Rice and Zelikow."[91] This hands-off behavior by these neocons suggests that they had full confidence that Zelikow shared their views.

Some insight into Zelikow's views before coming to this task might be garnered from an essay he coauthored in 1998 on "catastrophic terrorism." In this essay, which suggests that he had been thinking about the World Trade Center and a new Pearl Harbor several years prior to 9/11, Zelikow and his coauthors say:

> If the device that exploded in 1993 under the World Trade Center had been nuclear, or had effectively dispersed a deadly pathogen, the resulting horror and chaos would have exceeded our ability to describe it. Such an act of catastrophic terrorism would be a watershed event in American history. It could involve loss of life and property unprecedented in peacetime and undermine America's fundamental sense of security. . . . Like Pearl Harbor, this event would divide our past and future into a before and after. The United States might respond with draconian measures, scaling back civil liberties, allowing wider surveillance of citizens, detention of suspects, and use of deadly force.[92]

In any case, in light of Zelikow's authorship of *NSS 2002,* it is certainly no surprise that, as I reported in *The 9/11 Commission Report: Omissions and Distortions,* one of the omissions is any mention of imperial interests that might have served as motives for the Bush-Cheney administration to have orchestrated the attacks of 9/11. The Zelikow-led Commission did not, for example, mention that PNAC's *Rebuilding America's Defenses* had suggested that the transformation of the military, through which unipolarity could be enforced more effectively, could occur quickly if there were to be "a new Pearl Harbor"; it did not mention that the administration had had plans, to be discussed below, to attack both Afghanistan and Iraq prior to 9/11; and it did not mention that 9/11 had been described as presenting "opportunities" by Bush, Rice, Rumsfeld, and—yes—*NSS 2002.*

Moreover, once it is realized that Zelikow, who was in charge of the preparation of *The 9/11 Commission Report,* was also the primary author of *NSS 2002,* in which the post-9/11 foreign policy of the Bush-Cheney administration is officially stated, it is no surprise to see that *The 9/11 Commission Report* contains a chapter—"What to Do? A Global Strategy"—that provides propaganda for the Bush-Cheney administration's post-9/11 foreign policy.

The claim in the preface of the *9/11 Commission Report* that the Commission sought to be "independent, impartial, thorough, and nonpartisan" is absurd. The fact that the Commission was directed by Zelikow, combined with the fact that it was composed of people willing to be led by him, guaranteed that it would be none of those things.

In any case, after this interlude to reflect on the significance of Zelikow's authorship of *NSS 2002,* I return now to the discussion of possible imperial motives for 9/11 within the Bush-Cheney administration.

THE ATTACK ON AFGHANISTAN

Many times since the formal enunciation of the doctrine of preemptive-preventive warfare, the Bush-Cheney administration has defended it as necessitated by 9/11. In an address to the nation in 2004, for example, Bush said that the two lessons of 9/11 are that this country "must deal with gathering threats" and that it "must go on the offense and stay on the offense."[93] The first victim of this claimed right to "go on the offense" was Afghanistan.

Although the attacks of 9/11 were, according to the official story, planned and carried out by a nonstate organization, al-Qaeda, rather than by some state, the Bush-Cheney administration used the attacks as a pretext to launch attacks on *states*—attacks that had been planned *before* 9/11. The justification for this switch was provided by Bush's address to the nation on the evening of 9/11, in which he declared, "We will make no distinction between the terrorists who committed these acts and those who harbor them."[94] The attack on Afghanistan was then justified on the grounds that the Taliban was "harboring" Osama bin

Laden, the evil genius behind the 9/11 attacks, whom Bush on September 17 said he wanted "dead or alive" (after Cheney had said that he would willingly accept bin Laden's "head on a platter").[95]

But this was, of course, a pretext rather than the real reason for attacking Afghanistan—as illustrated by the fact that when the Bush administration had an opportunity to take bin Laden alive, it showed no interest. A week after 9/11, the Taliban said that it would hand OBL over—*if* the United States presented proof of his involvement in 9/11. But Bush refused to provide any such evidence, saying that there would be no negotiations or even discussion.[96] Again, four weeks after the U.S. attack on Afghanistan began, a Taliban spokesman said: "We will negotiate. But . . . we are not a province of the United States, to be issued orders to. We have asked for proof of Osama's involvement, but they have refused. Why?"[97]

There are probably two answers to this question. First, there is much evidence that the Bush administration did *not* want bin Laden, either dead or alive. One part of this evidence consists of several reports that the U.S. military in Afghanistan deliberately let bin Laden escape more than once.[98] A second reason is that the Bush administration, besides knowing that bin Laden was not responsible for the 9/11 attacks, evidently decided that it could not even marshal a convincing (albeit false) case that he was (as suggested by the fact that, after a White Paper presenting this proof was promised, it was never produced[99]).

To understand the real reasons for the attack on Afghanistan, one needs to look at some developments prior to 9/11. One such development was the publication in 1997 of Zbigniew Brzezinski's book *The Grand Chessboard: American Primacy and Its Geostrategic Imperatives.* As the subtitle shows, Brzezinski, while not a neoconservative, shared the neocons' concern to maintain and enhance U.S. "primacy." Portraying Central Asia, with its vast oil reserves, as the key to world power, Brzezinski argued that America, to ensure its continued primacy, must get control of this region, which would mean establishing several military bases there. However, Brzezinski added, American democracy posed an obstacle:

> America is too democratic at home to be autocratic abroad. This limits the use of America's power, especially its capacity for military intimidation. . . . The economic self-denial (that is, defense spending) and the human sacrifice (casualties even among professional soldiers) required in the effort are uncongenial to democratic instincts. Democracy is inimical to imperial mobilization.[100]

Brzezinski, however, then suggested a way in which this obstacle could be overcome. Having said that in the United States "the pursuit of power is not a goal that commands popular passion," he added, "except in conditions of a sudden threat or challenge to the public's sense of domestic well-being."[101] The American people *would* be willing to make the economic and human sacrifices needed for "imperial mobilization," he suggested, if there were "a truly massive and widely perceived direct external threat."[102] The kind of threat he had in mind was implied by his statement, earlier in the book, that the public was willing to support "America's engagement in World War II largely because of the shock effect of the Japanese attack on Pearl Harbor."[103] It is possible that Brzezinski's discussion here inspired the statement about a "new Pearl Harbor" in PNAC's 2000 document.

Be that as it may, a more specific motivation for the post-9/11 attack on Afghanistan was provided by the "pipeline war" that was going on.[104] The Bush-Cheney administration supported—as had the Clinton-Gore administration until 1999—UNOCAL's plan to build an oil-and-gas pipeline through Afghanistan, which was in competition with plans from oil companies based in other countries. What happened in 1999 was that UNOCAL, having become convinced that Afghanistan under the Taliban would never have the peace and stability needed for the pipeline project, decided to withdraw. Ahmed Rashid, finishing his book on the Taliban in mid-1999, wrote that the Clinton administration had shifted its support to the pipeline route from Azerbaijan through Georgia to Turkey, adding that "by now nobody wanted to touch Afghanistan and the Taliban."[105]

When the Bush administration came to power, however, it decided to give the Taliban one last chance. This last chance occurred at a four-day meeting in Berlin in July 2001. Representatives of the Bush-Cheney administration, trying to persuade the Taliban to share power with U.S.-friendly factions in a "unity government," reportedly gave the Taliban an ultimatum: "Either you accept our offer of a carpet of gold, or we bury you under a carpet of bombs."[106] When the Taliban refused, the Americans reportedly said that "military action against Afghanistan would go ahead . . . before the snows started falling in Afghanistan, by the middle of October at the latest."[107]

Given the fact that the attacks on New York and Washington occurred on September 11, the U.S. military had time to get ready, logistically, to begin its war in Afghanistan on October 7. By October 10, the U.S. Department of State had informed the Pakistani minister of oil that "in view of recent geopolitical developments," UNOCAL was ready to go ahead with the pipeline project.[108]

The contention that at least one of the purposes of the war was to support this project is suggested by the fact that the post-Taliban prime minister, Hamid Karzai, had previously been on UNOCAL's payroll, as had been PNAC member Zalmay Khalilzad, who in 2001 was appointed Bush's special envoy to Afghanistan and then in 2003 became the U.S. ambassador to Afghanistan. As Chalmers Johnson said in 2004, "The continued collaboration of Khalilzad and Karzai in post-9/11 Afghanistan strongly suggests that the Bush administration was and remains . . . interested in oil."[109] (In March 2005, Khalilzad would become the U.S. ambassador to Iraq.[110])

Still more evidence is provided by the placement of the military bases in

Afghanistan. As one Israeli writer put it, "If one looks at the map of the big American bases created, one is struck by the fact that they are completely identical to the route of the projected oil pipeline to the Indian Ocean."[111]

The concern to enable an American oil company to build this pipeline should not, however, be considered the only or even the primary motivation. The larger concern, suggests Chalmers Johnson, was "to establish an American presence in Central Asia." Evidence for this view is provided by the fact that the United States, besides establishing long-term bases in Afghanistan, had within a month after 9/11 arranged for long-term bases in Pakistan, Kyrgyzstan, and Uzbekistan.[112]

The new Pearl Harbor that occurred on 9/11, therefore, allowed the United States to support UNOCAL's pipeline project and, more generally, to fulfill the program, suggested by Brzezinski, of taking control of this region of the world.

The fact that 9/11 provided the necessary condition for the war in Afghanistan was stated by both Wolfowitz and Rumsfeld. In 2004, Wolfowitz told the 9/11 Commission that if the Department of Defense had asked Congress for permission to invade Afghanistan prior to 9/11, this request would not have been taken seriously. Rumsfeld, telling the Commission that "it can take a tragedy like September 11th to awaken the world to new threats and to the need for action," said that prior to 9/11 the president could not have convinced Congress that the United States needed to "invade Afghanistan and overthrow the Taliban."[113]

Afghanistan was not, however, the primary target in the sights of the Bush-Cheney administration. That target was Iraq.

THE ATTACK ON IRAQ

Several neocons, including some who became central members of the Bush-Cheney administration, had been wanting to bring about regime change in Iraq ever since Saddam Hussein's occupation of Kuwait in 1990. Leading voices for this policy included Cheney and Wolfowitz, who were then secretary and undersecretary of defense, respectively, and also Richard Perle, who chaired a committee set up by neocons called Committee for Peace and Security in the Gulf. But this idea was opposed by President George H. W. Bush along with General Colin Powell, then chair of the Joint Chiefs of Staff, and General Norman Schwarzkopf, the field commander, so it was not carried out.[114]

In 1992, Albert Wohlstetter, who had inspired Perle and Wolfowitz and other neocons, expressed exasperation that nothing had been done about "a dictatorship sitting on the world's second largest pool of low-cost oil and ambitious to dominate the Gulf."[115] (Wohlstetter's statement reflected his conviction, expressed back in 1981, that America needs to establish forces, bases, and infrastructure so as to enjoy unquestioned primacy in the region.[116])

In 1996, the "Clean Break" paper, written for Israel by Perle and other neocons, proposed that Israel remove from power all of its enemies in the region, beginning with Saddam Hussein. This 1996 document, in the opinion of Arnaud de Borchgrave, president of United Press International, "provided the strategic underpinnings for Operation Iraqi Freedom seven years later."[117]

In 1997, Wolfowitz and Khalilzad published a statement arguing that "Saddam Must Go."[118]

In 1998, Kristol and Kagan, in a *New York Times* op-ed entitled "Bombing Iraq Isn't Enough," called for "finishing the job left undone in 1991."[119] Wolfowitz told the House National Security Committee that it had been a mistake in 1991 to leave Saddam in power. Also, writing in the *New Republic*, he said: "Toppling Saddam is the only outcome that can satisfy the vital U.S. interest in a stable and secure Gulf region."[120] And the aforementioned letter to President Clinton from PNAC—signed by Cheney, Kristol, Perle, Rumsfeld, and Wolfowitz, among others—urged him to "take the necessary steps, including military steps," to "remov[e] Saddam's regime from power." Getting no agreement from Clinton, PNAC wrote a similar letter to Newt Gingrich and Trent Lott, then the leaders of the House and the Senate, respectively.[121]

In 2000, PNAC's *Rebuilding America's Defenses*, pointing out that "the United States has for decades sought to play a more permanent role in Gulf regional security," added, "While the unresolved conflict with Iraq provides the immediate justification, the need for a substantial American force presence in the Gulf transcends the issue of the regime of Saddam Hussein."[122]

In light of the fact that Cheney, Libby, Rumsfeld, Wolfowitz, and other neocons given central positions in the new Bush administration, it is not surprising to learn, from two former members of this administration, that it came into office intent on attacking Iraq. Paul O'Neill, who was secretary of the treasury and hence a member of the National Security Council, has said that within days of the inauguration, the main topic was going after Saddam, with the question being not "Why Saddam?" or "Why Now?" but merely "finding a way to do it."[123] Richard Clarke, who had been the national coordinator for security and counterterrorism, confirmed O'Neill's charge, saying, "The administration of the second George Bush did begin with Iraq on its agenda."[124]

Until the attacks of 9/11, however, no one had found "a way to do it." As neocon Kenneth Adelman has said: "At the beginning of the administration people were talking about Iraq but it wasn't doable. . . . That changed with September 11."[125] Bob Woodward makes the same observation in *Bush at War*, saying: "The terrorist attacks of September 11 gave the U.S. a new window to go after Hussein."[126]

However, even 9/11, by itself, was not a sufficient basis for getting the American people's support for an attack on Iraq. Not for lack of effort by Rumsfeld and Wolfowitz. On the afternoon of 9/11 itself, Rumsfeld said in a note to General Richard Myers—the acting head of the Joint Chiefs of

Staff—that he wanted the "best info fast. Judge whether good enough hit S.H. [Saddam Hussein] at same time. Not only UBL [Usama bin Laden]."[127] In the following days, both Rumsfeld and Wolfowitz argued that Saddam's Iraq should be, in Woodward's paraphrase, "a principal target of the first round in the war on terrorism."[128]

Colin Powell, however, argued that both the American people and other countries would at that time support an attack on Afghanistan, to do something about al-Qaeda, but not an attack on Iraq, since there was no evidence that it had anything to do with 9/11. He added, however, that after a successful campaign in Afghanistan, a war on Iraq would become more feasible. Bush accepted this argument.[129] In doing so, he was not rejecting the proposal to use 9/11 to justify an attack on Iraq, merely postponing its implementation: A plan for going to war in Afghanistan that Bush signed on September 17 also directed the Pentagon to begin planning military options for an invasion of Iraq.[130]

Stephen Sniegoski, explaining why the attack on Iraq could not be launched immediately, says, "Although the 9/11 atrocities psychologically prepared the American people for the war on Iraq, those horrific events were not sufficient by themselves to thrust America immediately into an attack on Iraq." A "lengthy propaganda offensive" would also be needed.[131]

This propaganda offensive involved convincing a majority of the American people of the truth of two false claims: that Saddam Hussein had been behind 9/11 and that he possessed, or soon would possess, weapons of mass destruction, including nuclear weapons, with which he could attack America. This part of the story is too well known to need much rehearsal. The point to emphasize here is that although this later propaganda was necessary, its success depended on 9/11. Halper and Clarke say that "it was 9/11 that provided the political context in which the thinking of neo-conservatives could be turned into operational policy."[132] Sniegoski, spelling out the point more fully, says:

> The 9/11 attacks made the American people angry and fearful. Ordinary Americans wanted to strike back at the terrorist enemy, even though they weren't exactly sure who that enemy was. . . . Moreover, they were fearful of more attacks and were susceptible to the administration's propaganda that the United States had to strike Iraq before Iraq somehow struck the United States. . . . It wasn't that difficult to channel American fear and anger into war against Iraq.[133]

Much of this channeling was done by the Bush-Cheney administration, especially Bush and Cheney themselves. In August 2002, Cheney declared that "there is no doubt that Saddam Hussein now has weapons of mass destruction . . . [and] is amassing them to use . . . against us."[134] In October 2002, Bush said that having "experienced the horror of September the 11th, . . . America must not ignore the threat gathering against us. Facing clear evidence of peril, we cannot wait for the final proof—the smoking gun—that could come in the form of a mushroom cloud."[135]

The administration was greatly aided in this propaganda offensive by neo-conservatives outside the government, who "linked their preexisting agenda (an attack on Iraq) to a separate event (9/11)."[136] Through their incessant propaganda—most widely spread in Lawrence Kaplan and William Kristol's *The War over Iraq: Saddam's Tyranny and America's Mission*—"Al-Qaeda and Saddam Hussein were morphed into the same enemy" and "the war on terror and war in Iraq were joined at the hip."[137]

This propaganda campaign was enormously successful. Shortly before the war on Iraq was launched, the two key ideas in the campaign—that Saddam Hussein had played a direct role in the attacks of 9/11 and that he was a threat because he had weapons of mass destruction—were accepted by 70 percent of the American people.[138] As a result, point out Halper and Clarke, the Bush-Cheney administration was "able to build the environment surrounding the terrorist attacks of September 2001 into a wide moral platform from which to launch a preemptive strike."[139]

That this propaganda campaign would be successful would have been predictable. As Hermann Göring, one of the top Nazi officials, said: "It is the *leaders* of the country who determine the policy and it is always a simple matter to drag the people along. . . . All you have to do is tell them they are being attacked."[140]

Accordingly, the fact that there were no Iraqis among the alleged hijackers does not mean that the desire for a pretext to attack Iraq could not have been one of the imperial motives behind the attacks of 9/11. The crucial precondition for the war in Iraq was a psychological state of mind in the American public—one of fear and anxiety combined with a desire for revenge—that would countenance the new doctrine of preemptive-preventive war. This state of mind was abundantly created by 9/11. Then, just as the ensuing propaganda offensive against Osama bin Laden, al-Qaeda, and the Taliban created almost unanimous acceptance of the war in Afghanistan, the propaganda offensive directed at Saddam Hussein was rather easily able to channel this fear, anxiety, and desire for revenge into a widespread feeling that a war to bring about regime change in Iraq was justified.

CONCLUSION: THE NEW ROME

The main point of this chapter is that, assuming that 9/11 was orchestrated by the Bush-Cheney administration (which includes, of course, the Pentagon under Donald Rumsfeld), the motives behind this false-flag operation were *imperial* motives, oriented around the dream of extending the American empire so that it is an all-inclusive global empire, resulting in a global *Pax Americana*.

People in office, to be sure, still feel the necessity to deny reality. Just as President Ronald Reagan in 1983 denied any imperial ambitions on the part of the United States—"We're not in the business of imperialism, aggression, or conquest. . . . We threaten no one"[141]—President Bush said in his highly imperialist address at West Point in 2002, "We don't seek an empire." Likewise, when Secretary of Defense Donald Rumsfeld was asked by an al Jazeera correspondent in 2003 if the Bush administration was bent on "empire-building," he replied: "We don't seek empires. We're not imperialistic. We never have been. I can't imagine why you'd even ask the question."[142]

As we have seen, however, commentators outside the government now freely admit the reality of American imperialism, with neocons even seeking to get this reality more widely acknowledged. For example, in an article entitled "American Imperialism? No Need to Run Away from Label," Max Boot, referring to Rumsfeld's just-quoted statement, wrote: "That's a fine answer for public consumption. The problem is that it isn't true."[143] What *is* true, as neoconservatives and others such as Andrew Bacevich and Paul Kennedy have emphasized, is that America has by far the most extensive empire ever created.

This fact has inevitably led to comparisons with the Roman Empire. Those by Krauthammer and Kennedy have already been quoted. Such a comparison has also been made by the well-known Harvard professor of international relations Joseph Nye, who served as an assistant secretary of defense in the Clinton administration. In 2003, Nye wrote: "Not since Rome has one nation loomed so large above the others. Indeed the word 'empire' has come out of the closet. Respected analysts on both the left and the right are beginning to refer to 'American empire' approvingly as the dominant narrative of the 21st century."[144] Nye's statement followed on the publication of Bacevich's 2002 book *American Empire*, which stated the comparison in an even more dramatic way. Pointing out that historian Charles Beard had argued in 1939 that "America is not to be Rome,"[145] Bacevich added that in the 1990s "most citizens still comforted themselves with the belief that as the sole superpower the United States was *nothing* like Rome." However, Bacevich says: "The reality that Beard feared has come to pass: like it or not, America today *is* Rome."[146]

Chapter 7

Jesus and the Roman Empire

Christians in America today have two reasons to know something about the Roman Empire. In the first place, we cannot understand why other peoples hate our country and what we might do about it unless we, as Chalmers Johnson has said, "grasp what the United States really is."[1] And if America now *"is* Rome," as Bacevich says, having some understanding of what Rome *was* can help us grasp what America now *is*.

A second reason for examining the nature of the Roman Empire is that Christianity arose during its heyday, and many scholars of the historical Jesus say that understanding the nature of the Roman Empire is crucial for understanding the message of Jesus. As Richard Horsley puts it: "Trying to understand Jesus . . . without knowing how Roman imperialism determined the conditions of life in Galilee and Jerusalem would be like trying to understand Martin Luther King without knowing how slavery, reconstruction, and segregation determined the lives of African Americans in the United States."[2]

So let us look at the Roman Empire as a basis for understanding both the nature of America's empire and the person our religious tradition has called the Christ—our central revelation of the God to whom we have pledged our ultimate loyalty.

THE ROMAN EMPIRE

Rome, after achieving dominance over the rest of Italy, became the dominant power in the western Mediterranean world by the end of the third century B.C.E. By the close of the second century, it had become the dominant power in the east as well, replacing the Macedonian empire established by Alexander. By the end of the first century, it had subjected most of the known earth to its rule, and the goal of Augustus Caesar was "to conquer what remained of the world."[3]

Students of empire have identified at least five features of the Roman Empire that are also exemplified, as chapter 9 will show, by the American empire: (1) the sense that the empire is divinely authorized; (2) the development and employment of overwhelming military power to spread and maintain the empire; (3) the use of terror, or simply the threat of terror, to intimidate; (4) rule through puppets backed up by the empire's pervasive military presence; and (5) the collection of taxes in order to enrich the empire's center and finance its imperial rule. I will look at these five features in general, then discuss their illustration in Palestine.[4]

Sense of Divine Authorization

After the decade of civil war that followed the assassination of Julius Caesar, his adopted son Octavian defeated Marc Antony in 31 B.C.E. Octavian took the name "Augustus," meaning "Revered," and was widely called the "savior of the whole human race" because he had brought "peace" to the whole world.[5] The adjectives, however, soon became even stronger, elevating him to the status of deity. He was called "the Divine Augustus" and "the most divine Caesar." Horace, referred to him as "god on earth."[6] Statues of him were erected next to those of traditional gods, and ritual sacrifices, shrines, and temples were established for him.[7] The official view of Augustus is illustrated by an inscription from 9 B.C.E., which reads:

> The most divine Caesar . . . we should consider equal to the Beginning of all things . . . [t]he beginning of life and vitality. . . . Whereas Providence, which has regulated our whole existence . . . has brought our life to the climax of perfection in giving us [the emperor] Augustus, whom it filled with strength for the welfare of men, and who being sent to us and our descendants as Savior, has . . . become [god] manifest, Caesar has fulfilled all the hopes of earlier times . . . , and whereas, finally, the birthday of the god has been for the whole world the beginning of good news (*euangelion*) . . . [therefore let a new era begin from his birth].[8]

Implicit in this description of Augustus as god and savior for bringing peace—the peace that came to be known as the *Pax Romana*—was the idea that the spread of the Roman Empire was the work of Divine Providence working through him.

For example, Virgil, having referred to Augustus Caesar as "son of a god," said that he "shall spread his empire . . . to a land that lies beyond the stars."[9]

The Development and Use of Overwhelming Military Power

The primary basis for the spread of the Roman Empire was the military power exercised by the Roman legions, which was so far superior to that of most other peoples as to make their defeat a foregone conclusion. By conquering peoples, Rome portrayed itself as pacifying them, bringing peace to them, by incorporating them within the *Pax Romana*. Indeed, one of the titles taken by the emperors was "Pacifier of the World."[10] But this was pacification through military might, which the Romans used ruthlessly. As a Caledonian chieftain at the time put it, "The Romans rob, butcher, plunder, and call it 'empire'; and where they make desolation, they call it 'peace.'"[11]

The Use of Terror to Intimidate

The Romans used their overwhelming power not merely to conquer but also to terrorize and thereby intimidate their conquered subjects to keep them in line. Whenever there was disobedience, Rome would not only retaliate but would do so disproportionately, often slaughtering vast numbers of people. They would do this even in regions with little strategic or economic value, in order to maintain what they called "honor" (which is similar to what U.S. leaders have called "credibility"). "What mattered most [to the Roman elite]," says Susan Mattern in her study of Rome's imperial strategy, "was how the empire [was] perceived by foreigners and subjects. . . . Terror and vengeance were instruments for maintaining the empire's image."[12] This view, incidentally, is not simply an inference by modern scholars. The contemporary historian Polybius, after viewing the corpses filling a city destroyed by the Romans, said, "It seems to be that they do this for the sake of terror."[13]

The security and endurance of Rome, its elite class believed, depended "on the image of the force it could wield and on its apparent willingness to use that force at whatever cost."[14] When the Roman legions were sent on expeditions, accordingly, their main mission was usually not defensive but "to punish, to avenge, and to terrify—that is, to reassert a certain state of mind in the enemy"—a state of "awe and terror."[15] This state of mind was supposed to bring what they called *fides*, that is, fidelity or loyalty.[16]

One of the chief means of terrorist intimidation was crucifixion, which both Cicero and Josephus called the worst form of death. The victims of this tactic of state terrorism were displayed in prominent places for all to see.[17] As one Roman put it: "Whenever we crucify the condemned, the most crowded roads are chosen, where the most people can see and be moved by this terror. For penalties relate not so much to retribution as to their exemplary effect."[18] The use of crucifixion was not unique to the Romans. It had been used by Alexander the Great and many prior hegemonial powers. By the time of the Jesus movement, however, it had become a distinctively Roman symbol of intimidation.[19]

The Use of Puppet Rulers

Upon conquering regions, the Romans generally did not exercise direct rule on the basis of military occupation.[20] Rather, they typically employed local strongmen as puppet rulers. The Romans maintained military garrisons somewhere in the general area, however, to make sure that these local leaders remained puppets and to put down any attempts to overthrow them.

Tribute and Taxation

One motive that some of the Roman rulers had for spreading and maintaining the empire was, of course, the enjoyment of power. Caesar, said Plutarch, had "an insatiable love of power and a mad desire to be first and greatest."[21] But the more general motive was to enrich Rome itself by laying the conquered regions under systems of tribute (a tax on the land) and other forms of taxation.

The price exacted by the Romans was severe enough not only to support the expense of maintaining the empire in its various regions but also to make the elite class of Roman society "obscenely wealthy."[22] It was also severe enough to lead to widespread poverty in the territories. The Romans themselves believed that "it was the empire's most onerous and deeply resented burden on provincials" and the one that most often led to rebellion.[23]

PALESTINE UNDER ROMAN DOMINATION

"The politics of first-century Palestine," say K. C. Hanson and Douglas Oakman in *Palestine in the Time of Jesus*, "must be interpreted in light of its domination by Roman interests." Having been under the control of successive empires for 600 years—with the exception of one interlude lasting less than a century—Palestine had been under Roman domination for almost a century by the time of Jesus' ministry.[24]

There was a difference between the way in which Galilee and Judea were ruled. Until 4 B.C.E., they had both been under rule from Jerusalem, first the rule of the Hasmonean high priesthood and then that of Herod the Great. Herod was a local military strongman who was appointed "king" of Palestine by Julius Caesar to be his client ruler—his puppet. But upon Herod's death, Galilee was put under his son Herod Antipas, designated "tetrarch," while Judea was, after problems with the original client ruler, put under a Roman governor, Pontius Pilate.

Both Galilee and Judea were, nonetheless, under Roman rule, and this rule was devastating militarily, culturally, and economically.

Militarily, the Romans had been brutal, employing systematic slaughter, the destruction of villages, and mass enslavement.[25] In Galilee, the Roman legions had, by the time of Jesus, killed tens of thousands of people and enslaved many more. One of the most traumatic attacks occurred in Magdala, evidently the home of Mary Magdalene, about fifty years before her birth. Another traumatic event was the burning of Sepphoris, only a few miles from Nazareth, at about the time of Jesus' birth.[26] To try to deter future challengers to Roman rule in Palestine, the Romans, of course, used crucifixions. For example, at about the time of Jesus' birth some 2,000 rebels were crucified.[27]

The Galileans were subjected as well to the violence of the Herods. After being appointed king, Herod the Great inflicted much death and destruction in the three years it took him, with help from Rome, to subdue his subjects. He then "established massive military fortresses and ruled with an iron fist"— indeed, a reign of terror employing ruthless secret police.[28] This system was continued by Herod Antipas.

Culturally, Roman imperialism meant flagrant violations of the people's traditions and sensibilities. Because the emperor was declared to be divine, any acknowledgment of him was considered idolatrous by the Jewish people. And yet King Herod, to curry favor, built temples and even whole cities named for Augustus Caesar. He also built numerous other pagan buildings and monuments and engaged in what was considered "the shameless worship of foreign gods." He even, after deciding to rebuild the Jerusalem Temple, had it built in grand Hellenistic style.[29] Herod's son Antipas continued this invasion of pagan architecture, building two Roman-style cities in Galilee within two decades. One of these cities, called Autocratoris (meaning "belonging to the Emperor"), was built on the ruins of Sepphoris (near Nazareth). The other city, called Tiberias (named for Tiberius, the successor of Augustus), was built at the opposite end of the Sea of Galilee from Capernaum (where Jesus evidently spent much of his time).

Even stronger cultural resentment was directed at the client rulers in Judea, the high priests of the Jerusalem Temple, who since the Roman subjugation of the region had been selected by representatives of Rome—first by King Herod, then by the Roman governor of Judea. The criterion for appointment was not piety and reverence for tradition but subservience to Roman rule. Herod, in fact, appointed Jews from the Hellenistic world, who had no prior relation to the Palestinian people. Their aloofness from the people was shown by the fact that, amassing great fortunes from the revenues they extracted from the people, they lived in great luxury in elegant villas overlooking Jerusalem.

Besides being regarded as illegitimate for these reasons, the high priests violated the Temple by offering sacrifices in honor of the Roman emperor. Their legitimacy was further undermined by the fact that it was their task to collect the tribute to Rome, which they did brutally, using hired thugs to do the collecting.[30] Given the emperor's claim to be divine, moreover, the tribute was regarded as "a direct violation of the Mosaic laws against idolatry."[31]

The volatile nature of this issue is shown by the fact that the issue of payments to the Roman Empire was involved in a revolt at about the time of Jesus' birth, another revolt when Jesus was about ten years old, and the big Jewish revolt about thirty-six years after his death, which led to the destruction of Jerusalem and its temple.[32]

Economically, the effects of incorporation into the Roman Empire were devastating to Galilee, as the region was "drawn into an increasingly centralized economy where some people prospered mightily and others sank into helplessness and debt."[33] The people not only had to pay tithes to the Temple but also taxes to Herod, which Herod made very high in order to pay for his massive building projects and his lavish lifestyle.[34] The idea that the taxes were oppressive should not, incidentally, be considered an exaggeration of certain scholars: Josephus, writing at the time, said that Herod had "reduced the entire country to helpless poverty."[35]

After Herod Antipas became tetrarch, furthermore, the tax-collection process became even more rigorous. From Autocratoris and Tiberias—which were built to be efficient administrative centers—Antipas dispatched "a veritable army of auditors, tax collectors, and soldiers to the groves, vineyards, and threshing floors of every village at harvest time to ensure that his share of the harvest . . . was duly handed over."[36]

Although most of the peasants were earning only a subsistence living, the overall tax burden took 40 percent or more of their total income.[37] To pay these taxes while retaining enough crops and animals to feed their families, many peasants were forced to borrow money, using their land as collateral. Their debts often became greater each year, until they were forced into foreclosure, so that more and more land passed into the hands of aristocratic families.

According to the Holiness Code of Leviticus, debts were supposed to be forgiven every seven years, so that this permanent loss of land would not occur. But the authorities had found a way to get around this statute.

This loss of land was a catastrophe, because like people in most agrarian cultures, the peasants of Galilee "cherish[ed] one goal above all others: family survival on the land of their ancestors." By the time of Jesus, say Horsley and coauthor Neil Asher Silberman, there was "a crisis of debt and dispossession that touched and transformed the lives of nearly every peasant family in Galilee."[38]

THE ANTI-IMPERIAL GOSPEL OF JESUS

By viewing the message of Jesus within this context, with its military, political, cultural, and economic oppression, we can see that, as Horsley puts it, Jesus preached an "anti-imperial gospel."[39]

In speaking of "the message of Jesus," I am referring to an understanding of this message that is based on conclusions of modern Jesus scholars. These scholars have devised several criteria for distinguishing the authentic sayings of Jesus himself from statements that, while attributed to Jesus in the four Gospels, reflect the theological and apologetic concerns of Christian communities at later times, forty or more years after the death of Jesus. Although I have drawn on several Jesus scholars, I rely here primarily on the writings of Richard Horsley.

The Reign of God

New Testament scholars have long known that Jesus' message was oriented around the idea of the reign, or kingdom, of God. The prayer that we call "the Lord's Prayer" is a modification of the Kaddish, a prayer for the establishment of God's kingdom that was recited regularly in Jewish synagogues at the time of Jesus. This fact is important, because it shows that Jesus' prayer, rather than being about a variety of topics, was focused around the petition "thy kingdom come"—which was an abbreviation of the Kaddish's petition: "May God establish his kingdom in your lifetime." But what kind of kingdom did Jesus have in mind? A good clue for answering this question is provided by the next lines: "thy will be done, on earth as it is in heaven."

Many scholars, on the basis of a too-literal reading of apocalyptic literature in general and apocalyptic passages in the Gospels in particular, have assumed that Jesus was talking about a dramatic end of this world brought about by overwhelming destructive power.[40] But the God of Jesus would have evidently been satisfied with a more modest development: a world in which God's will is done.[41]

A further clue to the nature of the kingdom Jesus had in mind is provided by the fact that the one ethical implication of the reign of God deemed important enough to include in this brief prayer was the injunction that we should "forgive our debtors."[42]

The word used in these lines really referred to debts and debtors, not "sins" or "trespasses." To understand what Jesus was about, we need to keep in mind that he was not providing a prayer to be recited by Christians two thousand years later. He was focused on the problems faced by his own people—the people of Israel—at that moment of their history, in which they were victims of Roman imperialism.

The anti-imperial nature of Jesus' message is implied in the central petition of the prayer he taught his followers: "Thy kingdom come."

> It is important to keep in mind [says Horsley] that "the kingdom of God" is a political metaphor and symbol. In Jesus' preaching and action the kingdom clearly includes the social-economic-political substance of human relations as willed by God. . . . Before it was spiritualized and etherealized in Christian discourse, "salvation" (*soteria*) meant the peace . . . and prosperity provided by the divine . . . emperor for his subjects. . . . For Jesus and many of his Palestinian Jewish contemporaries . . . , however, the blessings of

individual and social-political life would be provided by God as king, in contrast to the emperor. . . . Thus God's activity was political and Jesus' preaching of that activity was political—with obvious implications for the "imperial situation" then prevailing in Palestine.[43]

In proclaiming the coming kingdom of God, in other words, Jesus was proclaiming an end to the present subservience of the people of Israel to the Roman Empire and its local collaborators. This would not be a minor change. It would not only involve overcoming the religious problem of idolatry. It would also involve a complete change in social, political, and economic relations, which would henceforth reflect divine principles, rather than the demonic principles embodied in the present order.

The Present Demonic Rule

Jesus clearly believed, in line with widespread beliefs of the time, that the world was presently under demonic rule. This belief is reflected in the final petition of his prayer: "Save us from the Evil One."

But Jesus also believed that this demonic rule was coming to an end, as shown in his exorcisms. "If it is by the finger of God that I cast out the demons," he said, "then the kingdom of God has come to you" (Luke 11:20). The allusion to Exodus 8:19 in this statement, says Horsley, suggested that a new liberation from political-economic bondage was under way.[44]

The fact that people are possessed by demons was not unrelated to Roman rule. In the story in Mark 5:1–20, the exorcised demoniac identifies itself as "Legion," which the original hearers would have immediately recognized as a reference to the Roman troops, and the drowning of the troop of swine, after Legion entered into them, would have reminded them of the drowning of the troops of Pharaoh, the head of an earlier empire.[45] This view, incidentally, was not unique to Jesus and his followers: The Dead Sea Scrolls show that the Qumran community saw history as presently ruled over by two superhuman spirits, Light and Darkness, with the Romans being under the sway of the power of Darkness.[46]

"Jesus' overall perspective," says Horsley, "was that God was bringing an end to the demonic and political powers dominating his society so that a renewal of individual and social life would be possible."[47]

The New Social-Political-Economic Order

At the center of this new social life would be a just economic order, with sufficient food for everyone. The second petition of Jesus' prayer is for "our daily bread." This petition involves an allusion to Proverbs 30:8, which says (in the translation of the New International Version):

Give me neither poverty nor riches, but give me only my daily bread. Otherwise, I may have too much and disown you and say, "Who is the LORD?" Or I may become poor and steal, and so dishonor the name of my God.

The insight behind this proverb is that it is dangerous for people to have either too much money or too little, as either situation tempts them to reject God's rule in their lives. Implicit in Jesus' simple petition for daily bread, therefore, is a critique of an economic system that leads to a division between the very rich and the very poor.[48] Closely related to this critique, of course, is the petition about forgiving debts. Under the reign of God, the poor will not become even poorer by losing their property to the rich, who will thereby become even richer.

If we think that this concern with a political order that would bring about a just economic order is too prosaic to be what Jesus could have meant by the coming reign of God, we should look at Isaiah 65, in which the prophet has God speaking about creating "a new heaven and a new earth"—a phrase that would be repeated in Revelation 21:1. In this new situation, Isaiah's God says, "No more shall there be in it an infant that lives but a few days." Furthermore, the people "shall build houses and inhabit them; they shall plant vineyards and eat their fruit. They shall not build and another inhabit; they shall not plant and another eat. . . . They shall not labor in vain, or bear children for calamity."[49] In the time of Jesus, the situation criticized in this passage, in which the common people of Israel were forced into servitude to rich landlords, was even worse. This situation formed the background to the parable of the Wicked Tenants.[50]

Taxes and the Temple

Besides the fact that Jesus regarded the present situation, with its economic injustice and political servitude to foreign rulers, as controlled by demonic power, there are still other signs that his was an anti-imperial gospel. One of these signs is the evidence, embodied in the traditions, that Jesus had challenged the payment of the tribute to Rome[51]—which, as we have seen, was the most volatile of all issues.

Furthermore, given the widely held conviction that the Temple had become illegitimate and idolatrous through its subservience to Rome, a challenge to the Temple would also have anti-imperialist implications. And the evidence firmly supports the view that Jesus' final challenge, the one that led to his death, involved a challenge to the Temple and its high priests. Just as the parable of the vineyard suggests that he had indicted this ruling group,[52] the evidence also suggests that he had challenged the payment of the half-shekel tax to the Temple.[53]

Finally, and probably most important for understanding the reason Jesus was put to death, he evidently, besides prophesying that the Temple would be destroyed,[54] created a disturbance in the Temple in protest against the system set up there to collect money from the people. Whatever the exact nature of this disturbance, it was probably a symbolic action, with the primary antecedent being the prophet Jeremiah's acts symbolizing the imminent destruction of Jerusalem and its temple.[55]

The Trial and Crucifixion of Jesus

With regard to the crucifixion of Jesus, scholars point out that, for numerous reasons, the gospel accounts of the "trial of Jesus," especially their attempt to portray Jews rather than Romans as responsible for the death of Jesus, are surely fictional. For example, the actual Pontius Pilate, in extreme contrast with the indecisive, vacillating figure portrayed in the Gospels, was "not one to waste time on legal niceties." His administration was known, in the words of Josephus, for "frequent murders of untried prisoners."[56] But these scholars also agree that the high priests, who were made nervous by any threat to their system of privilege, were probably involved.

The responsibility for the crucifixion of Jesus, however, finally had to rest with the Roman authorities. The death penalty could be authorized only by them, and crucifixion was then and there an exclusively Roman manner of execution. It was also a manner used primarily for those regarded as challengers to Roman authority. "That Jesus was *crucified* by the Roman governor," summarizes Horsley, "stands as a vivid symbol of his historical relationship with the Roman imperial order."[57]

CHRISTIANITY AND EMPIRE

If Jesus' message of the kingdom of God was a direct challenge to the continued rule of the Roman Empire over his people, it would seem to follow that Christians down through history would have been radically anti-imperialistic. But this, especially since the age of Constantine in the fourth century of the Christian era, has seldom been the case. There are several reasons for this fact.

Changing the Enemies

For one thing, the complete opposition of Jesus and his early followers to the imperialism of their day has been largely hidden to readers of the Gospels. The main reason for this hiddenness is that the authors of the Gospels, seeking to present the message of Jesus so as to serve the needs of the Christian movement forty or more years after the death of Jesus, sought to make it appear that Jesus' message was directed against, and evoked opposition from, "the Jews," rather than the Roman Empire and those who collaborated with it.

This strategy was carried out most fully and effectively by the author of

Luke-Acts, which was written to show Roman authorities that Christianity was utterly harmless to the Roman Empire, because Christians, unlike Jews, were faithful subjects, and to convince Christians that the continued existence of the empire would facilitate, not hinder, the coming of the kingdom of God. For example, although Paul in reality, according to tradition, suffered the same fate at the hands of the Romans as did Jesus, the Book of Acts ends with Paul peacefully "proclaiming the kingdom of God . . . with complete freedom and without hindrance from anyone."[58] Given this picture, the Book of Revelation, which portrays the Roman Empire as the very embodiment of Satan, seems like a foreign body in the New Testament.

It is now well known that, whatever its merits at that time, this strategy of portraying Jesus' enemies as "the Jews" later contributed to the despicable history of Christian anti-Judaism, the deadly effects of which did not end with the Nazi holocaust. Also vitally important, however, is the fact that this strategy has led most later Christians to fail to understand the original thrust of their religion. Horsley and Silberman say that, for the early Christians, "Rome was the Beast, the Harlot, the Dragon, Babylon, the Great Satan. They knew that Rome's empire was made possible not by divine order but by the acquisition of vast territories through the deadly violence of the Roman legions and the self-serving acquiescence of their own local aristocracies."[59] This failure of later Christians to understand the beginnings of their religion has contributed to what is arguably the most fateful reversal in history: Christianity, in origin probably the most explicitly anti-imperial religious movement ever, has since the fourth century provided the religious foundation for the growth of empires even more extensive than Rome's.

The Idea of Unilateral Divine Action

A second reason for the fact that Christian faith has not been oriented against empire is the assumption, already evident at the time of Paul, that God would bring in the kingdom of God unilaterally. We do not know exactly what Jesus' view of this matter was—that is, whether he saw himself as merely proclaiming and dramatizing the inbreaking of the kingdom that God would bring about unilaterally, or whether Jesus believed that the activities of his movement would be the means by which God would bring the kingdom fully into existence.

But, whatever the view of Jesus himself may have been, his later followers clearly assumed that the replacement of demonic by divine rule would be effected unilaterally by God. As Horsley and Silberman say, Paul, expecting an "imminent divine intervention" that would result in "the utter destruction of 'this evil age,'" encouraged his followers to "separate themselves from the ways of the wicked and await the impending climax of a divine drama that had been unfolding for thousands of years." Given this stance of passive waiting for God to act, "The weekly meetings of the *ekklesiai* . . . and the ritualized reenactment of Christ's resurrection through baptism and the Lord's Supper became sacred ends in themselves," so the Christian movement "increasingly lost touch with its goal of forming a practical worldwide alliance against the forces of empire."[60]

Changing the Focus

Closely related to this development was the emphasis of some New Testament authors, especially Paul (at least as usually understood), on the cross and resurrection of Jesus to the neglect of his life and message, and on Jesus himself as the savior. As a well-known slogan among New Testament scholars puts it, "The proclaimer became the proclaimed," which meant a shift of emphasis from what God is going to do to what God has already done. This shift is implicit in the confession of Jesus as "the Christ," a term that was originally simply a translation of "the Messiah." For Jews, this term was to be applied to the person through whom the kingdom of God on earth would actually be brought about. From that perspective, it was self-contradictory to say that the Messiah had already come, given the fact that the world had not fundamentally changed.

Christians avoided this self-contradiction by understanding the "salvation" achieved by Jesus in a different way—a way implying that the idea of a reign of divine values on earth was at best a secondary dimension of Christian salvation. This dimension of complete salvation did not, of course, completely drop out of Christian thought and imagination. For one thing, its presence in the Lord's Prayer has made it too prominent to ignore. But the main focus shifted to the idea that we, as individual sinners, have been saved through the death and resurrection of Jesus. Jesus had thereby saved us from hell and for heaven. When Karl Marx called religion the "opiate of the masses," he had in mind primarily this otherworldly form of Christian faith, in which salvation does not require overcoming the evils of this world.[61]

Giving Caesar His Due

A fourth factor contributing to the misunderstanding of Jesus' message by later Christians is the traditional understanding of Jesus' statement in Mark 12:17, "Give back to Caesar the things that are Caesar's, and to God the things that are God's." According to this traditional interpretation, Jesus meant that, since the coin had Caesar's likeness on it, one should go ahead and pay the tribute. This text has therefore been seen as providing the basis for a dualism, especially emphasized by Luther, between "two kingdoms"—the divine and the secular, the eternal and the temporal—and for the later doctrine of the separation between religion and politics. Such a dualism, according to which there is no expectation that this world is to be ruled by divine principles, is often portrayed as the central difference between Christianity and Islam.

However, if Jesus' message was focused on the expectation of a divine rule on earth, that difference should not exist. Horsley argues, in any case, that the traditional interpretation of the passage in question is wrong. For Jesus and other Jews at that time, it was self-evident that *everything* belonged to God, so that *nothing* belonged to Caesar. With his ambiguous remark, therefore, Jesus was able to avoid being trapped into explicitly advocating nonpayment while still implicitly doing so.[62] Given this interpretation, which fits with the rest of Horsley's portrayal of Jesus as preaching the reign of God as the alternative to the reign of empire, this passage provides no basis for turning the present world over to be ruled by those with the most power, regardless of the principles being used to direct this power.

The Idea of Plenary Inspiration

Still another fact that has helped Jesus' anti-imperial gospel transmute into an empire-supporting religion is the doctrine of inerrant, plenary inspiration, according to which all parts of the Bible are equally inspired. Not all traditional Christian theologians have held this doctrine. Luther, for example, regarded the Bible as "the cradle of Christ," meaning that other parts are to be evaluated in terms of how well they conform to the gospel of Jesus Christ. On this basis, Luther felt quite free to criticize various parts of the Bible. Calvinism, however, taught that all parts of the Bible are equally inspired. This doctrine, in conjunction with the Protestant view that all parts of the Bible are to be given a literal interpretation, implied that the most bellicose passages in the Bible, including those ordering the Israelites to exterminate the Canaanites, actually reflected the divine will.

In earlier Christian thought, passages advocating warfare had been interpreted allegorically and anagogically (morally), rather than literally. In this way, the Bible's bellicose passages could be interpreted so that they did not conflict with a God of love and peace.

In any case, these bellicose passages, literally interpreted, were used by European Americans, seeing this land as "the New Israel,"[63] to justify the extermination of Native Americans. For example, John Quincy Adams, author of the Monroe Doctrine and one of the primary architects of territorial gains, believed, says Anders Stephanson, that "American expansionism derived its legitimacy from the imperatives of the Old Testament."[64]

The Traditional Doctrine of Divine Omnipotence

Underlying at least some of these factors contributing to the emergence of an empire-supporting Christianity is the traditional doctrine of divine omnipotence, according to which God can bring about events in the world unilaterally. Having this kind of power, God could inspire scriptures inerrantly and bring about a reign of God on earth unilaterally. This notion of divine power also created an insoluble problem of evil, as I have shown in many writings.[65] In the next chapter, I show that this conception of divine power has also contributed to still one more factor that has influenced Christians not to regard opposition to empire as part and parcel of Christian faith: the trivialization of the idea of demonic power.

Chapter 8

The Divine and the Demonic

After pointing out that the American empire is now often compared with that of Rome, I looked in the previous chapter at the Roman Empire as a basis for understanding not only the American empire but also the nature of the message of Jesus. Although Rome saw itself as divinely authorized to impose its *Pax Romana* on the world, the nature of this "peace" was far from divine. It was not even benign. Jesus regarded it as the very opposite of divine: as demonic. This fact raises the question of whether Christians today should regard the American empire as demonic. I discuss that question in chapter 9. The present chapter deals with a prior question: Is the notion of demonic power necessarily a mythological idea, which can no longer be taken seriously by modern (and postmodern) minds, or is it possible to develop a nonmythological notion of demonic power? I argue that the latter is the case.

Readers will, I should add, find this chapter very different from the previous ones. Whereas those prior chapters dealt with matters of fact, history, and politics, the present chapter is philosophical and theological. Working through it will, therefore, require a major psychological shift on the reader's part. A willingness to engage in a very different kind of discourse, involving radically different concepts, will be needed. I believe, nevertheless, that the concepts discussed in the chapter—the "divine" and the "demonic"—are of crucial importance in developing a form of Christian faith that is able to deal realistically with what America has become.

I begin with a discussion of the divine and the demonic in traditional Christian thought, then use that as a background for developing a new understanding of demonic power.

THE DIVINE AND THE DEMONIC IN TRADITIONAL CHRISTIAN THOUGHT

The contrast between the divine and the demonic is implicit every time Christians repeat the first petition of the Lord's prayer, "*Thy* kingdom come." The contrast is explicitly brought out by the final petition, "Save us from the Evil One." The contrast between divine and demonic power, including the fervent desire that the former will defeat the latter, is at the very center of Christian faith.

The New Testament's Mythological but Realistic View of the Demonic

This contrast is certainly central to the New Testament. Although the authors of the various New Testament writings surely believed that our world is essentially good, because created by God, they shared Jesus' view that it was at present under demonic control. The Gospel of Luke, for example, has the devil say that the kingdoms of the world are under his control (4:5–6). The Gospel of John speaks of the devil as "the ruler of this world" (14:30; 16:11). The First Letter of John says that "the whole world lies under the power of the evil one" (5:19). Paul speaks of "the present evil age" and of Satan as "the god of this world" (Gal. 1:4; 2 Cor. 4:4). And the New Testament view of this matter—that the world is the scene of a deadly battle between the divine and the demonic—is the theme of the book of Revelation in its entirety.

The New Testament, we can say, has a view of the demonic that is mythological but realistic. It is *mythological*, because it understands demonic power in terms of an individual creature with power, knowledge, and cosmic scope rivaling deity itself. Given the qualitative difference that must exist between the creator and any of its creatures, this view of the demonic must be regarded as mythological. No creature could approximate the omniscience, omnipresence, and universal power that belong to God alone.

And yet this picture is *realistic*, because it regards the demonic as a real power, with genuine autonomy, that is driving the world in a direction that is diametrically opposed to divine purposes.

Can we look at the past century of our world without thinking that the human race must be under the influence of such a power? The twentieth century was by far the bloodiest century in history, with unprecedented slaughter and genocide, and yet we have taken no steps to overcome the war-system of settling disputes. We created nuclear weapons and then, when we learned how deadly they were, built thousands more, until we had the world wired to be destroyed many times over. After we learned that a relatively modest exchange of nuclear weapons could initiate a "nuclear winter," leading to the death of human civilization and even most other forms of life, we still did not abolish them. Furthermore, we learned over three decades ago that, even if nuclear war is avoided, the continuation of our present trajectory, with its increasing population and pollution, would soon lead to extinction, but we have made no real efforts to change this trajectory. This has remained the case even after ozone depletion and climate change turned out to be occurring faster than predicted. Although the scientific consensus is that we must turn from a carbon-based to a solar-based energy system, with the rich countries reducing their emissions of carbon dioxide by 90 percent, and although the needed technologies are already available, the focus—especially in the United States, the global leader in pollution—is almost entirely on oil. We are, furthermore, a highly educated, smart people. It does seem that we are possessed by some demonic power that is leading us, trancelike, into self-destruction.

But is there any nonmythological way in which we can understand how this could be? To approach this question, let us look more closely at the biblical idea of the relation between the divine and the demonic. In the centuries prior to the New Testament period, the Jewish tradition had become thoroughly monotheistic. There is only one God, the creator of our world, who has acted in the history of Israel and that of other peoples and spoken through the prophets.

Monotheism is the doctrine that there is only one truly divine power, only one power worthy of worship. Monotheism does not, however, necessarily imply monism, the doctrine that there is only power, period. Monotheism is compatible with the belief in one or more centers of power that have some power of their own, and hence some autonomy, *vis-à-vis* divine power. Because a partially autonomous power could go bad, using its power to oppose the divine purposes, monotheism could be compatible with belief in a demonic power.

In fact, Jeffrey Russell, in his well-received volumes on the history of the idea of the devil, has argued that the New Testament view is best called "semidualistic monotheism."[1] In contrast with full-fledged dualism, a semidualistic position does *not* hold, as would a fully dualistic position, that the demonic is wholly autonomous and equal to God in cosmic scope and power. But it does allow some real autonomy to the demonic.

We can express this semidualism by saying that *the demonic is a creature and yet more than a creature.* To say that the demonic is a creature is to say that it, unlike the divine, does not exist eternally, but comes about only through the creative power of the divine. Once it has been created, however, it is not *merely* a creature, in the sense of being totally under the control of divine power. Rather, it can really oppose divine power and threaten its purposes. The demonic has potentially deadly consequences.

Something like this does seem to have been the view assumed in the New Testament. Such a view would, of course, presuppose that the creation has a degree of autonomy in relation to the creator. This was, indeed, the view of the Hebrew Scriptures, and this view was presupposed by New Testament writers. The crucial issue here is how the creation of our world was understood.

The Biblical View: Creation out of Chaos

Although it has long been assumed that the Hebrew Scriptures teach *creatio ex nihilo*, in the sense of creation out of absolute nothingness, biblical scholars have shown that this is not true.

Harvard's Jon Levenson has written a most important book on this issue called *Creation and the Persistence of Evil*. With regard to the opening verses of Genesis, he points out, the crucial question is how they are translated. Most translations, presupposing the idea of *creatio ex nihilo*, have rendered them, "In the beginning God created the heaven and the earth. The earth was without form and void." This translation, by indicating that the earth was "without form and void" *after* God's initial creative activity, rather than before, suggests that our universe was created out of nothing in the absolute sense.

Most scholars of the Hebrew Bible, however, agree that the best translation is: "When God began to create the heaven and the earth, the world was without form and void."[2] This translation suggests a version of the view articulated not only in most cosmogonies of the ancient Near East but also in Plato's *Timaeus*: the view that our universe was created out of a primeval chaos. This latter view, Levenson points out, is also presupposed throughout the rest of the Hebrew Bible, especially in its account of the Hebrew liturgical tradition.[3]

Getting clear on the biblical view is very important, Levenson emphasizes, because the assumption that the Bible teaches *creatio ex nihilo* has produced an overly optimistic picture of the universe, according to which God is in complete control.[4] The reference to "the persistence of evil" in the title of Levenson's book reflects the Hebrews' idea that primordial chaos was only circumscribed, not annihilated, with the result that it constantly threatens to break forth.[5]

The idea that the stuff from which God created the universe could offer resistance to the divine will was also implicit in Plato's statement that the creator willed that everything should be good "as far as possible."[6] The Hebrew and Platonic views on this subject were, therefore, similar.

The Doctrine of *Creatio Ex Nihilo*

If God, by contrast, had created our world out of absolute nothingness, then the stuff of which the world is made would be completely under divine control. It would have no autonomous power with which it could truly threaten divine purposes. Any evil that occurs would have to be understood as evil that God deliberately permits and can at some point unilaterally eliminate.

According to this view, no matter how bad things seem now, with over-population, resource shortages, global warming, growing terrorism, and weapons of mass destruction, we need not worry that anything will happen that will prevent God's purposes for our world from being fulfilled. This is what Levenson means by saying that the doctrine of *creatio ex nihilo* has made us overly optimistic. It has, in other words, made us complacent. We assume that we can go on with business as usual, even though destructive evil mounts on all sides, because we can leave it to God to prevent anything really disastrous from happening.

If this complacency-creating idea of creation is not biblical, why has it been considered the orthodox doctrine? This question is answered by another important book, *Creatio Ex Nihilo: The Doctrine of "Creation out of Nothing" in Early Christian Thought*, written by a German theologian, Gerhard May.[7] Besides agreeing with Levenson that this doctrine is nowhere to be found in the Hebrew Bible, May adds the additional point that it is also not found in the literature of intertestamental Judaism or in the New Testament.

The point that the idea of creation out of absolute nothingness is not found in intertestamental Judaism is extremely important, because scholars had long assumed that it was expressed in 2 Maccabees 7:28, which says that God created the world "out of non-being." May provides evidence to show that the use of this formula does not imply the doctrine of *creatio ex nihilo* in the strict sense, according to which the very stuff out of which this world is composed was itself created out of nothing.[8]

In the fourth century B.C.E., for example, the Greek philosopher Xenophon said that parents "bring forth their children out of non-being," and everyone knew, even back then, that babies do not simply materialize out of nothing. In other words, says May, the formula *creatio ex nihilo* was simply an "unreflective, everyday way of saying that through the act of creation something arose which did not previously exist."[9] As such, it did not imply *creatio ex nihilo* in the strict sense.

May's conclusion is even more strongly supported by the Hellenistic Jewish philosopher Philo, who lived in the first century C.E. Although Philo accepted the existence of a preexistent matter out of which God had created the world, he spoke of God as creating "out of non-being."[10]

This denial that *creatio ex nihilo* is found in the literature of intertestamental Judaism is crucially important, because it undermines the long-standing assumption that this doctrine is expressed in the New Testament. There are several passages, such as John 1:3, Romans 4:17, Colossians 1:16, and Hebrews 11:3, that, while not explicitly affirming the doctrine of *creatio ex nihilo*, have been taken to imply it. New Testament scholars and Christian theologians were able to read this doctrine into these passages because, as May says, they argued that "primitive Christianity found the doctrine ready-made in the Jewish tradition" so that "one would be able to presuppose it for the New Testament."[11] But if the New Testament authors did *not* find the doctrine of *creatio ex nihilo* in the tradition, then there is no basis for assuming that these ambiguous passages imply the doctrine.

I should add, incidentally, that May cannot be suspected of distorting the evidence to support his own theological position, because he, as a Christian theologian, accepts the doctrine of *creatio ex nihilo*.[12] I do not myself find his reasons for accepting it persuasive. But I admire his honesty in pointing out, as historian, that those who wish to support this doctrine cannot do so by appeal to the Bible.

In any case, besides undergirding Levenson's conclusion that this doctrine is not biblical, May explains why it nevertheless became accepted as the orthodox Christian position.

It did not become thus accepted, he pointed out, until the latter part of the second Christian century. Until that time, Christian as well as Jewish theologians accepted the Platonic view that our world was created out of unformed, eternally existing matter. We have seen that Philo, the most important Jewish theologian of the first century C.E., held this view. On the Christian side, many second-century theologians who are considered orthodox by later standards, including Justin Martyr, Athenagoras, and Clement of Alexandria, also held this view. Justin Martyr even argued that Plato "took over the doctrine that God made the cosmos out of unoriginate matter from the opening verses of Genesis."[13] In other words, Plato, in developing his doctrine that our world was created out of primordial chaos, plagiarized Moses! Nothing could better illustrate the fact that early Christian theologians did not believe that the Bible taught *creatio ex nihilo*. In any case, all of these theologians thought, May points out, that the "acceptance of an unformed matter was entirely reconcilable with biblical monotheism."[14]

The occasion for the change, which came about in the latter part of the second century, was a threat created by Marcion, who held a strongly dualistic view of the universe. In his theology, there were two divine beings—one good, the other evil. Our world is so filled with evil, Marcion said, because it was created by an evil creator, this being the deity of Hebrew Scriptures. The good and loving deity revealed in Jesus, Marcion maintained, was a different being.[15] On this basis, Marcion formulated a canon for Christians that excluded the Hebrew Scriptures. Church historians have long known that it was the crisis produced by Marcion's position that, by reaction, led the church to formulate a canon.

Now we learn that the crisis produced by Marcion also led, by reaction, to the doctrine of *creatio ex nihilo*.

What occasioned this reaction was Marcion's assertion that the primordial matter out of which our world was created was inherently evil. This doctrine made no sense philosophically. In Plato's view, uncreated matter in itself, being formless, is entirely "without qualities." It could not, therefore, be said to be *either* good *or* evil.[16]

Marcion was, therefore, evidently not a very clear thinker. But it is often unclear thinkers who make the biggest impact. And that was true in this case—thanks to some other unclear thinkers, who decided that the best way to fence the church off from Marcion's doctrine, according to which God created the world out of evil matter, was simply to deny that God had created the world out of *anything*.

The threat posed by Marcion's doctrine that the unformed matter was inherently evil could have been resolved simply by pointing out that he was confused. And the problem of evil, which rightly bothered Marcion, could have been overcome by emphasizing a point implicit in both Plato and the Hebrew Scriptures—namely, that the creatures, by virtue of having been created out of primordial stuff, had power to resist the divine will.

Both of these moves were, in fact, made by a second-century theologian named Hermogenes.[17] Against those who were rejecting the traditional view of creation out of chaos in favor of creation out of absolute nothingness, Hermogenes warned that this novel doctrine would create an insoluble problem of evil. If we say that God created our world out of nothing, he pointed out, we can have no coherent explanation of the existence of evil, "because as perfect Goodness [God] could only have created good, so the origin of evil would not be explained."[18] The idea of *creatio ex nihilo*, in other words, would lead people to deny the perfect goodness of God, because God, as the source of literally everything, would have to be the source of evil. Or it would simply lead people to deny the existence of God altogether. Hermogenes's prediction has, of course, proved to be all too accurate.

Those who were intent on fencing off the church's teaching from that of Marcion, however, would not listen to the clear-thinking Hermogenes. Tatian, one of Justin Martyr's pupils, began attacking the idea of an uncreated stuff, and Theophilus of Antioch, the earliest opponent of Hermogenes, explicitly affirmed the doctrine of *creatio ex nihilo*. Theophilus then influenced Hippolytus, Tertullian, and Irenaeus. Within decades, the novel doctrine of *creatio ex nihilo* was considered the fixed Christian position.[19]

It was primarily through the influence of Marcion and these other four theologians, therefore, that the doctrine of *creatio ex nihilo* came to be accepted as *the* Christian teaching. I suggested earlier that these other theologians, like Marcion, were less than clear thinkers. This conclusion is supported by May, even though he agrees with their conclusion. He calls the ideas of Theophilus "somewhat confused." And, having said that Theophilus's affirmation of *creatio ex nihilo* was bound to create "a philosophical problem" of evil, May adds, "But this is a question far beyond Theophilus."[20] Furthermore, although May praises Irenaeus for rejecting the Platonic view that God can will only "the best possible" in favor of the affirmation of "the absolute freedom and omnipotence of the biblical God," May admits that "Irenaeus did not discuss the problems of creation on the philosophical level of his time" and that his position was "only attainable because Irenaeus is quite unaware of philosophical problems."[21]

The importance of May's book cannot be overemphasized. It shows that the church, and thereby to a great extent Western civilization, was saddled with the unbiblical doctrine of *creatio ex nihilo* primarily through the influence of a handful of men who, besides not being in the mood for careful philosophical thought, were evidently incapable of it. The novel doctrine produced by these hasty and unphilosophical minds put Christian thinking about the God-world relation in opposition to the world's other religious traditions. It has, by supporting a doctrine of absolute divine omnipotence, given Christians an insoluble problem of evil.[22] And it has also—the point to be emphasized here—produced Christian complacency by undermining the New Testament's conviction that our world is the scene of a deadly battle between divine and demonic power.

St. Augustine on the Devil

A decisive figure in this development was St. Augustine, who at the beginning of the fifth century rigorously worked out the implications of the doctrine of *creatio ex nihilo*. His resulting doctrine of divine omnipotence required that all power belongs to God alone, so that nothing contrary to the divine will could happen. God, says Augustine, "is called Almighty for no other reason than that he can do whatsoever he willeth and because the efficacy of his omnipotent will is not impeded by the will of any creature. . . . Nothing . . . happens unless the Omnipotent wills it to happen."[23] Accordingly, it can be said even of evil wills, says Augustine, that they "are so entirely at the disposal of God, that He turns them whithersoever He wills, and whensoever He wills. . . . [God] does in the hearts of even wicked men whatsoever He wills."[24] The popular Christianity of the time thought of the devil as in some sense independent of God and as hostile to God's purposes, carrying on a life-and-death battle of cosmic proportions. But within Augustine's theology, the devil could no more oppose God's will than could any other creature. As Augustine said about Peter's denials: "By the power given to the devil . . . Peter was tempted so that he might not think too highly of himself. . . . God himself . . . did all things justly by the power he gave to the devil."[25] In this monistic theology, according to which all power belongs to God, the devil plays no essential role, being merely one more instrument through which the Sole Power unilaterally works its will.

This theology retains the mythological aspect of the New Testament's view of the demonic while giving up its realism. This view is mythological, to repeat, because it thinks of the demonic in terms of an individual creature who rivals God in cosmic scope, knowledge, and power. This view thereby attributes powers to a creature that no creature could have. But this view loses the New Testament's realism by depriving the demonic power of any shred of autonomy, regarding Satan instead as wholly under the divine thumb. Because all power is said to be ultimately God's, the battle between God and the demonic becomes a mock battle, not a real one. The demonic is safely domesticated, brought within the household of God's instruments. Christians could be complacent.

A NEW VIEW OF DEMONIC POWER: REALISM WITHOUT MYTHOLOGY

Implicit in the foregoing historical overview of traditional thinking about the divine and the demonic is a constructive suggestion: if we return to the biblical idea of creation out of chaos, we might be able to come up with a view of the demonic that is the opposite of St. Augustine's—a view that overcomes the mythological character of the New Testament view while retaining its realism.

God, Creativity, and the World

I am an advocate of the form of theology known as "process theology," which uses as its primary philosophical resource the philosophy of Alfred North Whitehead.[26] One of Whitehead's greatest gifts to theology is his doctrine that the basic stuff of which the world, including human life, is made is creative energy, which he called simply "creativity." This doctrine of creativity is part and parcel of Whitehead's view that our world was created out of chaos. This doctrine of creativity also turns out to provide a basis for a contemporary version of the semidualistic monotheism presupposed in the New Testament. It thereby provides the basis for a doctrine of demonic power as truly demonic—as truly threatening to divine purposes.

Creativity, like Plato's unformed matter, never exists by itself. It exists only as embodied in actual beings. God is the primordial embodiment of creativity. To say that God is primordial is to say that God has always existed. Creative power, therefore, has always existed as embodied by God. Thus far, process theology is in agreement with traditional theology.

Process theology rejects, however, the traditional view that creative power is primordially embodied *only* in God, which meant that God could completely control the creatures. The biblical tradition gave no clear answer to this question. On the one hand, there are passages suggesting that the creatures have no power *vis-à-vis* God, such as those passages saying that God molds human beings like a potter molds clay.[27] On the other hand, the idea that the world was created out of primordial stuff left open the possibility, emphasized by Hermogenes and Levenson, that the creatures, by virtue of embodying this primordial stuff, might have some power of their own with which they can resist the divine molding. The biblical tradition was, accordingly, ambiguous on this issue.

But this ambiguity was eliminated with the adoption of the doctrine of *creatio ex nihilo*. Monotheism became *monism*, according to which all creative power essentially belongs to God alone. If the creatures have any creative power, this is only because God has freely given them some. And, having been freely given, it can be withdrawn at any time. This is why traditional theists could be complacent about creaturely power, including that creaturely power called demonic.

In process theism, by contrast, creative power is primordially embodied in a world of finite beings as well as in God. But this does *not* mean that our particular world has always existed. Whitehead's view, like Plato's, is that our particular world started coming into existence at a particular time in the past.

This view is now also supported by scientific evidence, even if one accepts the currently dominant view, according to which our cosmos originated about 14 billion years ago.[28] The idea, widespread among physical cosmologists, that our world originated out of a vacuum, perhaps with a big bang, might seem to imply *creatio ex nihilo*. But the idea of a vacuum is really the idea of a condition in which, although there is no matter, there is tremendous energy.[29]

This view is similar to Whitehead's. His term for a situation with creative energy but no matter is "chaos." It was a chaotic situation because the embodiments of creativity, or energy, were simply momentary events, each one lasting perhaps a billionth of a second or less. There were, as Carl Sagan would have said, billions of billions of billions of these events. But none of them was channeled into enduring structures. Besides no electrons or neutrinos, there were not even any enduring individuals as simple as quarks. There were, by hypothesis, simply very brief energy events happening at random.

Creation of Our Cosmos out of Relative Nothing

Given this idea, there is a sense in which creation out of nothing can be affirmed. When we speak of "things," we normally have in mind *enduring* things, which retain their identity over time. In this sense of the term, there were no *things* in the chaotic situation out of which God created our world. God, accordingly, created our world "out of no-thing." Simply putting it that way, however, could cause confusion. This confusion can be avoided by using the language provided by Russian Orthodox theologian Nicolas Berdyaev. The Greek language, Berdyaev pointed out, has two terms for nothing, *ouk on*, which refers to *absolute* nonbeing, and *me on*, which refers to *relative* nonbeing.

On this basis, Berdyaev, who had a view of creation somewhat like Whitehead's, affirmed creation out of *relative* nothing.[30] This doctrine affirms that everything of value in our world is due to God. I cannot see why Christian faith in God as creator—of the heavens and the earth, of life, and of human life—requires any stronger affirmation than this.

This rejection of the doctrine of creation out of *absolute* nothingness means that the creation of our world did not involve the beginning of finite existence as such. It involved, instead, God's bringing order out of chaos. Our world started coming into existence when, out of this chaos, God evoked the most primitive forms of order at the base of our world. Instead of all events happening at random, some of them came to be ordered into enduring strings of events, in which each event in the string repeated the form of its predecessors. A more complex order emerged when these simplest enduring individuals combined to form compound individuals, perhaps quarks and gluons. Then these in turn merged in various combinations to form more complex enduring individuals, such as electrons, protons, and neutrons, which in turn merged to form atoms and molecules, then macromolecules, then living cells, and so on.

Self-Determination All the Way Down

This process of creation took a long time because God was not working with passive stuff, which could simply be manipulated. Rather, each enduring individual consists of a series of events, each of which has its own creativity, its own power. This creative power has two dimensions. It is, in the first place, the power of each event to respond to prior events with at least some iota of self-determination. We know of this responsive power from our own experience. In each moment, we are affected by all the events in our environment. But we decide precisely how to respond to them. For example, if a waiter accidentally spills scalding water on me, I will feel the pain; this is forced upon me. But I have the power to respond with either anger or forgiveness.

On the basis of this act of self-determination, I then exercise the second kind of creative power, which is usually simply called "causation." I cause my body to act in particular ways, so the waiter may hear me say, "You stupid idiot!" Or, if I use my freedom differently, he may hear, "That's OK. I realize you didn't mean to do it."

Whitehead's doctrine that all individuals embody creativity means that at least some iota of responsive, self-determining creativity, as well as some degree of outgoing, causal creativity, is exercised by all events, even those in the primordial chaos. In other words, freedom, like the lady's turtles, goes all the way down. Such a view would have been ridiculed in the nineteenth century, when science was heavily committed to a strict determinism. But since the discovery of quantum indeterminacy, this idea is not ruled out.[31] The idea is also increasingly supported by biologists who have discovered that bacteria make decisions.[32] Likewise, the scientist Robert Millikan, who was known as "Mr. Molecule" because of his intimacy with this form of existence, once said that if molecules were as big as dogs, we would unhesitatingly attribute the power of decision making to them.[33]

The idea that freedom goes all the way down might seem to be obviously false. There is surely no freedom in a rock or a pile of sand. But this apparent problem is avoided by the recognition, emphasized by Whitehead, that low-grade individuals can be organized in two basic ways. On the one hand, they can form things such as rocks and plants, in which there is no dominant center of activity to exercise self-determination. On the other hand, they can form "compound individuals," such as cells and animals, which do have a dominant center of activity through which the individual as a whole can act. The idea that some degree of freedom goes all the way down applies only to individuals—both simple and compound. This doctrine is not falsified, therefore, by the fact that things such as rocks and styrofoam cups have no freedom.[34]

Divine Power as Persuasive

Having explained the idea that our world was created out of things with some power of self-determination, I turn now to its theological implications. If God is the supreme but never the only embodiment of creative power, then power is always shared power. God never has a monopoly on power and hence can never unilaterally determine what will occur. Because the creativity embodied in finite beings is inherent to the realm of finitude—rather than freely bestowed—it cannot be withdrawn or overridden.

This view of shared power implies that divine power is persuasive, not coercive. God influences every finite event, but God cannot wholly determine how any event will use its own creativity and thereby its twofold power to exert self-determination and causal influence on others. Because living cells, viruses, bacteria, and DNA molecules have the twofold power to act with spontaneity and then to influence other things, for good or ill, we should not suppose that there is some level of the world that fully reflects the divine will—as if God for some mysterious reason wanted there to be cancer, AIDS, and genetically deformed babies. Rather, as Plato suggested, our creator at each level brought about the best order that was possible. The importance of this point to Whitehead is shown by his statement that Plato's view "that the divine element in the world is to be conceived as a persuasive agency and not as a coercive agency" should be considered "one of the greatest intellectual discoveries in the history of religion."[35]

Creation as Risk

Another theological implication of this view of the God-world relation is that the creation of a cosmos with very complex compound individuals is necessarily a risky business. This is so because the higher the form of existence, the greater its power of self-determination, with which it can resist the divine preferences, and also the greater its power to influence others, for good or ill.[36] Although electrons, atoms, and molecules have some power of self-determination, this power is surely vanishingly small. During most of the history of our universe, therefore, the freedom in the creation would have been trivial.[37] The rise of living organisms such as bacteria would have been the first truly significant increase in the power of self-determination. But even the freedom of these procaryotic cells was trivial in comparison with that of eucaryotic cells, which evidently emerged only a little over a billion years ago. Then about 550 million years ago, most of the basic life forms of today were created. This period, known as "biology's big bang," increased the freedom within the creation many times over.[38] The next major increase would have been the rise of the higher forms of mammals within the last 100 million years, especially the simians. Surely the greatest single increase in freedom, however, occurred when one line within the simians gave rise to human beings.

This very recent event in the history of our planet was God's greatest gamble, because creativity as embodied in human beings had the potential to become qualitatively more powerful than that of any other species. Because of our unprecedented power of self-determination, we can make decisions that run strongly counter to the divine influences upon us, which are always calling us to truth, beauty, and goodness. Because of our unique ability to understand these divine norms, furthermore, our ability to deviate from the divine will is our power to sin. Also, thanks to our distinctive minds, by means of which we can grasp and manipulate symbols, combined with our opposable thumbs, by means of which we can grasp and manipulate external things, we have far more power to exert coercive power than do other creatures. Our power to sin is, accordingly, matched by an equally unprecedented power to dominate.

Our unprecedented power of influence is not limited, moreover, to coercion: our linguistic power has given us an unprecedented form of persuasive power as well, a form of power that was greatly augmented with the invention of writing and more recently the technologies of mass communication. Because of the distinctive capacities of human beings, their emergence meant the rise of creatures who could, over time, come to exercise forms of power that could threaten God's present purposes for our world.

Creaturely Creativity and the Demonic

Whitehead's notion of creativity, I have suggested, provides a basis for reconceiving demonic power. Thus far I have spoken, as did Whitehead, simply of creativity, pointing out that it is embodied in both God and the world. Developing an idea of demonic power, however, requires that we distinguish clearly between these two embodiments.[39] We can make this distinction terminologically by calling creativity as embodied in God "divine creativity" and creativity as embodied in the world "creaturely creativity."

Making this distinction is important because these embodiments are qualitatively different. In one sense, to be sure, creativity as embodied in God is the same as that embodied in creatures: it involves the twofold power to exert both self-determination and then causal influence on others. In other respects, however, it is radically different. For one thing, every creaturely embodiment of creativity is a local embodiment, which is significantly influenced by only a small portion of the universe and has significant influence back upon only a small portion. Creativity as embodied in God, by contrast, is universal, because the divine experience encompasses the whole universe. Likewise, creaturely creativity is always directed by limited knowledge, even in the most informed human beings, whereas divine creativity is always directed by omniscience, the knowledge of everything knowable at the time.[40]

Because of these metaphysical differences, furthermore, divine creativity is—and this is the main point here—*morally* different from creaturely creativity.

Creativity as it is embodied in God is morally different from creaturely creativity in both of its dimensions. On the one hand, the responsive, self-determining creativity of God is always qualified by compassion for all sentient beings. The word "compassion," like its synonym "sympathy," literally means *feeling with*—feeling the others' feeling as one's own.

Abraham Joshua Heschel, in his great work *The Prophets*, argued that the God of the Bible, unlike the deity of some Greek philosophers, suffers with the suffering of the people. It was the prophets' experience of this divine *pathos*, Heschel suggests, that led them to cry for justice.[41] Marcus Borg, building on Heschel, has emphasized the centrality of divine compassion in the message of Jesus.[42]

Process theology provides philosophical support for this view, saying that it belongs to the very nature of God to feel the feelings of the creatures as God's own feelings, so that God suffers with our sufferings and rejoices with our joys. The divine knowledge of the world, therefore, is not neutral. It is *sympathetic* knowledge. We can call this the "responsive love of God."

To understand why God responds with sympathy or compassion for all sentient beings, even though humans do not, we can begin by reflecting on the fellow creatures to whom we most naturally respond with sympathy. These are, in my case, primarily the cells composing my own body. For these other beings, I have a natural sympathy, feeling their pains and enjoyments as my own, and this sympathy extends equally to all parts of my body. I will not, for example, take good care of one foot while deliberately causing pain to my other one. Nor do I have compassion for my feet while being indifferent to my hands. Given the fact that love in the most basic sense is being sympathetic with the feelings of others, feeling their feelings as one's own, and therefore wishing them well and doing what one can to help them, we can say that I have a natural and equal love for all parts of my body.

However, my natural compassion for my own bodily parts does not extend to the beings making up most of the rest of the world. I can remain indifferent to most of them. I may have a deep sympathy, which is partly natural and partly developed through intimate association, for a few other fellow creatures, such as my family members, close friends, and pets. But for the most part I do not have a natural sympathy or compassion for most of the life of the planet. Some degree of compassion can, to be sure, be cultivated, perhaps by regarding all other creatures as, like myself, sentient creatures loved by God. But this cultivated compassion will not lead me to feel the feelings of most other creatures with anything like the depth with which I feel the feelings of my own bodily members. As one honest observer put it, he was more preoccupied with the discomfort caused by a hangnail than he was with the starvation of millions of people around the world. Because we are very local beings, having a relation of direct sympathetic awareness of only, for the most, our own bodily members, we can be indifferent to, or even take delight in, the sufferings of others.

God, however, is not a localized being but the omnipresent one. And as Charles Hartshorne, the second founder of process theology, especially emphasized, we should think of God as the soul of the world, related to the world as a whole in somewhat the same way as we are related to our own bodies.[43] It is natural for God, therefore, to feel the feelings of all sentient beings with the same kind of sympathetic, compassionate awareness with which we feel our own bodily cells.

For Christians, this idea should come naturally, given our acceptance of Jesus' sufferings on the cross as God's own sufferings. And insofar as we take Jesus as the supreme revelation of God, the cross becomes revelatory of how God responds to the sufferings of creatures in general. As Matthew 25 suggests, insofar as we bring either joy or suffering to "one of the least of these," we bring either joy or suffering to God.

In any case, we can say that God's responsive creativity is always informed by compassion for the experiences of all the creatures. Unlike us, God cannot love some while hating or being indifferent to others. God naturally—by nature—responds to all creatures with responsive love.[44]

To reinforce this point, the importance of which will become more apparent below, we can look at the argument of some philosophers who have suggested that God might not be perfectly loving. For example, Henry David Aiken, arguing that "there is no logical connection between the metaphysical attributes [of God] and the moral attributes," added, "Logically, there is no reason why an . . . omniscient being might not be a perfect stinker." P. H. Nowell-Smith made a similar judgment, saying: "There is nothing in the idea of an . . . omniscient creator which, by itself, entails his goodness."[45] Both of these philosophers contend, therefore, that from the idea of God's omniscience, which means having perfect knowledge of all things, it does not follow that God would be perfect in goodness, having love for all things.

But for philosophers to say this is for them to forget about the kind of knowledge that we have of our own bodies. Many people, perhaps especially philosophers, are inclined to think of our most basic kind of knowledge as that which we obtain through sense perception, as when we see a deer. It is true that knowledge of that type does not necessarily involve sympathy. The deer hunter can, therefore, pull the trigger on his rifle, wounding or killing the deer, without feeling any pain himself. By analogy from this kind of knowledge, Aiken and Nowell-Smith can assume that, although God knows everything happening in the world, God might not be compassionate.

But the knowledge we get through our eyes is a very indirect kind of knowledge, mediated first by billions of photons, which carry information from the deer to the hunter's eye, then by billions of neurons, which mediate that information to his brain, from which his conscious experience derives it. We cannot imagine that God's knowledge of the world is this indirect, highly mediated form of knowledge. Rather, if God is omnipresent, then God's knowledge must be more like the knowledge that the hunter has of his own bodily cells, to which his experience is directly connected. And this knowledge, as pointed out above, is highly sympathetic.

Given this more adequate understanding of knowledge, which process theology provides, we can see that, contrary to Aiken and Nowell-Smith, the divine omniscience *does* imply the divine goodness. Or, to use the language of philosopher J. Brenton Stearns, we can say that, contrary to Stearns, God's "metaphysical eminence" *does* imply God's "moral eminence." Contrary to Stearns, therefore, it is *not* the case that a "metaphysically supreme being" might be evil. Once we see that direct, immediate knowledge is always sympathetic knowledge, we can see that an omnipresent, omniscient being would necessarily have compassion for all sentient creatures.[46]

This difference between God and the creatures with regard to responsive creativity leads to a parallel moral difference in *outgoing* creativity. Because we can feel hatred or at least indifference toward others, we can use our outgoing creativity—our creative influence in the world—in ways that are not intended to promote the welfare of most other creatures. Indeed, we can use our power to inflict pain upon or even destroy other creatures. But because of God's compassion for all creatures, God's influence on the world always aims to promote the good of all creatures. We can call this the "creative love of God."[47]

This doctrine—that it belongs to the very nature of God to have creative and responsive love for all the creatures because the relation of God to the world as a whole is analogous to our relation to our own bodies—is process theology's way of explaining the New Testament's insight that God *is* love.

The resulting understanding of God is trinitarian, with the three dimensions being the divine creativity, the responsive love of God, and the creative love of God.[48] The point here, however, is not the threeness but the fact that *the divine use of power is necessarily and hence always characterized by universal compassion and active goodwill.*

On the basis of this understanding of the divine reality, demonic power would involve creaturely power that is exercised in a way that is diametrically opposed to divine creativity. Therefore, demonic power would involve *creaturely creativity that is exercised on the basis of hate or indifference and therefore without the intent to promote the welfare of all those affected by it.*

Being diametrically opposed to divine creativity is, however, only one of the two characteristics creaturely creativity should have before we apply the term "demonic" to it. The other characteristic is that it be *powerful enough to threaten divine purposes.* The rise of human beings, I have suggested, introduced the potential for creaturely creativity to become this powerful.

With this account, we have a theoretical explanation of how demonic power is possible in a monotheistic universe. This position, I have said, can be called semidualistic monotheism. It is not *fully* dualistic, because demonic power is not eternal. The demonic is a creature that arose in time as a result of God's creative activity. If God had not stimulated the evolutionary process to bring forth humanlike beings, demonic power would not exist. The demonic, as the Bible and Christian tradition have held, is a creature. Although the power out of which the demonic arose—creaturely creativity—*is* eternal, it is not inherently evil. It is neutral, capable of becoming either good or evil.

Process theology, therefore, rejects Marcion's view that our world was created out of evil stuff, and also his view that demonic power is eternal. Many billions of years of evolution occurred in our universe and on our planet before demonic power arose. As Matthew Fox has emphasized, what has been called "original sin" is a latecomer in the universe.[49]

But this position, in contrast with monistic monotheism, is semidualistic, because it says that once the demonic power has emerged, it has its own power, so that it cannot be unilaterally controlled or eliminated by God.

Demonic Power as Uncontrollable by Divine Power

Because monistic monotheism has portrayed the demonic as ultimately under the control of divine power, it is important to emphasize that it cannot be unilaterally controlled by God. It *is* a creature of divine creative power: Without the influence of the divine persuasion in the evolutionary process, creatures with the powers now possessed by human beings would never have come into existence, and without these powers there would be no demonic power. Nevertheless, it is not *merely* a creature, as traditionally understood, because it arises not only out of Divine Creativity but also out of creaturely creativity, which is equally eternal. Now that demonic power exists, accordingly, it cannot be unilaterally controlled. The battle between divine and demonic power is therefore a real battle, with the outcome still undecided. The ideas developed thus far can explain only why demonic power is possible. They do not explain why it actually arose. The potential for demonic power may have existed for an indefinitely long period without becoming realized. Indeed, demonic power began to arise only a few thousand years ago, which means that the human level of creativity existed for a very long time before it started giving rise to demonic power. Why did this finally happen a few thousand years ago? The answer lies in the dynamic that has been called "the parable of the tribes."

THE PARABLE OF THE TRIBES

The phrase "parable of the tribes" is taken from the title of a book by Andrew Bard Schmookler.[50] His basic idea is that once the war-system arose, the various human societies—the various tribes—inevitably became locked in a competitive spiral that has led not only to increasingly lethal technology but also to many correlative developments. I will suggest that the emergence and increasing strength of demonic power has been part and parcel of this process.

The War-System

Schmookler's argument takes off from the fact that the war-system began within the past ten thousand years. It was closely related to the rise of civilization, with its cities and agriculture.[51] During the prior existence of human beings,[52] when they supported themselves by hunting and gathering, human life was, to be sure, filled with evils of various sorts. Desires for revenge and other motives would have led tribes to carry out savage raids on each other from time to time. But the hunting-and-gathering mode of existence would have provided no motive to develop a war-system as such. For example, captives, who could not be given enough freedom to share in the hunt, would have simply provided more mouths to feed. But the rise of civilization gradually changed all this. Slaves could be assigned the drudge work involved in agriculture and the building of walls and water canals. Women captives could, besides working in the homes and the fields, bear children to build up the city's defensive and offensive capacity. The cities, with their cultivated lands and their domesticated herds, provided additional motives for attack. The rise of civilization provided a precondition for the institutionalization of war.

Once the war-system began, everyone was forced to participate. Even if most societies wanted to be peaceful, any one society could force the rest to prepare for war or risk being subjugated or annihilated. As Schmookler says, "Nice guys are finished first."[53] Schmookler's perspective in many respects follows the classic analysis provided in the seventeenth century by Thomas Hobbes, which became the basis for the presently dominant approach to international relations, called "political realism."

The State of Anarchy

According to the Hobbesian-realist analysis, the interstate realm is a state of anarchy. The term "anarchy" is not used here in its popular sense, to mean a totally lawless, chaotic situation, but in its technical sense, to mean simply the absence of a superior power to regulate the behavior of the states to each other by declaring and enforcing moral norms.[54] In this anarchical situation, it is simply power—not power qualified by moral principles—that determines the relations between the tribes.[55] The classic formulation is provided by Thucydides, who has the Athenian general give other peoples only the choice of whether they want to be taken over peacefully or violently—adding that if they had the superior power, they would do the same to the Athenians.

Anarchy, according to this Hobbesian-realist analysis,[56] means "the war of all against all." The point is not that you actually fight against everyone else, but that every other society is at least potentially your enemy. War is brought on not only by the desire of one society's leaders for additional power, riches, and glory. It can be brought on simply by one society's fear that another society is amassing enough military power to attack. Thucydides again provides the classic statement, having his general say with regard to taking Sicily, "If we cease to rule others, we are in danger of being ruled ourselves."[57]

It is important to understand that the doctrine of political realism, strictly speaking, is limited to this analysis of the present situation, with its twofold point: (1) that the present world order is anarchical and (2) that this fact makes power the determining factor in international relations. For example, in a volume entitled *The Perils of Anarchy: Contemporary Realism and International Security*, the editors give this summary statement of the position of political realists: "Realists regard anarchy—the absence of any common sovereign—as the distinguishing feature of international life. Without a central authority to enforce agreements or to guarantee security, states must rely on their own means to protect their interests."[58]

Most realists, however, go beyond this descriptive analysis to include a prediction: that this is not only the way the international situation has always been but also the way it always will be. These realists, in other words, believe that it is part and parcel of realism to hold that it would be impossible to overcome anarchy through the free creation of a global government. They do recognize, to be sure, that a *de facto* global government might be created by a sufficiently strong imperial power, which could simply impose its own rule on the rest of the world. But they reject as unrealistic the idea that anarchy could be overcome by the free decision of the states or the peoples of the world to create a global democratic government. Those who hold otherwise they dismiss as "utopians."

However, even though the political realists who add this prediction about the future have surely been in the majority, this prediction does not belong to political realism as such. That this is so can be seen from the fact that there have been political scientists and political philosophers who completely accept the realist analysis of the past and the present while calling for the creation of a global government. For example, one well-known realist, Georg Schwarzenberger, who in 1941 published an otherwise orthodox realist book entitled *Power Politics: An Introduction to the Study of International Relations and Post-War Planning*, said, "Power politics, international anarchy and war are inseparable." But, he also said, "[war's] antidote is international government."[59] Likewise fellow realist Frederick Schuman, after publishing an essay in 1946 called "Toward a World State," later published a book entitled *The Commonwealth of Man: An Inquiry into Power Politics and World Government*, in which he made the same argument.[60] I emphasize this point because Schmookler calls for the creation of a global democratic government, through which global anarchy can be overcome, and yet he fully accepts the realist analysis, according to which global anarchy, as long as it lasts, will continue to make power politics inevitable.

The Selection for Power

The next crucial point of Schmookler's analysis, in fact, is that in the present anarchical state of civilization, coercive power inevitably grows. A new offensive weapon created by one tribe forces the other tribes to create new defenses against it. These defensive advances then lead to new offensive weapons, and so on. Likewise, each technological advance by any one tribe will soon spread to the other tribes within striking distance. Once this occurs, the advance no longer gives the first tribe an advantage, so it is impelled to develop still more deadly weapons. Furthermore, a move that may be intended defensively will often look offensive to others, evoking further efforts by them to increase their power, and there is no stopping point. Although the development of nuclear weapons might have occurred either sooner or considerably later than it actually did, the fact that it did eventually occur was made virtually inevitable by the dynamics of the system. Even the creation of this seemingly ultimate weapon did not slow down the drive to invent more weapons to get an edge over potential enemies, as the present drive to weaponize space shows.

The development of ever greater coercive power does not, however, involve only the development of new forms of weapons and defenses. The most obvious additional element is military strategy and tactics, to which a major portion of any history of warfare is devoted. But a society's ability to wage war is also to a great extent a function of its political and economic systems. Any development that gives a society a temporary military edge will tend to spread to the neighboring societies. For example, the success of an early form of capitalism in the Italian city-states in the fourteenth century gave them an edge over their rivals, because they had more money to buy weapons and pay their troops. It therefore soon spread to other countries.[61]

The main point of this analysis is that the evolution of civilization in the state of anarchy is necessarily shaped in large part by a principle similar to that of natural selection in Darwinian evolution, according to which only the fit survive. Schmookler calls this principle the "selection for power." This analysis is not reductionistic, as if the drive for power were at the root of all cultural developments. The point is, instead, that of those developments that do occur, those that increase a society's power *vis-à-vis* other societies will tend not only to survive but also to spread. In the long run, the direction of civilization has been shaped decisively by this selection for power. And, as civilization evolves, the need for power increasingly shapes every aspect of a society. In recent decades, for example, something like half of America's science has been devoted to military-related research. Anarchical civilization, with its war-system, results in a reign of power.

Implicit in this analysis is the idea that the reign of power in the realm between the states leads to the reign of power *within* each state. This is not to say that the rise of hierarchical, domination societies, historically associated with the rise of patriarchy, was motivated entirely or even primarily by the demands of the war-system. That interstate system did, however, provide the context in which hierarchical societies were virtually inevitable. As Gerda Lerner points out in her study *The Creation of Patriarchy*, nonhierarchical societies for the most part simply did not survive.[62] It is hard, furthermore, to argue with the claim that survival must take priority over all other considerations. But the argument from "necessity" in relation to external dangers has always, probably from the outset of the war-system, provided the excuse for the worst kinds of internal inequities. The war-system has also provided an ever-increasing basis for the human domination of nature.

Increasing Domination by the Demonic

Through this process, only briefly sketched here, demonic power, which the rise of human existence made possible, actually came to dominance on our planet. In recent millennia, human civilization has increasingly been oriented around the drive to increase human power, in the sense of the power to control, the power to destroy, the power to intimidate. Human beings in this context have wanted more power over nature in order to increase their power over other human groups in order to give them more power over nature, and on and on. Civilization has been significantly shaped by the drive to produce coercive power that would be used with hate or at least indifference. Civilization has especially and increasingly been in its grip during the past 5,000 years, since the rise of great empires.

Although the evolution of this dominance involved a step-by-step process, rather big steps occurred now and then, when significantly new inventions, ideologies, and institutions emerged. Perhaps the first great increase in demonic power occurred in the Bronze Age, some 6,000 years ago. The next big jump evidently occurred near the outset of the Iron Age, about 3,000 years ago, with the rise not only of empires but also of patriarchy and androcentric belief systems. It is, indeed, only here, when ideology became a central dimension of the parable of the tribes, that we can speak of the demonic as fully emergent.

In that respect, two fateful developments were the marriage of Christian theology with Greco-Roman forms of thought, which occurred in the early centuries of Christianity's existence, and the Constantinian exploitation of this resulting theology for imperialistic purposes in the fourth century. Subsequent crucial preconditions for the rise of the demonic to global dominance were the market economy, European colonization of the globe, the ideologies of Nationalism and Capitalism, the Industrial Revolution, and various late-modern ideologies, such as Social Darwinism. The grip of demonic power on our planet was further increased in the twentieth century by a number of developments, including Marxism-Leninism, Fascism, *Realpolitik,* the two world wars, nuclear weapons, the Cold War, the drive toward a totally global economy, the development of computerized weapons, and the drive for an all-inclusive empire.

Due to these developments and the consequences thereof, the demonic's domination of the planet, both in extent and intensity, now dwarfs that of its incarnation in the Roman Empire, the effects of which the New Testament writers had observed. Divine values, which as incarnated would lead to a peaceable, sustainable form of existence, are increasingly overridden by demonic values, which will inevitably lead to greater warfare against each other and the rest of the earth and thereby to unsustainability. The creator's hopes for this planet, which in principle could support the harmonious and joyous flourishing of human beings and other forms of life far into the future, will be thwarted. This will be, we can only suppose, one of the supreme tragedies of the universe.

We do not, of course, have to imagine this future tragedy in order to speak of divine purposes being threatened and even thwarted by demonic power. In looking back at human history from the time of the Bronze Age forward, the violations of our creator's will—that we have life and have it abundantly—have been massive. Hegel was not wrong to call this history a slaughterbench.

Hegel's view was that, as tragic as this history was, it was inevitable. We need not accept Hegel's rather monistic, pantheistic view of the relation between the divine and the human spirit to see an element of truth in his opinion. Creaturely freedom and therefore contingency are ubiquitous. The details of the trajectory of human civilization could have been enormously different. The parable of the tribes in conjunction with this worldview, however, suggests that in broadest terms our present crisis would have come about, sooner or later, in one way or another, once human beings had arisen. What is not inevitable, however, is that we continue to acquiesce in the trajectory that has brought us to this point. Now that we have the ability to understand what has happened, we could make the decision to break free from this trajectory.

DEMONIC POWER

Having now sketched an account of how demonic power is possible in a monotheistic universe and then an account of how it arose historically, I shall now flesh out the notion of the demonic more fully. I begin with the notion that the demonic involves an objective symbolic structure, which presupposes the idea, discussed previously, that creativity as embodied in humans is capable of becoming demonic in large part because of our linguistic power.

The Demonic as Objective Symbolic Structure

This dimension of the demonic can be approached through suggestions made by theologian Arthur McGill. Much discussion of human evil has suggested a voluntaristic and individualistic understanding of sin, according to which it is perversity of will originating from within the individual human being. McGill, however, pointed out that sin is understood in the New Testament as a state of subjugation to destructive, enslaving powers that seem to come "from beyond all human agency."[63] The most complete statement of the demonic as referring to transhuman powers occurs in Ephesians 6:11–12:

> Put on the whole armor of God, so that you may be able to stand against the wiles of the devil. For our struggle is not against enemies of blood and flesh, but against the rulers, against the authorities, against the cosmic powers of this present darkness, against the spiritual forces of evil in the heavenly places.

This passage reflects the idea that the New Testament authors saw the world, although created by God, as presently under virtual enslavement to demonic power. This picture also seems true of our contemporary world, seemingly rushing toward self-destruction in a hypnotic trance. Our battle seems to be against "flesh and blood" less than against some demonic power to which human civilization is in bondage. The demonic, therefore, would not simply be the destructive use by humans of their tremendous powers out of hate or indifference, but some objective, transhuman power that leads us to embody these attitudes and act in these ways.

Helpful in understanding the nature of this transhuman power is cultural theorist Ernest Becker, who offered this naturalistic account of the demonic's emergence: "The Demonic has a naturalistic basis. It comes into being on the basis of a real evolutionary development: man is the animal in nature who, par excellence, can create vast structures of power by means of his symbolic manipulation of the world of energy."[64] Although Becker is correct to focus on the symbolic power of human beings, he moves directly to the vast structures of power based on the "symbolic manipulation of the world of energy." As important as that is, even more basic are the "vast structures of power" based on the symbolic control of the world of human experience itself. We all live largely in terms of the symbolic world provided by the culture in which we are raised. Our psychic energy is largely channeled by this inherited symbolic world. I suggest, then, that the demonic can largely be understood as *symbolic structures that channel human creativity toward destructive activities based on hate or indifference.*

Our understanding of the effects of this symbol system can be aided by McGill's description of two ways in which the demonic has been understood to work:

> Sometimes it crushes and violates with overwhelming force. . . . In this mode the demonic is represented as a giant or a dragon, full of brutally destructive violence. At other times the demonic is experienced as securing its mastery over human beings, not by brute force, but by subtle insinuation . . . seducing people to give themselves over into its power. In this mode the demonic is presented as a wily serpent taking on the appearance of a lovely woman or handsome man, manipulating and enslaving the human ego by means of enticing forms.[65]

If this second form is literalized, the demonic becomes associated with the sexual. However, if we interpret the demonic out of our contemporary situation and the New Testament, we see this side of the demonic as the seduction to resort to destruction in the name of achieving good. Rather than having two forms, the demonic has two moments. Human destructiveness has become demonic, but an essential component of this demonic destructiveness is the whole symbolic framework of myths, images, beliefs, ideologies, traditions, and habits that seduce us to employ our power destructively.

The myths, images, and beliefs in the demonic cluster of symbolic structures contain a wide variety of ingredients, such as ideas of what it means to be a "man"; stories and myths of deliverance and regeneration through violence; ideas of superior and inferior peoples; notions of tribal pride; images of fulfillment through power, glory, and riches; stories and statues, even in churches, glorifying military heroes; national flags and anthems; religious scriptures or interpretations of them that provide divine sanction for military conquest and the domination of nature; interpretations of the universe implying that ultimate success and security come through coercive power; economic theories mandating the destruction of nature and traditional cultures for the sake of prosperity; and on and on. This cluster of symbolic structures can become an objective power by being incarnated in institutions, in public and private documents, in public and private habits, and now in the mass media.

The Demonic as the Quasi-Soul of a Culture

Although the previous elements descriptive of the demonic are essential, they do not explain why demonic power is so massive, why it appears to radiate from some all-pervasive demonic spirit, infiltrating every aspect of our lives and penetrating every dimension of our psyches. If the mythological idea of such a being is rejected and demonic power is instead understood entirely in terms of human agency, how are we to explain its seeming to radiate from a ubiquitous, transhuman source? The explanation, I suggest, involves the idea of a demonic soul of a culture.

It is important to be clear what is *not* implied by this idea. Human beings and other animals are genuine individuals because out of the organization of cells emerges a series of dominant experiences, which we call the mind or soul. The idea that a nation or a culture has a soul might be taken to mean that, out of a cohesive organization of human beings, a higher-level series of experience emerges, constituting the soul of that nation or culture, thereby turning that nation or culture into a true individual. Although some philosophers have endorsed some such idea, this is not what is intended here. There is no soul of a nation or a culture in this literal sense.

The idea of a national or cultural soul need not, however, be entirely metaphorical. We can say, instead, that a nation or culture has a *quasi*-soul. The meaning of this idea can be approached by reflecting upon the kind of unity possessed by a living plant. By being distinguished from an animal, a plant by definition has no *anima*, no dominating soul to make it a genuine individual. And yet every cell in the plant is what it is partly because it is part of that plant. Each cell is partly constituted by its relations to the other members of that plant. The identity of each cell is, therefore, significantly constituted by patterns pervasive of the whole plant. Although the plant does not have a literal soul, it has a quasi-soul—a pattern of interactions that acts to some extent as if it were a soul—which informs all its members.

By analogy, and in a more complex sense, we can speak of the quasi-soul of a nation. Because we are all internally related to each other, we enter into and help constitute each others' souls. Insofar as a nation has a set of shared symbols, memories, myths, ideologies, and habits that are often and widely rehearsed, these shared elements are reinforced. The quasi-soul of a nation is constituted only by those elements that are shared by most of its members, at least most of its dominant members, not those that are idiosyncratic to individuals or restricted communities. Of course, elements that were originally idiosyncratic to some individual or group can enter into the national quasi-soul, thereby changing it, but only by no longer being idiosyncratic. This process can now occur quite rapidly, thanks to the rise of the mass media.

Because this national quasi-soul is not a genuine soul, there is no unified national experience, in a literal sense, and no capacity for the nation to act as a unity. The quasi-soul of a nation is, nevertheless, objective to each of its members, confronting each of them with a pervasive set of beliefs, values, habits, mannerisms, and symbols. Most individuals make only a tiny contribution to the national quasi-soul, but it typically makes a massive contribution to each individual.

Only the individual soul has concrete existence and thereby intrinsic value; the notion of a national quasi-soul provides no justification for subordinating the individual to the nation. But the causal power of the national quasi-soul dwarfs that of the individual soul, because this quasi-soul is constituted by the causal power of millions of individuals, including those of past generations whose present effects are mediated not only through their objective symbolic products but also through members of the present generation.

This point provides the basis for a reconciliation of McGill's description, according to which the demonic is experienced as coming from transhuman agency, with my explanation of the demonic in terms of human agency. Insofar as the national quasi-soul is constituted by constantly repeated beliefs, images, symbols, and values that encourage us to use our awesome powers with hate or indifference, the national quasi-soul is demonic. Insofar as it is demonic, the individuals whose souls are formed in that society will tend to be ready servants of demonic evil. Insofar as they remain subject to this demonic pattern, their contribution back to the national quasi-soul will reinforce its demonic character, so that it will exert its influence undiminished, even strengthened, on the next generation of its members.

Although I have been illustrating the point by speaking of the quasi-soul of a nation, in the sense of a country, it is more true that it is a *culture* that is constituted by shared memories, stories, ideologies, beliefs, images, symbols, values, and habits, and a culture may or may not be coterminous with a country. On the one hand, a country may embody two or more cultures. On the other hand, a culture may be largely common to two countries. For example, although their political structures and histories differ, England, the United States, and other Anglo-Saxon countries have to a considerable extent a shared culture, so that one could speak of an Anglo-Saxon quasi-soul. Likewise, although the various nations of Europe are very different in many ways, with, for example, the quasi-soul of Germany being very different from that of France and Italy, we can also speak of a European quasi-soul, although it exists at a more abstract level and has a far more tenuous hold on its members than do the quasi-souls of their more immediate cultures. The power of a quasi-soul at any level depends upon the intensity of memories, beliefs, myths, symbols, attitudes, emotions, and habits that constitute it. The degree to which a cultural quasi-soul is demonic depends upon the content of those beliefs, myths, and so on. Children in some cultures inherit a more bellicose soul than do children in other cultures.

Ideological Selection

Because the power of a society is determined partly by its ideology, the selection for power operates with regard to it as well as the other determinants of its power.[66] We should expect, accordingly, that the history of civilization's ideologies will involve the gradual ascendancy of those that are most effective in producing a warrior-mentality and thereby a warrior-society. An effective ideology of power will, for example, lead people to believe that by being warriors they are obeying the will of, and even imitating the behavior of, the deity of the universe; it will lead them to believe that by dying in the service of this deity, they will be especially rewarded; it will lead them to hate, or at least be indifferent to, the welfare of people in other societies; it will convince them that they are a chosen people, so that by subjugating others they are actually bringing about divine rule on earth; and so on. An effective ideology of power will tend to promote political and economic systems that increase a society's military capacity; it will also tend to produce philosophies, sciences, and technologies through which nature can be effectively dominated. The growth of such ideologies of power has been an intricate part—in many ways the most important part—of the growth of demonic power over the past few thousand years.

Walter Rauschenbusch, in his great book *A Theology for the Social Gospel*, emphasized this psychical or spiritual dimension of what he called "the kingdom of evil." Pointing to the structures and habits of modern society that promote sin, Rauschenbusch showed how people are seduced into sin, through the power of authority and imitation, long before they have reached the age of accountability.[67] In offering this account as a nonmythical way to understand the traditional view that people are led into sin by "supra-personal forces of evil," Rauschenbusch made a valuable contribution to the rediscovery of the reality of demonic power.

Rauschenbusch's discussion of the "supra-personal forces of evil" and the "kingdom of evil" provide a helpful way of understanding the doctrine of "original sin." As many theologians have said, it should really be called "originating sin," because it is a disposition to feel and act in ways to which the term "sin" is usually applied. But even the term "originating sin" is problematic, insofar as people tend to think of sin as something for which the individual is primarily responsible. But insofar as children are born into cultures with a more or less demonic quasi-soul, their own souls will be shaped by these beliefs, images, attitudes, and feelings long before they have reached the age of accountability. There is, to be sure, always at least a slight degree of freedom, even at the youngest age. But at this age the freedom is too slight to be made the focus of attention, as the term "sin" does. By speaking instead of "the demonic," we can better convey the idea of a power to which people are subjugated and from which they need help to break free.

This demonic power is now, even more completely than in New Testament times, in effective control of the trajectory of civilization. This control is now so complete that although we are on the verge of destroying human civilization and much of the rest of the planet's advanced forms of life, our leaders are, rather than changing course, actively fanning the flames of conflict.

The trajectory through which demonic control of civilization has grown has

run primarily through the history of empire. Two thousand years ago, that trajectory was embodied in the Roman Empire. Although Rome saw itself as
divinely authorized, the authors of the New Testament saw it as the ultimate
embodiment of the demonic to date. Today, the trajectory of empire is embodied in the United States, which, as discussed earlier, has an empire that dwarfs
Rome's in both power and reach.

CONCLUSION: A WAY OUT?

The condition that not only gave rise to the war-system and hence imperialism
but has also allowed them to continue, Schmookler emphasizes, is the anarchical state of civilization. Like many other thinkers, he believes that the spiral of
violence will be overcome only when civilizational anarchy has been overcome
by a global government.

There are two paths through which such a government could be created.
One path would be for the peoples of the world to form a global democracy.
The other path would be for one country to become the de facto government
of the world. The United States, which since its inception has been increasing
the scope of its empire, has since the end of the Cold War and especially since
9/11 been seeking to rely primarily on its military superiority to move closer to
that goal. The ideology advanced by the neocons says that a truly global American empire, a *Pax Americana*, would be a good thing for the world, not only
bringing universal peace by bringing the reign of anarchy to an end, but also
bringing about regimes around the world that are committed to freedom,
democracy, and human rights. In its most extreme form, this ideology prom-
ises that American rule will bring "an end to evil."[68] That apocalyptic notion
suggests, of course, that a global empire run by America would be an approxi-
mation of the reign of God on earth desired by Christians, Jews, and Muslims.

In the next chapter, I present reasons to believe that an all-inclusive American empire would be more an embodiment of the demonic than of the divine.

Chapter 9

The American Empire, Demonic Evil, and 9/11

In chapter 6, we saw that many American commentators, at least outside the government, now openly discuss a fact that the rest of the world has long known—that America now has by far the most extensive empire the world has ever seen.

In chapter 7, we saw that Jesus and early Christians, especially as represented by the final book of the New Testament, considered the Roman Empire demonic, embodying values that diametrically opposed divine values. We also saw that this view was based on good reasons, because of five characteristics of the Roman Empire: (1) it claimed that it was divinely authorized and even, in fact, that its emperor was divine; (2) it developed and then deployed overwhelming military power to spread and maintain its empire; (3) it used terror, or simply the threat of terror, to intimidate its subjects and enemies; (4) it ruled other peoples through puppets backed up by its pervasive military presence; (5) it collected exorbitant taxes to enrich its center and finance its imperial rule, thereby impoverishing its subjects.

Chapter 8, presenting a nonmythical view of demonic power, suggested that it is best thought of as creaturely power that, besides being diametrically opposed to divine values, is also powerful enough to threaten divine purposes. Creaturely power has become this strong only in human beings and, in fact, only after human beings created civilization, which led to a war-system, which led to the development of ever-increasing power to dominate nature and other human beings. This war-system gave rise to empires, which became the principal embodiments of demonic power, because they not only had enormous power— both military and economic—but also generally exercised this power with hate or, more generally, indifference to the welfare of their subjects and enemies.

Maintaining the primacy of the empire was the supreme value. The empire's subjects, such as the peasants of Galilee, had value only insofar as they served this supreme value. From the perspective of the empire, the values taught by the prophets of Israel as divine values—justice, mercy, compassion for the poor—were nonvalues. The empire, being the embodiment of divinity, was the true measure of value. From the biblical point of view, however, the empire was the chief embodiment of demonic values: besides flagrantly and massively violating the truly divine values, it was idolatrous, claiming that its emperor, with his perverted system of values, was divine and hence deserved the people's ultimate loyalty.

In the present chapter, I ask whether this evaluation of the Roman Empire by Jesus and early Christians applies to the American empire. Or is America the exception to the general rule, having created a benign and even benevolent empire, which can be regarded as furthering the divine purpose for the world?

I begin by looking at this latter view, America's preferred view of itself, which has recently been promulgated by neocons. I then examine various types of evidence suggesting that this view is the exact opposite of the truth. In the course of this discussion, the reader will see that the American empire embodies the five features of the Roman Empire mentioned above. Of course, the second of these features—the development of overwhelming military power—has already been discussed in chapter 6. The present chapter illustrates the other four.

THE AMERICAN EMPIRE AS BENIGN AND DIVINE

There have been various ways in which Americans in earlier centuries expressed the view that their empire-in-the-making was divinely authorized. One of these ways was to refer to America as the "new Israel."[1] But the phrase that really caught on was "manifest destiny," which John O'Sullivan coined in 1845 to signify the mission of the United States "to overspread the continent allotted by Providence for the free development of our yearly multiplying millions."[2] In 1850, the idea that this destiny was to create a universal empire was expressed by an editor named James Dunwoody Bronson DuBow in the following words:

> We have a destiny to perform, a "manifest destiny" over all Mexico, over
> South America, over the West Indies and Canada. The Sandwich [Hawai-

ian] Islands are as necessary to our eastern, as the isles of the gulf to our western commerce. The gates of the Chinese empire must be thrown down . . . and the haughty Japanese tramplers upon the cross be enlightened in the doctrines of republicanism. . . . The eagle of the republic shall poise itself over the field of Waterloo, after tracing its flight among the gorges of the Himalaya or the Ural mountains, and a successor of Washington ascend the chair of universal empire![3]

Such ideas were, in fact, expressed from almost the founding of the United States. David Humphreys, a protégé of George Washington's, wrote in a poem:

Our constitutions form'd on freedom's base,
Which all the blessings of all lands embrace;
Embrace humanity's extended cause,
A world of our empire, for a world of our laws.[4]

But this kind of talk, common in the eighteenth and nineteenth centuries, was heard much less in the twentieth century. Early in that century, imperialism took on negative connotations, so it became taboo in respectable circles to speak of "American imperialism" and, by association, of "American empire." These terms were, for the most part, used only by left-wing critics of American foreign policy.[5] There were, however, a few exceptions.

One of these exceptions was Ronald Steel, who in 1967 published a book entitled *Pax Americana*. Writing as the criticism of the Vietnam War was heating up, Steel acknowledged that "by any conventional standards for judging such things," America is "an imperial power," having an empire "the scope of which the world has never seen."[6] However, Steel argued, "America has been engaged in a kind of welfare imperialism, empire building for noble ends rather than for such base motives as profit and influence"—the chief noble end being "permitting other nations to enjoy the benefits of freedom, democracy, and self-determination."[7] When America intervenes, Steel said, it does so with "the most noble motives and with the most generous impulses." Steel has since recanted this view.[8] But his previous position has become one of the central points in the neocons' promotion of a truly global American empire.

Charles Krauthammer was one of the earliest ones to start trumpeting this theme. In his famous 1991 essay, "The Unipolar Moment," he said that although people usually "recoil at the thought of a single dominant power for fear of what it will do with its power . . . [,] America is the exception to this rule," because "the world generally sees it as benign," as a power that "acts not just out of self-interest but a sense of right."[9]

In that same year, Ben Wattenberg, in a book entitled *The First Universal Nation*, wrote: "The American empire is not like earlier European imperialisms. We have sought neither wealth nor territory. Ours is an imperium of values."[10]

In 1996, William Kristol and Robert Kagan, arguing that America needed a foreign policy that did not bore Americans, proposed a policy of "benevolent global hegemony." This proposal was not unrealistic, they assured their readers, because America's moral ideals and its vital interests are "almost always in harmony."[11]

In 1998, Kagan developed this notion further in an essay entitled "The Benevolent Empire." Saying that "the benevolent hegemony exercised by the United States is good for a vast portion of the world's population," Kagan argued that this is no surprise, because, "Ever since the United States emerged as a great power, the identification of the interests of others with its own has been the most striking quality of American foreign and defense policy."[12]

In 2002, Krauthammer took up the theme again, saying that America's claim to being a benign power is not mere "self-congratulation" but is verified by its "track record."[13] Dinesh D'Souza, in that same year, described America as "the most magnanimous imperial power ever."[14]

Max Boot, in an essay published in May 2003, after the apparently easy victory in Iraq, argued that America's primary foreign policy goal should now be to preserve and extend what Krauthammer had called "the unipolar moment." Saying that "that moment has now stretched into a decade and shows no sign of waning," he asked why the general rule that "any hegemon will call into being an opposing coalition . . . hasn't happened to America." The answer, he suggested, is obvious: "America isn't like the empires of old. It does not seek to enslave other peoples and steal their lands. It spreads freedom and opportunity." The war in Iraq, Boot adds, should be seen as simply one important step "in a larger campaign to make the world safe for democracy."[15]

This latter idea, that the purpose of the American empire is to bring about global democracy, has been a central theme of most neocons. In 1991, Joshua Muravchik published a book entitled *Exporting Democracy: Fulfilling America's Mission*. Ben Wattenberg wrote, "Americans have a missionary streak, and democracy is our mission."[16] For most neocons, Dorrien says, "The crusade for world democracy and the struggle to preserve America's unipolar dominance were the same thing."[17]

The idea that America is in the business of spreading freedom and democracy, and thereby serving a universal cause, has often been articulated by President Bush. His address to the nation on September 7, 2003, closed with these words: "We are serving in freedom's cause—and that is the cause of all mankind."[18] In his State of the Union address earlier that year, he explicitly declared this cause also to be God's cause, saying, "The liberty we prize is not America's gift to the world; it is God's gift to humanity."[19] In the inaugural address at the outset of his second term in 2005, Bush said that "it is the policy of the United States to seek and support the growth of democratic movements and institutions in every nation and culture."[20] The next day, Krauthammer wrote, "The great project of the Bush administration [is] the strengthening and spread of democracy."[21]

Vice President Cheney, even implying that the American empire has divine blessing, sent out a Christmas card in 2003 that asked, rhetorically: "And if a sparrow cannot fall to the ground without His notice, is it probable that an empire can rise without His aid?"[22]

In sum, the neocons and their president, reinvigorating rhetoric from an earlier time, have argued that the emergence of an all-inclusive empire would be the best possible result for the world, because the American empire, besides being benign and even benevolent, acts to promote values that are universal, because they are prized by all people. Insofar as religious language is used, this empire can be described as not only benign but also divine, in the sense that it is being used by God to bring divine values, especially freedom, to the whole world. Unlike other empires, according to this view, America can be trusted with sufficient power to bring these values to other peoples by force, if necessary, because there is no conflict between American interests and its ideals: its primary interest is to spread these ideals.

This view of the nature of America's empire is, however, challenged by many commentators. Krauthammer, as we saw, said that America's claim to be a benign empire is supported by its "track record." But Bacevich, having recently reexamined this track record,[23] rejects the claim "that the promotion of peace, democracy, and human rights and the punishment of evil-doers—not the pursuit of self-interest—[has] defined the essence of American diplomacy." He says instead that "unflagging self-interest and large ambitions underl[ie] all U.S. policy."[24] Pointing out that the aim of the U.S. military has been "to achieve something approaching omnipotence," Bacevich mocks the idea that such power in America's hands "is by definition benign" because the leader of the free world "does not exploit or dominate but acts on behalf of purposes that look beyond mere self-interest."[25] Against those who justify American interventions in other countries on the grounds that America's foreign policy is to promote democracy, Bacevich points out that in previous countries in which America has intervened, "democracy [did not] flower as a result." America intervenes not for altruistic purposes, he adds, but "to sustain American primacy."[26]

Many other intellectuals have similar views. Chalmers Johnson, who like Bacevich was once a conservative who believed that American foreign policy aimed at promoting freedom and democracy, now describes the United States as "a military juggernaut intent on world domination."[27] A book written some years ago by Noam Chomsky, the second edition of which was published a year after Muravchik's *Exporting Democracy*, was entitled *Deterring Democracy*. A more recent book by Chomsky is subtitled *America's Quest for Global Dominance*.[28] Richard Falk has written of the Bush administration's "global domination project," which, far from promising to usher in global democracy, poses the threat of "global fascism."[29]

To have a basis for deciding which of these diametrically opposed views is closer to the truth, we need to look at some representative examples of American foreign policy in practice and some of its effects on the general good of the planet.

Evaluating these examples, however, presupposes some agreement about moral principles, because each of the two views involves a moral argument. The neocons argue that although exercising imperial leadership necessarily involves the United States in various violations of traditional moral principles, the overall general good of the world will be advanced insofar as American dominance becomes more complete, because the United States is committed, as its track record shows, to promoting freedom, democracy, and human rights. And—those neocons who use theistic language and their president can add—we can assume that because America is the only country with the power as well as the commitment to advance freedom, democracy, human rights, and the general good, God supports the growth of the American empire.

The critics of the American empire argue that all the evidence supports the opposite conclusion: that the expansion of the American empire will not promote freedom and democracy, that it will not advance the protection of basic human rights, and that it will not serve the overall, long-term good of the world. And—those critics who use theistic language can add—we can thereby assume that God does *not* support the further extension or even maintenance of the American empire.

To adjudicate between these two positions, we need, besides some representative examples of U.S. foreign policy in action and some measures of the overall fruits of American dominance in recent decades, also some agreement on moral principles. I discuss moral principles in the next section, then in following sections provide examples relevant to the question of whether U.S. foreign policy has been devoted to the promotion of freedom, democracy, and human rights and has, in fact, served the global good.

CHRISTIAN AND UNIVERSAL MORAL PRINCIPLES

Because this book is written from a Christian perspective, the moral principles employed obviously must be Christian. At the same time, however, we live in a pluralistic world and even an increasingly pluralistic country, in which there is increasing interaction between peoples from different religious traditions. For Christians in America to evaluate their country's foreign policy in a way that can be received as relevant by peoples of other traditions, both inside and outside of the United States, we need a moral position that, while being Christian, is also shared by peoples of other religious traditions.

Some moral philosophers believe that such a position is unattainable. Part of them hold this view because of their acceptance of atheism, which leads them to conclude that there can be no "natural law," in the sense of a set of moral principles rooted in the nature of things that can be known by peoples in various traditions. We must, they conclude, accept moral relativism, which means that there are no common moral principles in terms of which, for example, U.S. foreign policy could be declared immoral.

However, whatever be the merits of the argument that atheism implies relativism,[30] it would not, in any case, be relevant to Christianity and other religious traditions, all of which are theistic in the broad sense, meaning that they *do* believe that moral principles are rooted in the very nature of things. Accordingly, presupposing for present purposes that philosophers and theologians have shown the viability of a cosmology that is broadly theistic,[31] we can dismiss this first argument.

Religious Pluralism and Moral Universalism

A second argument against the possibility of an ethic that is both Christian and global points to the fact that all the religious traditions are different from each other, some of them radically so.[32] From this fact, some thinkers argue that the search for a Christian ethic that is simultaneously universal would be futile.

Philosophers and theologians actually involved in interreligious dialogue, however, have concluded that this is not true. One Christian theologian who has led the way toward the articulation of a global ethic is Hans Küng, who has pointed out that at least most religious traditions affirm some version of what Christians have called the golden rule—at least in its negative formulation, sometimes called the "silver rule": Do not do to others what you would not want them to do to you.[33] Immanuel Kant enunciated this principle in different language: Do not treat others as mere means to your ends, rather than as ends in themselves.

From either of these general formulations, we can derive a large number of more specific rules, which refer to things that people universally would not want others to do to them or their loved ones, such as:

> Don't murder other people.
>
> Don't cause other people to starve.
>
> Don't steal other people's natural resources, such as their land, water, and oil.
>
> Don't steal other people's personal property.
>
> Don't deprive others of their basic freedoms.
>
> Don't cause others needless pain.
>
> Don't terrorize other people.
>
> Don't rape other people.
>
> Don't humiliate other people.

Thick and Thin Morality

A third argument that is often made against the idea of a universal ethic, at least implicitly, appeals to the existence of a growing school of thought known as "communitarianism." According to this argument, the leading communitarian philosophers reject the position known as "cosmopolitanism," which affirms universal moral principles. The existence of this communitarian school of thought, the argument seems to go, provides strong evidence against the view that the various communities, with their different traditions, share any common moral principles. We must, therefore, accept relativism.

This argument is, however, based on a false premise. Most of the philosophers who are generally considered the leading communitarians are *not* relativists. They instead affirm the reality of basic moral principles that are universal. They are, in other words, *cosmopolitan* communitarians.[34]

This position is developed at some length by Michael Walzer in a book called *Thick and Thin*. Although in earlier writings, Walzer's concern with difference and particularity had seemed to lead him to a relativistic position, he in this later book defends "a certain sort of universalism." Using the notion of a "thick" morality for some community's actual moral position with all its particularities, he argues that every thick and particularist morality has within it "the makings of a thin and universalist morality."[35] This thin morality "consists in principles and rules that are reiterated in different times and places, and that are seen to be similar even though they are expressed in different idioms and reflect different histories and different visions of the world."[36]

Whereas a thick morality is "maximalist," consisting of everything a particular tradition wants to say, the thin morality is "minimalist," being the absolute minimum that must be insisted on always and everywhere. However, Walzer emphasizes, to call the universal element "thin" and "minimalist" is not to say that it is unimportant. In fact, he says:

> The opposite is more likely true: this is morality close to the bone. There isn't much that is more important than "truth" and "justice," minimally understood. The minimal demands that we make on one another are, when denied, repeated with passionate insistence. In moral discourse, thinness and intensity go together.[37]

Every attempt to formulate this universal moral minimum, Walzer suggests, will probably be stated in terms of negative injunctions, such as "rules against murder, deceit, torture, oppression, and tyranny." Moreover, Walzer suggests, in the West "these standards will probably be expressed in the language of rights, which is the language of our own moral maximalism." However, he quickly adds, "That is not a bad way of talking about injuries and wrongs that no one should have to endure."[38]

Basic Rights

This rights-based approach to morality is especially natural for Americans, since it is rooted in the American Declaration of Independence, which speaks of entitlements founded on "the laws of nature and of nature's God" and says that all people "are endowed by their Creator with certain unalienable rights."

One American philosopher who has developed the rights-based position in great detail, and specifically in relation to U.S. foreign policy, is Henry Shue. As the title of his book *Basic Rights* indicates, he has focused on those rights that are most basic in the sense that they are common to all human beings because the "enjoyment of them is essential to the enjoyment of all other rights."[39] Shue focuses in particular on "minimal economic security, or subsistence," by which he means "unpolluted air, unpolluted water, adequate food, adequate clothes, adequate shelter, and minimal preventive public health care."[40]

This approach is grounded in the United Nations' Universal Declaration of Human Rights, which says in Article 3 that "everyone has the right to life" and in Article 25 that "every man, woman and child has the inalienable right to be free from hunger and malnutrition."[41] As James Nickel has said, the unifying idea behind the Universal Declaration is "the idea of a decent or minimally good life for all people."[42]

Although the approach to morality in terms of human rights is not the only one, it is, as Walzer says, "not a bad way of talking about injuries and wrongs that no one should have to endure." Thanks in large part to the U.N.'s Declaration of Rights, moreover, this approach has become increasingly universal. A recent book entitled *Prospects for a Common Morality* points out, in fact, that although some people in the world of theoretical philosophy have lost confidence in the possibility of any universal moral consensus, there is now in the practical world of international relations "a remarkable kind of cross-cultural moral agreement about human rights."[43]

This agreement has come about through dialogue. Although members of each tradition tend to begin with the assumption that their own moral code should be accepted as the universal one, they soon learn that they need to distinguish between those elements in their tradition that are truly universal, shared with all the other traditions, and those that are not. Through this process, Christians, for example, can articulate a set of moral principles that is both Christian and universal. Muslims can articulate an ethic that is both Islamic and universal. And the same with Judaism, Buddhism, Hinduism, and other traditions.

Through this process we can, even in our pluralistic world, develop a set of moral criteria that can be universally recognized as valid for judging matters of public policy, such as U.S. foreign policy. For example, if those who carry out this foreign policy did not do to people of other countries what they would not want done to them; if they did not treat other people as mere means to U.S. ends rather than as ends in themselves; if they did not, more concretely, act so as to deprive people of adequate food, water, shelter, and minimal health care; if they did not steal the oil and other natural resources of other peoples; if they did not engage in murder, deceit, torture, oppression, and tyranny; if they did not deprive other peoples of their right to self-determination—if U.S. foreign policy did not lead its agents to do any of these things, then few if any people would criticize it.

The problem is that U.S. foreign policy leads its agents to do *all* of these things, as illustrated in the following sections.

SOME EXAMPLES OF U.S. FOREIGN POLICY DURING THE COLD WAR

During the Cold War, we saw in chapter 1, the United States, working through the CIA and NATO (and hence the Pentagon), supported various kinds of clandestine operations, including false-flag terrorist attacks, to prevent the rise of any Communist governments in Europe. These operations were part of a much broader strategy aimed at extending the American empire.

Planning for this strategy started, in fact, within weeks after World War II began in Europe in 1939, at which time the Council on Foreign Relations, in collaboration with the U.S. Department of State, formed a committee to devise strategy for the war and the ensuing peace. Laurence Shoup and William Minter, who refer to this committee as the "imperial brain trust," say that it "worked out an imperialistic conception of the national interest and war aims of the United States" that "involved a conscious attempt to organize and control a global empire."[44]

The basic idea was that the United States, which was struggling to come out of the Great Depression, was not self-sufficient, even though, thanks to its interpretation and enforcement of the Monroe Doctrine, it already had the rest of the Western Hemisphere as a source of markets and raw materials. In addition, these strategists decided, America needed a "Grand Area" that included China, Japan, the Dutch East Indies (now Indonesia), the British Empire, and the British Commonwealth. Control of this Grand Area was, moreover, only a temporary measure. "The preferred ideal," in the words of Shoup and Minter, "was even more grandiose—one world economy dominated by the United States," with "international political and economic institutions" that would "integrate all of the earth's nations under the leadership of the United States."[45]

Besides setting these goals, the brain trust also recognized that U.S. policy makers, while privately formulating these actual war aims, needed to formulate different war aims for public consumption. "Formulation of a statement of war aims for propaganda purposes," the brain trust pointed out, "is very different from formulation of one defining the true national interest."[46] In particular, the authors said:

If war aims are stated which seem to be concerned solely with Anglo-American imperialism, they will offer little to people in the rest of the world, and will be vulnerable to Nazi counter-promises. . . . The interests of other peoples should be stressed, not only those of Europe, but also of Asia, Africa, and Latin America. This would have a better propaganda effect.[47]

In practice, this policy of the Grand Area meant not only preventing as many countries as possible from aligning themselves with the Soviet Union and, later, with China, but also preventing countries from developing a socialist economy or any form of nationalist economy, in which a country's raw materials would be used for its own people rather than being offered up to the global capitalist economy led by the United States. I look now at a few interventions based on this policy.

Iran 1953

During the 1940s, the Anglo-Iranian Oil Company, which was owned by Great Britain, was exploiting Iran, giving it only 20 percent of the profits when the going rate was 50 percent. After failing to budge Britain during negotiations, Iran in 1951 nationalized the company. This move was led in the parliament by Mohammad Mossadegh, who after that was elected prime minister. Although the British government was given a generous settlement, it organized, with American support, an economic blockade, which plunged the already impoverished country into destitution. The British then in late 1952 approached the CIA about organizing a coup, believing that the incoming Eisenhower administration would be amenable. They were right.

The Eisenhower administration had reasons to bring about regime change. Iran's nationalization of a foreign oil company, if allowed to stand, might inspire similar seizures elsewhere.[48] Also, if there were a friendly government in Tehran, Iran could be used for surveillance of the Soviet Union and otherwise protecting U.S. interests in the Gulf region.[49] Furthermore, Eisenhower's secretary of state, John Foster Dulles, and his brother Allen Dulles, the new director of the CIA, had both previously worked for the law firm representing Standard Oil of New Jersey.[50] Finally, although Mossadegh was not a Communist, the claim had been made that he was, and the Eisenhower administration had swept into office by charging the Democrats with having lost both China and Korea to the Communists.[51]

The CIA planned a coup with the young shah of Iran, along with General Fazlollah Zahedi, a former Nazi collaborator. Zahedi's forces, having been supplied by the U.S. Army, were easily victorious.[52] The shah then became America's puppet ruler of Iran.

Although the U.S.-backed ouster of Mossadegh was bitterly denounced by the people of Iran, the young shah gave thanks to Allah and the CIA[53]—as presumably did Standard Oil, which started receiving 40 percent of Iran's oil profits. The *New York Times*—in spite of having earlier pointed out that Mossadegh had "acquired a reputation as an honest patriot"[54]—declared that his ouster would be a good learning experience: "Underdeveloped countries with rich resources now have an object lesson in the heavy cost that must be paid by one of their number which goes berserk with fanatical nationalism."[55] "Fanatical nationalism" is, of course, the idea that a country's resources should benefit its own people, rather than the corporations of America and its allies. This object lesson provides an example of the way in which the U.S. government has, like Rome and other empires, used terror to intimidate.

The aftereffects of this object lesson were even more deadly. Although Allen Dulles declared that Iran had been saved from a "Communist-dominated regime,"[56] democratic freedom was not to be the result. The shah's regime instituted, in the words of Amnesty International, "a history of torture which is beyond belief."[57] This torture was the work of the shah's secret police, SAVAK, which was trained by Americans.[58]

Guatemala 1954

The next year, the Eisenhower administration, seeking to duplicate its success in Iran, overthrew what Piero Gleijeses, who has written the definitive study of this event, called "the first truly democratic government in Guatemala's history" and "the best government it has ever had." The United States thereby returned Guatemala, for the remainder of the century and beyond, to the condition that has led it to be called "the land of eternal tyranny."[59] In doing so, the Eisenhower administration also destroyed the man most responsible for the ten years of democracy that Guatemala enjoyed from 1945 to 1954, Jacobo Arbenz.

In 1944, Arbenz, a military officer, prevented a military takeover of the government and insisted on a free election, which was won by a "spiritual socialist" who introduced some reforms that helped workers but did not seriously threaten U.S. interests. Then in 1951, after having saved democracy from another military coup, Arbenz himself became president.

In a speech articulating his moral vision, Arbenz said:

> I grant great importance to economic policy, but only as a means to achieve our social goals. All the riches of Guatemala are not as important as the life, the freedom, the dignity, the health and the happiness of the most humble of its people. How wrong we would be if—mistaking the means for the end—we were to set financial stability and economic growth as the supreme goals of our policy, sacrificing to them the well-being of our masses. . . . Our task is to work together in order to produce more wealth. . . . But we must distribute these riches so that those who have less—and they are the immense majority—benefit more, while those who

have more—and they are so few—also benefit, but to a lesser extent. How could it be otherwise, given the poverty, the poor health, and the lack of education of our people?[60]

This rhetoric did not bother U.S. leaders—until a year later when they realized that he was serious, having begun to implement a plan for agrarian reform.

Although it was a moderate program, expropriating only uncultivated land from larger estates, it was extremely successful: it was implemented with little violence; it resulted in an immediate increase in production (rather than a temporary decrease, as in most such programs); and it helped a large percentage of Guatemala's people.[61] Arbenz, points out Gleijeses, had "accomplished a unique feat: the first true agrarian reform of Central America. . . . For the first time since the Spanish conquest, the government returned land to the Indians."[62] The landed elite, the American-owned United Fruit Company, and the U.S. government, however, had a different perspective.

Although the complaints by United Fruit, made central in previous accounts of this coup, were important, the main thing that led to the Eisenhower administration's decision to remove Arbenz was the very fact that the agrarian reform was successful. It was a classic case of "the threat of a good example." As a letter to the assistant secretary of state for inter-American affairs put it:

> Guatemala has become an increasing threat to the stability of Honduras and El Salvador. Its agrarian reform is a powerful propaganda weapon; its broad social program of aiding the workers and peasants in a victorious struggle against the upper classes and large foreign enterprises has a strong appeal to the populations of Central American neighbors where similar conditions prevail.

American leaders did not, of course, use this reason in their public discussions. The expressed concern was that Arbenz's government constituted a "Soviet beachhead" in Central America.[63] This, however, was not true.

Although Arbenz had indeed become a Communist, he had done so by finding that Marx's analysis illuminated the situation of Guatemala and by discovering that the Communist intellectuals in Guatemala were hardworking, incorruptible people who were, like Arbenz, genuinely concerned to help their country, especially the poor.[64] There was no connection to the Soviet Union whatsoever; the two countries did not even have diplomatic relations.[65]

However, the mere fact that Arbenz was a Marxist, combined with the fact that he was carrying out a successful program of land reform, led Washington to orchestrate a coup.[66] It did so by bribing and intimidating the Guatemalan army, telling it that the army of Castillo Armas, which was going to enter Guatemala from Honduras, was simply a proxy for the Americans, so that if it was defeated, the U.S. military would invade the country in full force. So when Armas led a little band of soldiers across the border, the Guatemalan army simply did not fight.[67]

This successful intimidation provides an example of the way the United States, with its overwhelming power, needs simply to use the *threat* of force to get its way. And the overthrow of Arbenz was clearly intended, like the overthrow of Iran's government, as a means to intimidate other countries not to try to nationalize the companies exploiting their natural resources.

In any case, after the removal of Arbenz, a puppet government was installed by U.S. officials; land reform was scuttled; labor unions were outlawed; labor organizers were killed; and political parties and opposition newspapers were banned.[68] Longer term, the American overthrow of Guatemala's fledgling democracy resulted in decades of state terror, much of it carried out by death squads. It also resulted in widespread poverty, with some 20,000 Guatemalans, mainly children, dying of hunger each year, and many other children avoiding this fate only through prostitution.[69]

Although Guatemala was listed as a democratic country, it was actually, due to the intervention of 1954 and the ensuing American support, a military dictatorship, with elected officials subservient to the army. From the perspective of the U.S. government, however, what counted was that Guatemala had been saved for "the free world." It could be so counted because, as one U.S. official said about Latin America in general, it provided strategic materials for the United States and was a major purchaser of U.S. goods, so "notwithstanding the imperfections which mar the actual practice of democracy, the area is to be regarded as an effective part of the Free World."[70]

The "land of eternal tyranny" had, beginning in 1944, experienced ten years of hope. But thanks to the United States, the hope of the Guatemalans became, as the title of the book by Gleijeses says, a "shattered hope." In Eisenhower's memoirs, nevertheless, the overthrow of Arbenz is listed as one of his proudest accomplishments.[71] Most Americans, including American Christians, agreed at the time with the campaign slogan, "We like Ike." They would have liked him less, however, if they had known what he and the Dulles brothers were doing in Iran, Guatemala, and other countries around the world.

Greece 1964 and 1967

It is also instructive to see how the United States treated democracy in Greece, generally considered the land of its birth. George Papandreou became prime minister in 1964, shortly after Lyndon Johnson had become president of the United States. The Johnson administration tried to persuade Papandreou to accept its solution to a dispute involving Cyprus, but Papandreou had his ambassador explain to Johnson that this solution would be unacceptable to Greece's parliament and in violation of its constitution.

"Then listen to me, Mr. Ambassador," Johnson reportedly replied,

fuck your Parliament and your Constitution. America is an elephant.

Cyprus is a flea. If these two fleas continue itching the elephant, they may just get whacked by the elephant's trunk. . . . We pay a lot of good American dollars to the Greeks. . . . If your Prime Minister gives me talk about Democracy, Parliament and Constitutions, he, his Parliament and his Constitution may not last very long.

They did not. In 1965, the CIA helped King Constantine bribe enough members of Papandreou's party to topple his government.[72]

One reason Washington wanted to remove Papandreou was because of his son, Andreas, who was in the cabinet. Having discovered that the Greek secret service, the KYP, was serving as the CIA's means to control Greek policy, Andreas Papandreou had George Papadopoulos, who was serving as the KYP's liaison with the CIA, transferred.

In April 1967, George and Andreas Papandreou were about to be returned to power by the voters. Two days before the election, however, a military junta, led by Papadopoulos, staged a coup, claiming that the action was necessary to prevent a Communist takeover. Papadopoulos, who had been on the CIA payroll for fifteen years, was widely considered "the first CIA agent to become Premier of a European country."[73]

As a result, Greece experienced a seven-year nightmare, with thousands of people subjected to extreme forms of torture, some for merely criticizing the government. American leaders, however, defended Greece's military junta, which one U.S. general called "the best damn Government since Pericles." The Papadopoulos regime appreciated this support, with one notorious torturer regularly telling his victims: "You can't fight us, we are Americans."[74]

Indonesia 1957–1965

After World War II, Indonesia won its independence from the Netherlands, which had tried to recolonize it. Sukarno, the hero of Indonesia's battle for independence, was elected president. But America found him insufficiently obedient to its wishes. The basic problem was that Sukarno—although he was not a Communist, did not allow any members of the Communist Party (the PKI) into his cabinet, and even ruthlessly suppressed Soviet-oriented Communists—did not persecute *nationalistic* Communists, who had sided with him against the Soviet-oriented ones.[75]

The Eisenhower administration became obsessed with the possibility that because of Sukarno's tolerance of the PKI, it might become strong enough "to take power through legal . . . means" (even though it was the smallest of Indonesia's four major parties). Washington hence decided on a covert policy, in the words of Secretary of State Dulles, "to bring about a new government on Java."[76] The plan was to exploit the dissatisfaction of the outer islands with the central government in Java, thereby turning their movement for a federal system into a full-blown civil war.

This war, which occurred in 1957, was supported by massive military assistance and generous funding, courtesy of American taxpayers, who were not informed that their money was being used to foment war against a democratically elected government. The idea was to establish a pro-American government on the island of Sumatra, which has Indonesia's oil, then use it as a base for taking over the whole country.[77] However, in spite of the massive American support given to the rebels, Java's forces held them off, partly because they foiled an American plan for a false-flag operation. (The plan was to burn the U.S.-owned oil fields on Sumatra, then blame it on the Javanese, to provide, in the words of a U.S. soldier, "a pretext to send in marines.")[78]

One result of this imperialist adventure, which fulfilled Sukarno's prediction that American support for the rebels would be the "way to hell," was the loss of some 40,000 Indonesian lives.[79] But that was merely a foretaste of the hell to come.

Fearing that Indonesia's parliamentary system would allow the PKI to win the 1959 elections, Washington bribed the army to postpone the elections and then to eliminate the parliamentary system altogether.[80] Later, in 1965, the U.S. ambassador to Indonesia, in view of the fact that the PKI had become stronger, told President Johnson that "an unsuccessful coup attempt by the PKI might be the most effective development to start a reversal of political trends."[81]

Within months there was such an attempt, fabricated by the CIA and the Pentagon in collusion with army strongman General Suharto, who blamed it on the PKI. Suharto then used this "failed coup attempt" as a pretext to begin a general slaughter, for which the Johnson administration provided arms and "shooting lists."[82]

The ensuing holocaust resulted in the deaths of 1 to 2 million people; the CIA itself compared it to the Nazi and Soviet mass murders.[83] Many of the victims were simply peasants, schoolteachers, and union organizers accused of being Communist sympathizers. In addition, hundreds of thousands of people were put in jail or concentration camps, many for the rest of their lives.[84]

The long-term consequences were also devastating. Indonesia would not enjoy free elections or representative government for the rest of the century.[85] Landlessness increased, wages fell, and Indonesia became the poorest nation in Southeast Asia, with much of the population living in stark poverty with insufficient food.

America's 1965 intervention in Indonesia did, however, serve a few interests. Suharto, who ruled the country dictatorially until 1999, being careful not to upset the United States, became "a fabulously wealthy man." And Indonesia, having been saved, like Iran, from the nationalists, became a "paradise for investors."[86] The CIA was extremely proud of the 1965 intervention, regarding it as a model for future operations.[87]

In the light of these illustrations, we can see the absurdity of the neocons' statements that America's ideals and its vital interests are "almost always in harmony," that "the identification of the interests of others with its own has been the most striking quality of American foreign and defense policy," and that "democracy is our mission."

These interventions in Iran, Guatemala, Greece, and Indonesia illustrate, moreover, that if, as Ben Wattenberg says, the American empire is an "imperium of values," then the values of those who have been running U.S. foreign policy are diametrically opposed to the basic values shared by Christianity and other religious traditions. These agents of American foreign policy have acted so as to deprive people in other countries of basic rights, such as food, health care, and an adequate income; they have stolen oil; they have supported systems of torture and terror; they have supported the murder of hundreds of thousands of civilians; and they have engaged in massive deceit, claiming to protect freedom and democracy while doing the exact opposite. More generally, they have treated others as mere means to their ends, not as ends in themselves, and in so acting they have done to others what they absolutely would not want done to themselves, their loved ones, and their country.

The illustrations here, to be sure, all come from roughly the same period. But these are *representative* examples. U.S. foreign policy has embodied essentially the same principles in earlier decades and subsequent decades, as many studies show. In *Killing Hope*, for example, William Blum chronicles some fifty "U.S. Military and CIA Interventions Since World War II"— including Brazil, Bulgaria, Cambodia, Chile, China, the Congo, the Dominican Republic, El Salvador, Haiti, Iraq, Nicaragua, the Philippines, and Vietnam—most if not all of which left the countries worse off than they would have been without the interventions.[88] As these studies by Blum and many others amply show, U.S. foreign policy has not, any more than Rome's foreign policy, aimed at the promotion of freedom, democracy, and human rights.

However, some neoconservatives have suggested, even though it is true that the American commitment to these values was less than it should have been in prior decades, the installation of the Bush-Cheney administration brought about a significant change. Even though national self-interest still plays an important part in foreign policy decisions, the commitment to using U.S. power to replace tyrannical regimes with democratic governments is much greater in this administration, partly because it realizes that a world of democratic governments is a world that is good for America. In this administration, accordingly, American ideals and interests really are largely identical.

This view can be best tested by means of an examination of the foreign policy adventure that had been at the top of the agenda of the neocons: the war in Iraq.

THE WAR IN IRAQ

In spite of the widespread claims that the war in Iraq was carried out for noble ends, an actual examination of the planning for, and the execution of, the war undermines these claims.

For Democracy and Human Rights?

One claim, as we have seen, is that the decision to go to war against Saddam Hussein's Iraq reflected the neoconservative commitment to global democracy. One problem with this claim is pointed out by Halper and Clarke in a section entitled "The Humanitarian Cloak." In discussing the architects of the Project for the New American Century, they say:

> The democratizing sympathies of Kristol, Perle, Wolfowitz, and other neo-conservatives referred only to the Middle East. . . . When discussing the spread of democracy, they were not referring to the increased authoritarianism and severe political repression in Central Asia or Zimbabwe. In their book about "America's mission," Kaplan and Kristol do not mean Cuba or North Korea. Widespread torture, severe restrictions on the media, arbitrary imprisonment of citizens, harassment and incarceration of opposition leaders, closure of opposition newspapers, and elections that are neither free nor fair are not an issue to neo-conservatives when they take place in Uzbekistan or Kyrgyzstan. Kristol's case for "human dignity" and "human freedom" is not related to the forcible relocation of civilians and the widespread use of forced child-labor camps in Myanmar or to the Bhutanese government's atrocities involving village raids, gang rapes, torture, and forced evictions against its southern Nepali-speaking population. The infamously despotic regime of Equatorial Guinea and the President of Turkmenistan who granted himself presidency for life in a country known for its arbitrary imprisonment and torture of citizens is not referred to in the "great moral cause" and the "great strategic goal" of the Bush doctrine.[89]

When looked at in this light, the foreign policy of the Bush-Cheney administration appears to be no different from that of prior administrations: It pursues its own interests while cloaking them in humanitarian rhetoric.

This conclusion is reinforced when we recall that the neocons' preoccupation with the Middle East in general and Iraq in particular always had to do primarily with oil. As Robert Dreyfuss has put it, "The real reason for the American invasion of Iraq was the most obvious one: Oil." This does not mean, Dreyfuss adds, that the Bush administration went to war for the benefit of U.S. oil companies. Rather, to refer to "oil" here is to refer to "the strategic commodity that is the single most important world resource. Even a novice geostrategist knows that who controls oil controls the world."[90] In other words, the United States intervened in Iraq for the same reason that it has intervened in most places: to sustain and enlarge American primacy.

One might reply, however, that the fact that the Bush administration is not trying to bring about democracy everywhere at once, along with the fact that it operates partly out of self-interest, does not necessarily mean that it is not genuinely seeking to promote democracy in Iraq. And there is, in fact, a sense in which this is true. This sense is suggested by the fact that when the administration and its neocon supporters speak of promoting democracy, they often speak of "market democracy." That qualification brings up the question as to which of these two goals, a democratic government or a capitalistic economy integrated into the global economy, is the most important. Insight into this issue can only be gained, of course, by looking at what the administration has actually done since it began its occupation of Iraq.

The most important thing about Iraq, aside from its oil, for understanding U.S. planning to occupy it was the fact it had a socialist and nationalist economy, which was dominated by some 200 state-owned companies. Much of U.S. foreign policy, as we saw in chapter 6, has been directed to the destruction and prevention of such economies. (Recall the statement by the *New York Times* in 1953 that the U.S. overthrow of the [democratically elected] government in Iran was justified in light of the fact that that government had gone "berserk with fanatical nationalism.")

It is not surprising to learn, therefore, that two months before the United States attacked Iraq, it had worked out a comprehensive privatization plan.[91] This plan would, in Naomi Klein's words, turn Iraq into "a gleaming showroom for laissez-faire economics, . . . a laboratory for the neocons."[92]

This plan was to be put into effect by Paul Bremer, who in May 2003 was put in charge of the Coalition Provisional Authority (CPA). Bremer rather immediately "enacted a radical set of laws unprecedented in their generosity to multinational corporations," then announced that he would begin privatizing the state-owned firms.[93]

These plans did not proceed very far. The plan to privatize the oil industry was blocked by U.S. oil companies.[94] And the plan to privatize all the other firms was slowed down by the fact that it was illegal, then hindered by the insurgency, which convinced most companies that Iraq was too dangerous and unstable to invest in.[95] However, the time, energy, and money put into formulating and then trying to carry out this plan, combined with the fact that all the decisions about the economy were to be made by the occupiers, not the Iraqis, show that the administration was more interested in marketizing Iraq's economy than in democratizing its polity.

Removing Regimes That Harbor Terrorists?

If the rhetoric of democracy and human rights did not reveal the administration's true motives behind the war in Iraq, perhaps, we might think, the administration was really serious about going after governments that harbored terrorists. In this way, the effort to bring about regime change in Iraq could be seen as a genuine response to the attacks of 9/11, aimed at preventing such attacks in the future.

One problem with this view, of course, is that if 9/11 was orchestrated by the Bush administration, this rationale is a lie. Even apart from this consideration, moreover, there is abundant evidence that the real reason for attacking Iraq was not that it was harboring terrorists.

For one thing, prior to the American-led attack on it, Iraq was not harboring or spawning terrorists, as our government knew full well.

A second problem with that rationale has been revealed by General Wesley Clark, the former supreme commander of NATO. He has reported that a three-star general in the Pentagon told him in 2002 that the Pentagon had a five-year plan to attack Iraq, Syria, Lebanon, Libya, Iran, Somalia, and Sudan, adding, "We're not that good at fighting terrorists, so we're going after states." After hearing this list of states, Clark says, he remarked that the states that harbored the most terrorists—Saudi Arabia, Egypt, and Pakistan—were not on the list. America's allies, the three-star general explained, were exempted from the Bush doctrine.[96] The rhetoric about going after states that harbor terrorists, in other words, was simply, like the rhetoric about promoting democracy, a pretext to attack enemies.

Removing Weapons of Mass Destruction?

However, a defender of the Bush-Cheney administration might reply, the basic reason for entering Iraq was the administration's belief that Saddam had, in violation of U.N. declarations, weapons of mass destruction, which he, or terrorists with which he might share these weapons, could use against his neighbors or even the United States. It is true, of course, that no such weapons were found. But this does not mean the Bush administration was dishonest. It means only that they were victims of bad intelligence.

There are, however, many problems with this defense, the most basic of which is that the administration was not the victim but the instigator of the false intelligence. Suspicions that this had indeed been the case had been voiced almost from the beginning and resulted in several investigations. These investigations, which absolved everyone of intentional fabrication, did not quell the suspicions, which continued to be voiced through the early months of 2005.[97]

These suspicions were then proved true on May 1, when the *Sunday Times* of London published a memo that contained the official minutes from a briefing given by Richard Dearlove, then head of MI-6 (Britain's equivalent of the CIA), to Prime Minister Tony Blair and other members of his cabinet. This briefing had been given on July 23, 2002, about eight months before the attack on Iraq. Dearlove, having just returned from a meeting with members of the Bush administration, reported to Blair that President Bush had decided to bring about regime change in Iraq by launching a war, and that this war was to be "justified by the conjunction of terrorism and WMD [weapons of mass destruction]." As to how the Bush administration could be certain that intelligence reports would support this justification, Dearlove said that "the intelligence and facts were being fixed around the policy."[98]

The problem was not, therefore, intelligence failure; it was intelligence *fabrication*. The entire war was, therefore, based on a premeditated lie.

This revelation fits, of course, with facts that were discussed in chapter 6. Paul O'Neill and Richard Clarke had both revealed in 2004, as we saw in chapter 6, that the Bush-Cheney administration came into office with an attack on Iraq at the top of its agenda, with the only question being "finding a way to do it." The way settled on was, after carrying out the attack on Afghanistan, to convince the American people that Saddam was connected to 9/11 and that he possessed weapons of mass destruction. On August 26, 2002, almost exactly a month after the meeting with Dearlove, Cheney declared that "there is no doubt that Saddam Hussein now has weapons of mass destruction . . . [and] is amassing them to use . . . against us."[99] On October 7, Bush made his statement that "we cannot wait for the final proof—the smoking gun—that could come in the form of a mushroom cloud."[100]

Three days later Congress voted to authorize the war against Iraq. But the propaganda offensive, based on cooked intelligence, continued. In his State of the Union address on January 28, 2003, Bush said: "The British Government has learned that Saddam Hussein recently sought significant quantities of uranium from Africa," intelligence that was clearly fabricated. Then on February 5, Colin Powell presented cooked evidence to the U.N. Security Council[101]— a presentation that he has since regretted as a "blot" on his record.[102] Although Powell did not admit that the intelligence used to justify the war had been deliberately fixed, independent analysts have shown that it was.[103]

All the attempts to rationalize the war in Iraq, to show that it was a noble effort, or at least a defensive necessity, have been exposed as false. This war has from the first been based on lies, greed, and imperial lust. To see it accurately is to see that it is an unmitigated evil.

GLOBAL APARTHEID

The two previous sections have given examples of U.S. violations of the rights of individual people and countries. I turn now to some effects of U.S. imperialism—or "leadership," as its advocates like to call it—on the world as a whole. These advocates of American empire might pose the issue thus: "We can grant that U.S. imperialism has required the violation of the rights of some people, even millions of people, and also violated the sovereignty of many countries. After all, as the saying has it, 'You can't make an omelet without breaking some eggs.' Is it not true, nevertheless, that U.S. leadership, especially as exercised since World War II, has contributed to the general good of the world so that, overall, that leadership can be considered benign, even benevolent?"

In many ways, the most important event of the twentieth century occurred during and after World War II, when the United States replaced Great Britain as the leader of the global capitalist economy. From that point onward, the United States bears increasing responsibility—and hence credit or blame—for the overall welfare of our world. The best way to predict whether an even more inclusive American empire would be good or bad for the planet as a whole is to look at some dimensions of planetary trends from 1945 to the present. I look here at some trends that must be regarded as most crucial, especially from the perspective of Christian faith. In the present section, I examine the growth in the division between the rich and the poor, which has come to be called "global apartheid." In the following section, I look briefly at several other dimensions of American imperialism that bear on the question of the general good of the world.

The Reality of Global Apartheid

The term "global apartheid" was introduced into the discussion of global inequality primarily through a booklet of that title published in 1978 by Gernot Köhler.[104] Writing long before apartheid in South Africa was dismantled, Köhler defined global apartheid as "a structure of world society" in which "a minority of whites occupies the pole of affluence, while a majority composed of other races occupies the pole of poverty," and in which "the affluent white minority possesses a disproportionately large share of world society's political, economic, and military power. . . . [G]lobal apartheid is thus a structure of extreme inequality in cultural, racial, social, political, economic, military and legal terms, as is South African apartheid."[105]

Köhler did, however, point to one major difference—that "global apartheid is even more severe than South African apartheid."[106] In particular:

> Income inequality is even worse: In South Africa, the poorest 40% of the population receive only 6.2% of the national product, while the poorest 40% of the world receive . . . [only] 5.2% of the world product. . . . [T]he richest 20% of South Africa's population take 58.0% of the income, while the richest 20% of the world take . . . 71.3% of world income.[107]

Köhler's moral conclusion: "Just as the world community opposes apartheid in South Africa, it should also oppose the global apartheid."[108]

In 1992, the concept was discussed, somewhat surprisingly, by Thomas Schelling, a Harvard economist who had focused on strategic and national security affairs. Asking which country the world as a whole most closely resembled, he said: "I find my own answer stunning and embarrassing: South Africa." Spelling out the implications, Schelling, while not mentioning Köhler's discussion, gave a similar analysis: "We live in a world that is one-fifth rich and four-fifths poor; the rich are segregated into the rich countries and the poor into poor countries; the rich are predominantly lighter skinned and the poor darker skinned. . . . There is no systematic redistribution of income."[109]

In 1993, Richard Falk, referring to the discussions by both Köhler and Schelling, pointed out that since Schelling is a well-known military strategist, he should have extended his analysis to include the fact that "the rich, light-skinned countries enjoy a decisive military superiority and engage in frequent interventionary operations against the poor, dark-skinned countries."[110] Falk's point was that, as we saw above, these countries with military superiority, especially the United States, often use that superiority to prevent the poor countries from improving their economic situations.

Another feature of Schelling's discussion that has evoked criticism is his failure to draw the same moral conclusion as had Köhler, namely, that global apartheid should be condemned and dismantled. Rather, Schelling said to his fellow Americans, we must safeguard what we possess, including "our material standard of living."[111]

In any case, 1992, which brought Schelling's study, also brought the first book-length discussion of the topic: *Unraveling Global Apartheid*, by Titus Alexander. In explaining the parallel between global and South African apartheid, Alexander said:

> Three-quarters of the land [in apartheid South Africa] and all its natural resources could only be owned by whites, a sixth of the population. The West also has a sixth of the world's population and commands over three-quarters of global resources. . . . [In South Africa,] democracy for a few meant oppression for the many. So it is for most people in the global economy. . . . Free trade and consumer choice for a few means low incomes, long hours and a struggle for subsistence among the many.[112]

After citing these and several other parallels, Alexander concluded:

> The profound parallels between apartheid and the global system mean that people in the West are as much part of institutional injustice towards the world's majority as white South Africans were towards their non-white neighbours.[113]

Given the fact that apartheid as practiced in South Africa "was declared illegal and a 'crime against humanity' by the U.N. General Assembly in 1973," Alexander added, "Inequality between the West and the world's majority . . . is just as immoral and illegitimate. It deserves the same condemnation."[114]

Historical Origins of Global Apartheid

People in the affluent world have tended to assume that the great disparities between their societies and those in poor countries are "natural," perhaps because they have always existed, due perhaps to differences in character. Recent studies have shown, however, that the disparities arose rather recently as a result of a famous historical development, colonialism. In a statement quoted with approval by well-known economist Robert Heilbroner, Paul Bairoch said that in the 1750s "living standards in what we today call the North were not notably higher than those in the South." Bairoch, who wrote these words in 1980, then added, "Over the next 230 years, the average citizen in the capitalist world grew to be eight times richer than one in the noncapitalist world." Why? Primarily because of "the drainage of wealth from the underdeveloped Periphery to the developed Center."[115]

This drainage of wealth occurred in the period of European expansion, during which it colonized most of what is now often called the "third world." As Colin Parkins has explained, "The European powers' expansion profoundly affected the local economic and social structures in these areas and tied them into global economic relationships that shaped their subsequent development." The impact of this colonial relationship took several forms:

> the disruption of indigenous processes of development, the imposition of market relations, the consolidation of authoritarian political structures, and above all the formation of an international division of labour in which the colonized areas acted as primary commodity producers and labour reserves for the industrialized world.[116]

What this "division of labour" meant is that the economies of the colonized countries were structured not to meet their own people's needs but to serve the desires of the colonizers. One result "was an unprecedented accumulation of wealth and capital in the metropolitan countries."

So, rather than being natural and eternal, "the patterns of global apartheid are a product of this history."[117]

Recent Developments

When the United States took over leadership of the global economy after World War II, the nature of this history did not significantly change. America was, in other words, no less exploitative than had been Great Britain and the other European colonial powers. Indeed, the United States was determined to maintain the great disparity that obtained at that time.

In 1947, George Kennan, who was director of the policy planning staff in the U.S. State Department, said in a "top secret" memo that has since been quoted countless times:

> We have about 50% of the world's wealth, but only 6.3% of its population. . . . In this situation, we cannot fail to be the object of envy and resentment. Our real task in the coming period is to devise a pattern of

relationships which will permit us to maintain this position of disparity without positive detriment to our national security.[118]

Kennan thereby expressed the same attitude that had been manifested by the "imperial brain trust."

The chief instruments for carrying out this policy, aside from the CIA and the U.S. military, were the so-called Bretton Woods Institutions[119]—namely the International Monetary Fund (IMF), the World Bank (technically known as the International Bank for Reconstruction and Development), and the General Agreement on Tariffs and Trade (GATT), which has recently turned into the World Trade Organization (WTO). There was again, as David Korten has explained, a difference between public and private aims:

> The public purpose of what became known as the Bretton Woods system was to unite the world in a web of economic prosperity and interdependence that would preclude nations' taking up arms. Another purpose in the eyes of its architects was to create an open economy unified under U.S. leadership that would ensure unchallenged U.S. access to the world's markets and raw materials.[120]

The best indicator of which of these two purposes was most important is, as Korten points out, provided by the results.

> If measured by contributions to improving the lives of people or strengthening the institutions of democratic governance, the World Bank and the IMF have been disastrous failures—imposing an enormous burden on the world's poor and seriously impeding their development. In terms of fulfilling the mandates set for them by their original architects—advancing economic globalization under the domination of the economically powerful—they both have been a resounding success.[121]

Commenting further on what the World Bank and the IMF have done to the poor around the world, Korten says: "They have arguably done more harm to more people than any other pair of non-military institutions in human history."[122] This harm has been especially great since the 1980s, when loans to borrowing countries resulted in enormous debts, which were followed by "structural adjustment programs," which forced the countries to spend less and less money on programs for their own people and more and more money simply to pay the interest on the loans. The way this has worked has been described in many works, such as Walden Bello's *Dark Victory: The United States, Structural Adjustment, and Global Poverty* and various writings by theologian John Cobb, including one entitled "Imperialism in American Economic Policy."[123] In *Confessions of an Economic Hit Man*, moreover, John Perkins explains how he, while working on behalf of U.S. interests while saying he was working to alleviate poverty in other countries, used deceptive development loans and other means to further impoverish them while further enriching U.S. interests.[124]

As a result of these and related processes, the disparity between the rich and the poor of the world has continued to increase. Cobb has written:

> The disparity in per capita income between the US and the undeveloped nations is estimated as having been about thirteen to one in 1947. In 1989, . . . the disparity had reached around sixty to one. Even more troubling is that disparities within the developing countries have grown, with hundreds of millions of people living in a kind of destitution that was rare in earlier times.[125]

Another way to quantify the growing disparity is in terms of the gap between the richest fifth of the world's population and the poorest fifth. In 1960, people in the richest fifth were thirty times wealthier than the poorest fifth. By 1997, they had become seventy-four times wealthier.[126]

This disparity increased even further in the following years. Using still another method of measuring it, the *Human Development Report* of 2005 says that the richest 10 percent of the world's population receives 54 percent of the world's total income, while 40 percent of the world's population—meaning 2.5 billion people—receive only 5 percent of the world's total income.[127]

One consequence of this absolute poverty is lack of sufficient food, clean water, and even the simplest medical care by over a billion people. Primarily as a result of these deficiencies, about 18 million people die from poverty-related causes every year, 11 million of whom are children under the age of five. This would mean, at the present rate, 180 million people, including 110 million children, dying from poverty-related causes every decade.[128]

Accordingly, whereas the United States, especially under the present administration, has portrayed itself as the great champion of the right to life, it has been presiding over, and using its power to enforce, an economic system that denies the right to life to people on a massive scale, by denying them the means even to a subsistence living. This global economic system does not merely allow billions of human beings to sink below what Henry Shue calls "the line beneath which no one [should] be allowed to sink." It *pushes* them under.

The fact that the United States is fully conscious of what it is doing, and intends to keep doing it, is expressed in "Vision for 2020," which was discussed in chapter 6. Having said that the mission of the U.S. Space Command is to "dominat[e] the space dimension of military operations to protect US interests and investment," this 1997 document added, "The globalization of the world economy . . . will continue with a widening between 'haves' and 'have-nots.'"[129] In other words, just as George Kennan's 1947 memo said that, because of the disproportionate share of the world's resources that we in the United States use, "we cannot fail to be the object of envy and resentment," this document, written fifty years later, recognizes that the increasing disparity between the rich and the poor, caused by the U.S.-led global economy, will make the "have-nots" of the world increasingly resentful, so the U.S. military will need ever more sophisticated weapons to keep them in line. In 2005, the head of the Space Command, General Lance Lord, was quoted as saying that by putting weapons in space, the United States, employing a strategy called "Global Strike," will have the "incredible capability" to destroy things "anywhere in the world . . . in forty-five minutes."[130]

In light of the facts discussed in this section, one can only wonder how Robert Kagan can write about "the benevolent hegemony exercised by the United States," saying that this hegemony "is good for a vast portion of the world's population."[131]

EVIL EMPIRE

During the Cold War, American leaders characterized the Soviet Union as an "evil empire." This characterization was based on several factors, especially the Soviet Union's mass murder of some 50 million of its own citizens during the Stalinist period, its brutal interventions in Eastern European countries, and its (alleged) desire to create an all-inclusive global empire. "Throughout the Cold War," Dorrien says, "American political leaders maintained that Soviet Communism was evil because it was ideologically driven to rule the world."[132]

The other regime that Americans regularly call evil, even demonic, is the Nazi regime, partly because it brutally attacked other countries, partly because it murdered some 6 million Jews in its genocidal holocaust, and partly because World War II, which it initiated, resulted in the deaths of some 60 million people. We rightly consider the Nazi regime demonic.

But if we apply the same criteria to the American empire, how can we withhold the judgment that it, too, is an evil, even demonic, empire? America has overthrown the governments in more countries than Germany and the Soviet Union combined. The United States, especially now that it is under the sway of neocon thinking, seems "ideologically driven to rule the world." During the Cold War, Dorrien points out, U.S. political leaders claimed that "America built a global military system and fought proxy battles with the Soviet Union not because it aspired to dominate the world, but to keep the Soviet Union from doing so."[133] But the fact that American leaders did not dismantle this global military system after the Soviet Union crumbled, and even continued to expand it, showed that this claim was false (this being the fact that drove Bacevich to rethink the true goals behind U.S. foreign policy). And now neocon thinkers and U.S. military documents openly proclaim that a global *Pax Americana* is the goal. If it would have been evil for the Soviets to want to dominate the world, is it not evil for Americans to seek this kind of domination?

According to neocon ideology, of course, this does not follow, because the

Soviet Union was inherently evil, whereas America is inherently good. So whereas a Soviet-imposed global empire would have been evil, an American-imposed global empire would be good. As Wattenberg has put it: "A unipolar world is a good thing, if America is the uni."[134]

We have, however, seen that this part of neocon ideology is patently and massively false. U.S. foreign policy does not act on behalf of civil and political rights; it does not honor the basic economic right to subsistence; it does not respect the results of democratic elections when the "wrong" candidates win; it does not promote freedom and the general good. There is no reason to expect a world with an American "uni" to be much if any better than a world with a German, a Chinese, a Japanese, or a Russian "uni."

This conclusion is partly because of the next point: whereas Soviet and Nazi leaders were each responsible for over 50 million deaths, American leaders, besides being responsible for millions of deaths through their interventions in Central America, Indonesia, Vietnam, Iraq, and elsewhere, are, by virtue of their leadership of the global economy, ultimately responsible for some 180 million deaths from poverty-related causes *each decade*.

In the early decades after World War II, to be sure, one could not pin much of the responsibility for these deaths on the United States, except for those that occurred in countries in Latin America, whose economies the United States had largely controlled for many decades. The millions of people who died from poverty-related causes in other parts of the world were primarily the responsibility of imperial powers in Europe, especially the British Empire. Processes had been set in motion by them that could not have been changed overnight, or even in a few years. As the years wore on, however, the responsibility of the United States increased, insofar as it, besides not creating structures to decrease global poverty, actually took measures to sustain and even increase it. For the most part, to be sure, U.S. leaders did not consciously want other people to get poorer. But the preservation and even increase of global poverty was a consequence, and a predictable consequence, of their policies.

U.S. leaders, in other words, did not hate the people whose economic hopes they dashed. They were simply indifferent to their welfare. U.S. policies and actions were, accordingly, demonic, because U.S. leaders used their enormous power with indifference to the welfare of those upon whom it was exercised.

In 2002, South African President Thabo Mbeki, in speaking of the "social behaviour [that] has produced and entrenches a global system of apartheid," described it as "social behaviour that has pity neither for beautiful nature nor for living human beings."[135] A social-economic system that was in harmony with the will of God, who has compassion for all people, would be one that did have pity for the poor—that is, one that would be aimed at overcoming their poverty.

The conclusion that the American empire is evil, and in fact the principal location of demonic power in our time, follows from other dimensions of its behavior as well. I will mention three.

Nuclear Weapons

One of these dimensions has been America's development of a nuclear arsenal that could destroy the earth, in the sense of that it would no longer be capable of supporting human life and, in fact, most other forms of life as well. The official rationale during the Cold War, of course, was that this arsenal was purely for the sake of deterring the Soviets from launching a first strike on America. The dissolution of the Soviet Union, however, disproved that claim. In any case, the deterrence strategy itself, insofar as it was seriously intended, showed an amazing indifference to the fate of the earth. The whole idea was that if the Soviet Union launched a first strike, we would retaliate with a massive strike on its population centers. This program was not given up even after scientists predicted that even a small nuclear exchange, involving only a few weapons, could trigger a "nuclear winter," meaning a dust cloud all over the planet that would keep out sunlight for so long that virtually everything would die. The policy of nuclear deterrence has been repeatedly condemned as immoral by individuals and bodies, including Christian bodies, with moral authority.[136]

There has also been massive discussion of four other problems with the production and possession of nuclear weapons. One is the possibility that the production process could result in horrendous accidents. A second problem is that there is no safe way to dispose of spent nuclear materials, which continue to give off radiation for hundreds of thousands of years. A third problem is that with various countries, including the United States, having nuclear weapons on a "hair trigger" (meaning they are ready to be launched immediately after a perceived first strike against one's own forces or population centers), an "accidental" nuclear war could result simply from misperception or miscommunication.[137] A fourth problem, which is the one that has been most discussed recently, is that terrorists—whether terrorist states or nonstate terrorists—might get possession of one or more nuclear weapons, which they might then use to blackmail some nation or even to cause great devastation.

In spite of these problems, which could result in the death of hundreds of millions of people or even the end of civilization, the United States has not been willing to do what it alone is in position to do: bring the era of nuclear weapons to an end. U.S. leaders have from the outset found the strategic advantage brought by their nuclear superiority more important than removing the possibility of a nuclear end to civilization. If this is not demonic evil, it is hard to know what would be.

This refusal is especially odious in light of the double standards the United States has been employing in relation to the Nuclear Non-Proliferation Treaty, which entered into force in 1970.[138] The basic ideas in this treaty were outlined by President Kennedy in an address to the United Nations General Assembly in 1961, in which he said:

> Today, every inhabitant of this planet must contemplate the day when this planet may no longer be habitable. Every man, woman and child lives under a nuclear sword of Damocles, hanging by the slenderest of threads, capable of being cut at any moment by accident or miscalculation or by madness. The weapons of war must be abolished before they abolish us.[139]

The purpose of the treaty was to prevent nuclear weapons from spreading beyond the five countries who already possessed them: the United States, Russia, Great Britain, China, and France. The methods to be used by the nuclear powers were to try to get all other nations to sign the treaty, to refuse to share nuclear technology with nations that refused, and to work toward nuclear disarmament.

The effort by the United States to lead the enforcement of this treaty, however, has been doubly problematic. First, its enforcement is selective, employed only against nations regarded as enemies. The United States has not seriously objected to the secret creation of nuclear weapons by two allies, Israel and Pakistan.[140] More recently, the Bush administration, after it had invaded Iraq on the charge that it possessed nuclear weapons and at the same time that it was threatening Iran with sanctions or worse if it proceeded with its plans to develop nuclear energy, worked out a bilateral agreement to share nuclear technology with India, which had acquired nuclear weapons and refused to sign the treaty.[141]

The second problem is that the United States is not living up to its side of the treaty. The goal of preventing others from joining the nuclear club is only one part of the treaty. All signers in addition declared "their intention to achieve at the earliest possible date the cessation of the nuclear arms race and to undertake effective measures in the direction of nuclear disarmament."[142] The United States, besides not moving in this direction, is increasing its nuclear arsenal (with, for example, the addition of "bunker busters") and planning to put nuclear weapons in space.

Global Warming

A second major issue that threatens not only the general good of the human race but its very survival is global warming. And again, the United States, far from using its extraordinary power to overcome or at least mitigate the problem, has been its primary cause. It has not only been the primary source of carbon dioxide and other greenhouse gases going into the atmosphere. It has also been the chief impediment, by far, to the achievement of any global agreement, with teeth, to reduce this route to civilization's suicide. It has consistently, for the decades during which scientists have been aware of the problem, failed either to sign enforceable treaties to curtail the emission of greenhouse gases or to undertake a voluntary program to do so. Although the scientific consensus now is that if civilization is not to be destroyed by global warming within the next 100 years or so, then the highly industrialized nations, and especially the

United States, need to reduce emissions by about 80 percent, the United States has even refused to agree to keep emissions at the present level. The attitude has been that, as the first President Bush notoriously put it at the Earth Summit in Rio de Janeiro in 1992: "The American way of life is not negotiable."

The U.S. government, especially during the present Bush administration, has even justified its inaction by casting doubt on the scientific evidence that global warming is occurring and that its effects will become increasingly catastrophic.

The most frightening possibility is "runaway global warming," which will occur if some kind of positive feedback cycle begins. That is, if variable A causes an increase in variable B, which in turn causes an increase in variable A, then global warming will be unstoppable and will quite quickly put an end to the planet's viability for most forms of life. There are several possible variables through which this process might begin. Some scientists believe that there is a real chance that, if present trends are not drastically altered, some version of runaway global warming will occur within the present century, perhaps as early as 2050.

However, in spite of an extremely widespread scientific consensus that, unless drastic changes are made, especially by the United States, human civilization may be destroyed through global climate change even if it manages to avoid destroying itself by means of nuclear weapons, American political leaders have done essentially nothing—except to thwart the efforts of others to do something helpful.[143]

The American behavior in regard to these two issues—nuclear weapons and global warming—demonstrate as clearly as possible that demonic power is now firmly lodged in the United States, especially in its government, its corporate heads, the "defense" industries, its plutocratic class more generally, and its ideologues.

The other crimes of the U.S. government that we have examined here—the interventions in other countries to override their decisions, including their democratic elections, which violate their sovereignty and their people's civil and political rights; and the direction of the global economy so as to produce widespread poverty, often so severe as to cause some 18 million deaths, including over 10 million children's deaths, per year—all these crimes are sufficiently evil to call the American empire demonic. America is using its unprecedented power for purposes that are diametrically opposed to the will of our creator, who loves all its creatures, wanting them to survive and thrive.

But in risking the extinction of human and other higher forms of life through nuclear holocaust or global warming, the United States is threatening the long-term divine purpose for this planet—that it continue to bring forth and nurture a great variety of forms of life, especially very high forms of life, which can actualize the highest values possible for creatures, such as truth, beauty, and goodness. It has taken our creator billions of years to bring the planet to this point. By threatening to bring about the grossly premature death of this planet—a planet that could without nuclear holocaust or global warm-ing or some other catastrophe probably continue to support life for millions of more years—the United States is threatening to defeat the divine will for this world in the most extreme way imaginable. Nothing, therefore, could be more demonic.

Many theists, to be sure, have been taught that our creator is omnipotent in the traditional sense, so that it would be impossible for us to threaten the divine purposes. From this perspective, whatever God wills, God can bring about uni-laterally. If we sin, we can do so only because God permits it. But there is no evidence for this view, and abundant evidence against it, such as the insoluble problem of evil that would exist if it were true, and the very fact that our world has been created through a long, slow, evolutionary process, which is consistent with the idea that the divine power is persuasive, not coercive or all-controlling.

A theism that is consistent with the facts, therefore, provides no grounds for complacency—no grounds for the assumption that if things get bad enough, divine power will step in to save the day, and the planet. As chapter 8 argued, the battle between divine power and demonic power is a *real* battle, which means that the outcome is not predetermined. There are, to be sure, arguably respects in which the divine purposes cannot be defeated, as I have suggested elsewhere.[144] But there is no good reason to believe that these respects include the divine purposes for this planet.

Insofar as we accept the idea that the divine purposes *can* be threatened by creaturely power, we can maintain our definition of the demonic—that it is creaturely power that, besides being strong enough to threaten divine purposes, is exercised in ways that are diametrically opposed to those purposes. From this perspective, we must conclude that the United States is today the chief embod-iment of demonic power.

This perspective, to be sure, requires an enormous shift in our understand-ing of the relation between our country and our God. Most Americans who believe in God have been brought up assuming that America is at least basi-cally on God's side, perhaps even the chief instrument of divine purposes in the world. To go from that understanding to the view that our country is instead the chief embodiment of demonic power, hence the primary threat to divine purposes on our planet, is not an enjoyable conversion. But it is, I believe, a conversion that is necessary if our beliefs are to correspond to real-ity and if we are to be in position to turn our country, and hence our world, in a different direction.

The Demonic and 9/11

In this final section, we consider, in light of the ideas discussed in the previous section, the relation between the demonic and 9/11. The attacks of 9/11, under-stood as a false-flag operation orchestrated by forces within the U.S. government, can be taken, I suggest, as the chief revelation of our time. Not a divine revelation, to be sure, but the chief revelation of the demonic—of the extent to which it has taken control of the American government.

To some extent, the interpretation of 9/11 as a manifestation of demonic evil is self-evident. The attacks of 9/11 have been described as unspeakably evil by members of the Bush-Cheney administration. President Bush himself, on the evening of 9/11, said: "Thousands of lives were suddenly ended by evil, despicable acts of terror. . . . Today, our nation saw evil, the very worst of human nature."[145] No explanation of why the attacks were despicable was necessary. The proposition was rightly taken to be self-evident. And if the attacks were orchestrated by our own government, the proposition is even more self-evident. It will be useful, nevertheless, to reflect on various reasons *why* the false-flag attacks can be taken as a demonic revelation.

For one thing, to begin with the most obvious point, leaders of the government take a solemn oath to protect their own citizens. This is their first duty. To launch an attack on their own citizens is a violent breach of this oath of office. According to Article 3, Section 3, of the Constitution, moreover, the very definition of treason is for an American citizen to engage in "levying war" against the United States, and the Bush administration has itself defined the attacks as acts of war. For such an act of war to be orchestrated by members of the government would be treason of the worst sort.

This treason is made especially destructive by the fact that it apparently involved many parts of the executive branch, including the CIA, the FBI, and the Department of Justice, and the resulting cover-up apparently involved, besides all these agencies, members of the U.S. Congress. Burns Weston, a professor of law, has said that the "disparity between official 9/11 'spin' and independently researched 9/11 fact [is] so glaring as to suggest the possibility of a constitutional crisis unlike anything our country has ever known."[146] Facing up to this crisis could be the most traumatic experience ever undergone by our country. But if we do not face up to it, then our constitutional form of government will be essentially over, leaving no checks on the executive branch's power to do as it wills. A demonic value system within the executive branch is revealed by the fact that it, for the sake of its imperial goals, would create this foreseeable dilemma for our country by engineering the treasonous attacks of 9/11.

Second, the evil of the attacks becomes even worse insofar as they were orchestrated in order to pave the way for launching unprovoked wars on two countries that provided no threat, whether imminent or long-term, to the people of the United States. The administration and its Pentagon even planned to use 9/11 as a pretext, as we saw earlier, to attack still more countries. The U.S. government was planning, therefore, to use the deaths of some three thousand people (whom itself had killed) to justify wars that would most likely kill and maim many hundreds of thousands of people, perhaps millions.

A third reason to regard 9/11 as a manifestation of demonic evil is that it has been used, numerous denials notwithstanding, to launch the kind of "clash of civilizations" that Samuel Huntington had predicted.[147] As illustrated by the fact that all the countries on the Pentagon's hit list are predominantly Muslim, this war pits the predominantly Christian West (along with its ally Israel) against the Islamic world. Members of the military-industrial complex had long wanted a replacement for the Cold War, often called World War III, once it started winding down. There had been attempts to get the American public and Congress behind a "war on terror" since 1981.[148] But they had not been successful. Only with 9/11 did such a war get public backing. The description of it as World War IV points to its role in providing a new global enemy to replace the ubiquitous Communist enemy as a pretext for enlarging the American empire.

One of the evils of this civilizational war is that it has implanted in Western minds an association between "Muslim" and "terrorist," so that Muslims tend to be regarded as guilty until proven innocent. This description of America's targeted enemies as "terrorists," moreover, serves to provide a justification for killing them, or at least incarcerating them without trial, because the label strips them of their humanity and hence their rights. The term "terrorist," in other words, serves the same function as did the label "commie" in the Cold War and "gook" in the Vietnam War in particular. People thus labeled could be killed with indifference and impunity. If this deliberate creation of a global clash of civilizations in our time is not demonic, then it is hard to know what would be.

A fourth demonic dimension of 9/11 was the intention to use it to instill fear in the American public. This fear, which is similar to the fear of a nuclear attack that was instilled in Americans during the Cold War, has served, as observed earlier, to make Americans ready to acquiesce in the attacks on Afghanistan and Iraq, the doctrines of preemptive-preventive warfare, the weaponization of space, the increased funding for military purposes, and even to give up, through their congressional representatives, many of their civil liberties. British novelist John Le Carré, in an article entitled "The United States Has Gone Completely Mad," suggested that 9/11 had been used to create a national neurosis based on ignorance and fear.[149] The 9/11 attacks were, thereby, examples of the "strategy of tension" used during the Cold War to create fear in the hearts of Italians, Belgians, and other Europeans, only on a much bigger scale. In this respect as in many others, therefore, 9/11 was a violation of Kant's fundamental moral doctrine: members of the U.S. government had treated its citizens as mere means to their ends, not as ends in themselves.

Fifth, rage created around the world by this civilizational war has increased the possibility that some organization will acquire and employ nuclear weapons against America simply for revenge. And, with our own nuclear weapons ready to fire very quickly,[150] there is no predicting what the response would be. Accordingly, the administration's war, while allegedly aimed at preventing terror, has increased the likelihood that the most terrifying and destructive of all possibilities will occur.

A sixth destructive consequence of the attacks was their use to focus the public and congressional mind almost exclusively on terrorism, thereby distracting it from the ecological crisis, which is the overarching issue of our age. For the first time in history, one species, our own, is on a trajectory that, if not radically altered, will soon bring our planet's life, at least in its higher forms, to an end. The preeminent issue of our day, therefore, should be whether human civilization can learn to live in a way that is sustainable. Politicians, scientists, educators, and the mass media should be united in working to this end. With the demise of the Cold War, it appeared—partly because the fact of global warming was becoming increasingly obvious—that this issue might start to get the attention it had long deserved.

But the violence of 9/11, along with the official narrative thereof, distracted our primary attention away from the relation between humanity and nature and forced it back to human-vs.-human issues. Given the fact that much valuable time has been lost since the attacks—time that might have been used to slow global warming before it is too late—this dimension of 9/11 may turn out to be the most destructive from the divine perspective. The very fact that this foreseeable possibility exists makes 9/11 an extreme example of the demonic.

I conclude this chapter with the observation that the relation between 9/11 and the American empire goes both ways. On the one hand, the American empire plays an explanatory role with regard to 9/11. Only if we understand the nature of the American empire, along with ideas for extending it that were developed in the 1990s, can we understand why the attacks of 9/11 occurred. On the other hand, the attacks of 9/11 play a revelatory role in relation to the American empire. For it is only when we realize that the attacks of 9/11 were carried out and covered up for the sake of America's global domination project that we can, as I have suggested elsewhere, "*fully* grasp the extent to which this project is propelled by fanaticism based on a deeply perverted value system."[151] That judgment follows, at least, if one views these matters from the perspective of a Christian value system.

Chapter 10

A Call to Reflection and Action

Learning the truth about 9/11 should, I believe, lead the church into a process of reflection and action. I suggest in this chapter some topics for reflection, then some possible actions.

REFLECTIONS

Prior to reflection upon the *implications* of this book's thesis should be, of course, reflection on the question of the *truth* of this thesis—that 9/11 was a false-flag operation carried out by forces within our own government in order to advance the American empire. One way to approach this question would be simply to ask whether, given the facts laid out in this book and elsewhere,[1] any other interpretation can plausibly handle all these facts. Having worked on this question for over three years now, I have concluded that no other interpretation is possible. The rest of what I say presupposes this conclusion.

Truly reflecting on the implications of 9/11 as a false-flag operation could lead individuals and groups into literally hundreds of topics. I suggest a few that should, I think, be near the top of the list.

1. One of these topics is the implication of the fact that the theses about 9/11 presented in this book are never seriously discussed in the mainstream media in the United States. This blackout applies not simply to the claim that 9/11 was a false-flag operation, which of course would generate great resistance, even outrage, if presented sympathetically. It applies even to details of the cover-up that, by themselves, would not be explosive. Take, for example, the discrepancy, revealed in chapter 4, between the time the 9/11 Commission said Vice President Cheney went down to the shelter conference room, and the time he must have actually gone down, according to all prior reports, including Secretary of Transportation Norman Mineta's eyewitness account. This discrepancy could be presented as simply a factual error on the part of the 9/11 Commission, but even such details are excluded from coverage.

How can the mainstream media's failure to report obvious discrepancies such as these be explained other than by supposing that they are willingly complicit in the cover-up of the truth about 9/11 and have decided that they will not expose any falsehoods in *The 9/11 Commission Report*, at least none that could appear to be part of a systematic cover-up? In referring to the mainstream media, I refer not, of course, to the reporters but to the editors behind the scenes and the corporate owners for whom they work. These are the people who decide what does and does not make it into our newspapers, magazines, and radio and television shows.

2. Reflecting on this failure to report on facts that would undermine the official story about 9/11 could then lead to the question of what other facts have been excluded. One of those was the evidence, reported in the previous chapter, that at least eight months before the attack on Iraq in March 2003, the Bush administration had decided to "fix the intelligence" about Iraqi weapons of mass destruction in order to match the Bush administration's policy, already determined, to go to war.

This revelation, which was made in London's *Sunday Times* on May 1, 2005, was stunning. It should have been the stuff of headlines and editorials in every major paper in the country. It should have been the lead story on every radio and TV news broadcast. It should have been discussed on CNN every night for months. But it was not.

The mainstream media in this country seemed determined to ignore or belittle the memo. The next day, it was mentioned in a *New York Times* story, but the memo's statement that the facts and the intelligence would be "fixed" was buried in the fifteenth paragraph and not further discussed. The *Washington Post*'s first story on the memo did not appear until May 13, after readers had complained about lack of coverage, and even then was buried deep inside the paper. *USA Today* did not mention the story until June 8. On June 13, the *New York Times* finally ran a full-length story on the memo but this story, by distorting the memo, portrayed it as insignificant.[2] By June 15, six weeks after the story first appeared in London, many major papers, including the *New York*

Times, had not yet run an editorial about the memo and some other major papers, including the *Washington Post* and the *Los Angeles Times,* had published editorials dismissing the memo as unimportant.[3]

Had it not been for bloggers on the Internet, even this minimal coverage might not have occurred. The monumental nature of this failure by the mainstream media can be best expressed by quoting a few of these bloggers, who expressed their dismay and disbelief at this failure.

David Michael Green, a professor of political science, wrote that the U.S. crime in attacking Iraq has been turned into "an astonishing demonstration of the depth of American democracy's decay [by] the complicity of the media establishment in hiding the original crime." In support of this claim, Green, writing on May 13, 2005, asked, rhetorically:

> Apart from 9/11, has there been a more important story in the last decade than that the president lied to the American people about the reasons for invading Iraq, and then proceeded to plunge the country into an illegal war which has alienated the rest of the world, lit a fire under the war's victims and the Islamic world generally, turning them into enemy combatants, . . . cost $300 billion and counting, taken over 1600 American lives on top of more than 15,000 gravely wounded, and killed perhaps 100,000 Iraqis?[4]

Ten days later, Robert Dreyfuss, writing about "the stunning lack of editorial comment on the Downing Street memo," asked: "Where are the thundering editorials demanding that the White House explain itself? That Congress investigate?"[5]

We must conclude that Green was right: that this episode clearly revealed the major media's complicity in covering up the truth about the war on Iraq.[6]

Something else that would seem to be of national importance is evidence that the presidential election of 2004 was stolen by Bush backers. In a well-written article entitled "None Dare Call It Stolen," New York University professor Mark Crispin Miller presented abundant evidence for this conclusion in August 2005 in *Harper's* magazine, usually considered a reputable publication.[7] However, although television news shows are supposed to like explosive stories, they did not pick up this one, so it did not become part of the conversation. Miller then presented this evidence more extensively in a book entitled *Fooled Again,*[8] but as far as the mainstream media was concerned, it might as well not have been published. A book was also put out containing Congressman John Conyers's report on problems in the election,[9] but that too was not considered newsworthy by the mainstream media. Peter Phillips, who as the head of Project Censored puts out a book each year with the most important stories that had been censored by the mainstream media the previous year, included this story in *Censored 2006.*[10]

This lack of coverage is suspicious at the least. There had been much discussion about whether Bush fairly won the 2000 election, with much of it concluding that Al Gore should have become president.[11] The issue of whether that election had been stolen became recognized as especially important after the Bush administration's post-9/11 behavior, especially the attack on Iraq, and the reaction thereto. Also, America presents itself as the country most concerned with democratic elections, sometimes sending representatives to monitor elections in other countries to make sure that they are reasonably fair. Reports about the fairness of such elections are often considered important enough to make the evening news. And yet virtually no coverage was given to solidly researched reports that America's own presidential election, perhaps for the second time in a row, had been stolen.

There appears to be a pattern here. Although the mainstream media often do carry negative reports about Bush and Cheney, the evidence for fixing the intelligence and stealing the election is, like the evidence that 9/11 was a false-flag operation, in another class. It is evidence for crimes so big that widespread knowledge about them would, besides leading to demands for impeachment, undermine the confidence of average Americans in their country, something that the corporate owners of the mass media surely do not want.

All of this should be food for thought for Christians who regularly repeat the Lord's Prayer, with its hope for a reign of God on earth. If we want to align ourselves with the divine purpose to replace the rule of demonic values with the rule of divine values in our country and our world, we need a realistic understanding of the ideological role played in American political life by the mainstream media. There are many good books that lay out the conflict between the corporate ownership of the mainstream media, on the one hand, and the media's responsibility to provide citizens with information needed to vote wisely, on the other.[12] These books should be studied in the churches.

3. Another issue raised by 9/11 is the long tradition of American exceptionalism, according to which America is qualitatively different from countries in the old world (Europe).[13] This notion is reflected in the idea that the American empire, unlike all previous ones, is an empire devoted to spreading freedom and democracy. This notion also lies behind the idea that no important political events, such as assassinations, election results, or attacks on Americans, could be the result of conspiracies within the government. To be a "conspiracy theorist" is to be un-American, because it is to deny the idea that we are the exceptional nation, in which such things simply do not happen.

In seeking to understand what might be the real relation between God and our nation, we Christians in America might begin by reflecting on the question of whether there is any truth in the idea of American exceptionalism, or whether it has simply been a means by which this country's official ideology has served to make the immoral seem permissible, perhaps even divinely mandated.

4. Chapter 7 discussed Jesus' message that God's will is to replace the present reign of demonic values with a reign of divine values in which, for

instance, all people would have their daily bread. Chapter 8 presented a contemporary way of understanding the nature of demonic power. Chapter 9 showed that in our present world, demonic power is not only real but in the driver's seat. The church, if it finds helpful this way of understanding demonic power, might reflect on its implications for understanding the church's very purpose.

In my own view, the church should understand itself as a community of faith devoted to freeing both individuals and institutions from subjugation to demonic power. Classes, sermons, reading-and-discussion groups, pastoral counseling, and spiritual direction could be used to help members become aware of various routes through which they may have been led into adopting ideas, images, and stories that have shaped their feeling and thinking in ways that further the control of demonic power in their lives and their various communities. A difficult but necessary task would be to reflect on the degree that the church community itself has been subjugated to demonic power. And then, in light of the concern of the God of Jesus to overcome the subjugation of the public sphere to demonic values, we need to reflect on the subjugation of local, national, and international political and financial institutions as preparation for acting effectively in relation to those institutions.

5. In the previous point, I referred to the church as a "community of faith." This conception can lead, however, to very different understandings of the church and the very nature of being a Christian, depending on how "faith" is understood. Many people, especially outside the church, assume that faith means believing things for which there is little if any evidence. Some people understand faith as trusting that God will make everything come out all right. I find most helpful, however, those who have pointed out that *fides,* the Latin word for faith, means "fidelity." The basic religious question to us would then be: to whom or what do we give ultimate fidelity, to whom or what are we ultimately loyal? A Christian community of faith would be one that is loyal to God as revealed in Jesus, the creator of us all who loves us all.

On this understanding, the idea that we are "justified by faith" would be that we are justified, in the sense of being made just, by developing ultimate fidelity to God, the creator and lover of all creatures. Understanding faith as ultimate fidelity to God would make clear why Christian faith is incompatible with Nationalism. The nation, in the sense of the state, seeks to instill in us ultimate fidelity to it ("I pledge allegiance . . ."). Insofar as it is successful, we are Nationalists. But Nationalism, understood as ultimate fidelity to one's country, is incompatible with Christian faith, understood as ultimate fidelity to the whole. One cannot give ultimate fidelity to the creator and lover of the whole creation while giving ultimate fidelity to one part of the whole. Nurturing Christian faith in this sense would provide an inoculation against Nationalism, perhaps the most potent of modernity's demonic ideologies, the most extreme form of which is nationalistic imperialism.

ACTIONS

Many kinds of action on the part of the church and individual Christians would be appropriate if 9/11 is understood as a revelation of the demonic nature of American imperialism. I suggest a few.

1. One of the chief reasons for the demonic nature of the American empire is that, as Bacevich says, the U.S. military has been seeking "to achieve something approaching omnipotence."[14] This observation should set off alarm bells in Christians who understand that, given the universal tendency to sin, no person or organization can be trusted with anything approaching omnipotence.

Lord Acton, a Roman Catholic who did understand this point, immortalized it in his famous axiom: "Power tends to corrupt, and absolute power corrupts absolutely."[15] Acton's wording is important. He does not simply say, unlike many misquotations of his dictum, that power of any sort necessarily corrupts. He says only that power *tends* to corrupt. When he speaks of *absolute* power, however, he does not use that phrase. He says simply, "Absolute power corrupts absolutely."

If Acton was correct, and I believe he was, then we should expect the leadership of the Pentagon to have become absolutely corrupt. And the suspicion that it has would certainly be consistent with much that we know about, including Abu Ghraib, Guantánamo, and 9/11.

The best solution would be to turn the U.S. military into what we call it: the Department of Defense. As Bacevich points out, it has instead been transformed into "a Department of Power Projection," with "defense per se figur[ing] as little more than an afterthought."[16]

The fact that the U.S. military is equipped to project power to every part of the globe is a large part of the reason that it believes it needs such a huge budget. U.S. military spending is now equal to, if not greater than, the military spending of the rest of the countries of the world combined.

If the U.S. military existed purely to defend the American homeland, it would not need anywhere near that much. I suggest that one good project for the church in America to take on would be to bring about a great reduction in military-related spending. Perhaps a good goal for the first phase of this project would be to cut spending by 75 percent. At that level, America would still be spending one-fourth of what the rest of the world combined spends. That would surely be enough for us to defend ourselves.

An integral part of this project would be for the church to educate itself, and then educate the rest of the country, about the actual proportion of the federal budget that goes for military-related affairs. One fact is that military-related spending is far greater than the budget for the Defense Department. The expenditures for nuclear weapons, for example, are in the budget of the Energy Department. Economics professor Jurgen Brauer, who has taken account of this and many other factors, has concluded that the widespread idea that only nineteen cents of every tax dollar goes for military spending is a gross distortion. He says, instead, that sixty-eight cents of every dollar goes for military-related expenses, leaving only thirty-two cents for everything else. In other words, "Defense is not one-fifth of federal spending but two-thirds of it."[17]

2. Under present arrangements, to be sure, the church would have difficulty educating the public about these and other matters because of the corporate control of the media, discussed above. The corporations tend to appreciate having the American taxpayers fund the world's most powerful military machine so that it is available to protect U.S. corporate interests. (As we saw, the U.S. Space Command understands its mission to be protecting the interests of the "haves" while they continue to increase their advantage over the "have-nots.") But this problem simply points to another task the church needs to take on: reversing the corporate control of all the mass media or finding some other way for the American people to be informed about such matters as stolen elections, fixed intelligence, and false-flag operations.

3. For the church to succeed with either of these projects, the U.S. Senate and House of Representatives would have to be very different from what they are now. They would need actually to represent the people of the United States, rather than the corporations who pay lobbyists to get their wishes turned into laws. The problem here is that although America likes to think of itself as a democracy—which means, in Lincoln's words, "government of the people, by the people, for the people"—it has instead become a plutocracy—which means government of the rich, by the rich, for the rich. This plutocratic control of the government explains why the gap between the rich and the poor is becoming greater not only in the world as a whole but also in the United States in particular.[18]

The problem of plutocratic control, with regard to the presidency as well as the U.S. Congress, can be solved only through public financing of elections (along with requiring television networks to give free airtime to candidates). At present, the cost of winning elections is so great, primarily because of the enormous cost for television time, that presidents, senators, and representatives must spend much of their time raising money. The consequence is that, besides having less time for the people's business, they become beholden to the special interests who have supplied the money, and if they do not vote the way those special interests wish, at least most of the time, they will not receive money from them next time.

It might be thought that public financing of elections would be too expensive. If, however, military spending is reduced by several hundred billion dollars a year, there will be plenty of money available to take care of this relatively small expense (as well as many other things, such as health, education, welfare, and the environment).

4. The three tasks already mentioned, while being extremely important in themselves, should also be understood as necessary steps toward a larger goal:

genuine global democracy (as distinct from the phony global democracy promised by some of the neocons). As discussed earlier, the move to global democracy will be necessary if we are to overcome the war-system of settling disputes and hence overcome the precondition for military imperialism. By overcoming this war-system, even the need for the size of military envisioned above would be removed. The military, organized to fight wars, could be replaced by a police force, designed to protect the public.

Although such thinking sounds utopian, in the sense of impossible, the individual states making up the United States of America, which are about the same size as European states, do not have their own armies to attack and defend themselves from other states (as if California, for example, might send its army over to Arizona, Nevada, and Utah to take control of more of their water, which would mean that they would need big armies to protect themselves from California). The need for each state to have its own army was removed when the early federated system was changed to a federal system, with a federal government. In the same way, creating a government at the global level would obviate the need for each country to have its own army. Disputes would be solved through legislation and the courts, as are disputes between the states in America.

This move to global democracy will be necessary not only to overcome war and imperialism, but also to solve the two other problems discussed earlier: global apartheid and the global ecological crisis, especially global warming. With regard to the former issue, the previous chapter quoted South African President Thabo Mbeki's statement that the "global system of apartheid" has no pity for human beings. After making that statement, he added, "The suffering of the billions who are the victims of this system calls for the same response that drew the peoples of the world into the struggle for the defeat of apartheid in this country."[19] He is right. But defeating global apartheid will simply be impossible apart from the creation of a global government with the power to regulate the global economy and the mandate to overcome, slowly but surely, the obscene inequality that exists today, with millions of people dying of starvation while a few people control billions of dollars.

The idea of creating a global government is, to be sure, a huge and extremely controversial idea, any satisfactory discussion of which would require a good-sized book. Even the most basic pros and cons cannot be discussed here. But I have elsewhere explored some of these questions, including the most difficult problem: how the creation of a democratic government at the global level, which would turn the world as a whole into a democracy, might be possible. As I envisage it, this is a process in which Christianity would, in cooperation with other religions of the world, play a major role.[20]

As with the other issues mentioned, in any event, I am not trying to lay out a convincing case here but simply to suggest some possible courses of action to be explored.

5. The final action to be suggested here is actually the one that needs to be considered first. The church in America needs to disassociate itself, fully and explicitly, from America's imperial project.

There are different ways in which this disassociation might be effected. At the lowest and easiest level, local congregations could simply choose to take this step, announcing that it finds any cooperation with the American empire incompatible with its understanding of Christian faith. At a higher level, various denominations could take this step.

Another possibility would be the formation of an anti-imperial church movement, for which the rejection of America's imperial project is considered a necessary implication of Christian faith. Such a movement would be analogous to the movement of "Confessing Christians" formed in Germany in 1934, a year after the Nazis had come to power. The Confessing Christians, two leaders of which were theologians Karl Barth and Dietrich Bonhoeffer, opposed the movement known as the "German Christians," which treated Hitler as a new messiah who would bring Germany the greatness that it deserved. In their famous Barmen Declaration, the Confessing Christians said that support for National Socialism violated basic principles of the Christian faith. One had to choose either Christian faith or National Socialism. One could not affirm both.[21]

Later in the century, some Christian bodies decided that rejection of the system of apartheid in South Africa was a necessary implication of Christian faith. For example, in 1977, the Lutheran World Federation declared that although with regard to most political questions, "Christians may have different opinions," the system of apartheid in South Africa was an exception. This system was "so perverted and oppressive," these Lutherans said, that it "constitutes a *status confessionis*"—that is, a confessional situation. The Christian faith, they declared, required that "churches would publicly and unequivocally reject the existing apartheid system."[22]

An analogous question before churches in America today is whether the American empire is "so perverted and oppressive" that the public rejection of it should be regarded as an implication of fidelity to God as revealed in Jesus of Nazareth, who died on a cross of the Roman Empire.

A way to begin this conversation at the national level would be for the national social ministry offices of the various Protestant denominations, along with the Social Development of World Peace Department of the U.S. Conference of Catholic Bishops, to convene a meeting to discuss whether the contrast between the *9/11 Commission Report* and the available evidence is such that the church should initiate a new, truly independent, investigation of 9/11, to see if the attacks were, as suggested here, orchestrated on behalf of U.S. imperial interests.

Notes

Preface

1. Quoted and discussed in Ray McGovern, "God on Their Side," TomPaine.com, December 30, 2003 (http://www.tompaine.com/feature2.cfm/ID/9678/view/print).
2. This term had become well known prior to 9/11 thanks to Chalmers Johnson, *Blowback: The Costs and Consequences of American Empire* (New York: Henry Holt, 2000).
3. The Web site was www.wanttoknow.info; this site then led me to www.cooperativeresearch.org, where Paul Thompson's timeline was originally posted. His work has since been published as *The Terror Timeline: Year by Year, Day by Day, Minute by Minute: A Comprehensive Chronicle of the Road to 9/11—and America's Response* (New York: ReganBooks [HarperCollins], 2004).
4. David Ray Griffin, *The New Pearl Harbor: Disturbing Questions about the Bush Administration and 9/11* (Northampton, MA: Interlink, 2004), xxiii.

Chapter 1—9/11 and Prior False-Flag Operations

1. On the Mukden incident, see Walter LaFeber, *The Clash: U.S.-Japanese Relations throughout History* (New York: Norton, 1997), 164–66; Louise Young, *Japan's Total Empire: Manchuria and the Culture of Wartime Imperialism* (Berkeley: University of California Press, 1999), 40; "Mukden Incident," *Wikipedia* (http://en.wikipedia.org/wiki/Manchurian_Incident); "Mukden Incident," *Encyclopedia Britannica*, 2006 (http://www.britannica.com/eb/article-9054193).
2. The question of responsibility for the Reichstag fire had long remained controversial. But the dominant view, that the fire was set by the Nazis themselves, was confirmed in 2001 with the publication of *Der Reichstagbrand: Wie Geschichte Gemacht Wird*, by Alexander Bahar and Wilfried Kugel (Berlin: Edition Q, 2001). This book presents ample evidence of Nazi responsibility, including the testimony of a member of the SA, who said that he was in the subterranean passageway that night and saw other SA members bringing explosive liquids from one building to the other. Bahar and Kugel have, accordingly, substantiated the position contained in William Shirer, *The Rise and Fall of the Third Reich* (New York: Simon & Schuster, 1990), 191–93.
3. Wilhelm Klein, "The Reichstag Fire, 68 Years On" (review of Alexander Bahar and Wilfried Kugel, *Der Reichstagbrand*), World Socialist Web site, July 5, 2001 (http://www.wsws.org/articles/2001/jul2001/reic-j05.shtml).

4. Ibid.

5. See Ian Kershaw, *Hitler: 1936–45: Nemesis* (New York: Norton, 2001), 221; "Nazi Conspiracy and Aggression, Vol. II: Criminality of Groups and Organizations" (http://www.nizkor.org/hweb/imt/nca/nca-02/nca-02-15-criminality-06-05.html); and "Gleiwitz Incident," *Wikipedia* (http://en.wikipedia.org/wiki/Gleiwitz_incident#References). Although there was only one dead man at the scene, the incident is often said to have involved several men. This idea evidently originated with the Germans themselves, as the BBC said, in a bulletin broadcast later that evening: "There have been reports of an attack on a radio station in Gleiwitz, which is just across the Polish border in Silesia. The German News Agency reports that the attack came at about 8:00 p.m. this evening when the Poles forced their way into the studio and began broadcasting a statement in Polish. Within a quarter of an hour, say reports, the Poles were overpowered by German police, who opened fire on them. Several of the Poles were reported killed, but the numbers are not yet known" (http://www.bbc.co.uk/history/war/wwtwo/countdown_390831_thur_05.shtml).

6. Howard Zinn, *A People's History of the United States* (1980; New York: HarperPerennial, 1990), 150; Richard Van Alstyne, *The Rising American Empire* (1960; New York: Norton, 1974), 143.

7. Van Alstyne, *The Rising American Empire*, 146.

8. Walter LaFeber, *The American Age: U.S. Foreign Policy since 1750*, 2nd ed. (New York: Norton, 1993), 83.

9. Philip S. Foner, *The Spanish-Cuban-American War and the Birth of American Imperialism*, 2 vols. (New York: Monthly Review, 1972), 1:xv–xvi, xxviii.

10. Ibid., 145, 179–87.

11. Ibid., 213, 229, 248.

12. Ibid., xxx, 209, 229, 258.

13. Stuart Creighton Miller, *"Benevolent Assimilation": The American Conquest of the Philippines, 1899–1903* (New Haven, CT: Yale University Press, 1982), 11.

14. Geoffrey Perret, *A Country Made by War: From the Revolution to Vietnam—The Story of America's Rise to Power* (New York: Random House, 1989), 280n.

15. Foner, 1:304, 309; Van Alstyne, *The Rising American Empire*, 132, 188; and Thomas McCormick, *China Market: America's Quest for Informal Empire, 1893–1901* (Chicago: Quadrangle Books, 1967).

16. Miller, *"Benevolent Assimilation,"* 57–62.

17. Quoted in Zinn, *A People's History*, 307.

18. Gabriel Kolko, *Anatomy of a War: Vietnam, the United States, and the Modern Historical Experience* (New York: Pantheon Books, 1985), 124; George McT. Kahin, *Intervention: How America Became Involved in Vietnam* (Garden City, NY: Anchor Press, 1987), 217–19.

19. Kahin, *Intervention*, 221; Marilyn B. Young, *The Vietnam Wars, 1945–1990* (New York: HarperCollins, 1991), 116–17.

20. Kahin, *Intervention*, 221.

21. Ibid., 222–23; Young, *The Vietnam Wars*, 118–19.

22. Kahin, *Intervention*, 220.

23. Young, *The Vietnam Wars*, 119.

24. Daniele Ganser, *NATO's Secret Armies: Operation Gladio and Terrorism in Western Europe* (New York: Frank Cass, 2005), 53–54.

25. Ibid., 27–29.

26. Ibid., 16.

27. Ibid., 2, 13, 16, 91–97, 227, 241, 245–46.

28. Ibid., 119, 3.
29. Ibid., 79–80.
30. Ibid., 5.
31. Ibid., 3, 119–20.
32. Ibid., 7, quoting Casson on *Newsnight*, BBC-1, April 4, 1991.
33. Ibid., quoting the *Observer*, June 7, 1992.
34. Ibid., 9–11.
35. Ibid., 82, 120. On the evidence linking NATO and the United States to the Bologna massacre, see ibid., 25, 81.
36. Ibid., 234–35.
37. Ibid.
38. U.S. Department of State, "Misinformation about 'Gladio/Stay Behind' Networks Resurfaces: Thirty-Year-Old Soviet Forgery Cited by Researchers," USINFO, Identifying Misinformation, Jan. 20, 2006 (http://usinfo.state.gov/media/Archive/2006/Jan/20-127177.html).
39. Allan Francovich, "Gladio: The Foot Soldiers," BBC-2, June 24, 1992, cited in Ganser, *NATO's Secret Armies*, 235.
40. The only other support the State Department provides for its claim is this statement: "In April 1992, journalist Jonathan Kwitny wrote in *The Nation* that, 'evidence so far hasn't supported initial allegations that the secret armies used their hidden C.I.A.-supplied caches of weapons and explosives to carry out political violence that killed civilians.'" It is interesting that this was evidently the strongest evidence the State Department could find, especially given the fact that Kwitny's statement, about what evidence has emerged "so far," was made thirteen years before Ganser's well-researched book appeared.
41. Former CIA agent Philip Agee, describing the CIA's attempt to prevent any participation of Communists in the executive branch of government, wrote: "For the CIA this is evidently the priority of priorities" (Philip Agee and Louis Wolf, *Dirty Work: The CIA in Western Europe* [Secaucus, NJ: Lyle Stuart, 1978], 182; quoted in Ganser, *NATO's Secret Armies,* 85).
42. Ganser, *NATO's Secret Armies*, 86.
43. Ibid., 88; this is Ganser's summary statement.
44. Ibid., 90.
45. Ibid., 98.
46. Ibid., 115–18.
47. Ibid., 225–30.
48. Ibid., 239.
49. Ibid., 241–43.
50. Ibid., 241.
51. Ibid., 138–39.
52. Ibid., 144–47, citing Allan Francovich, "Gladio: The Foot Soldiers," BBC-2, June 24, 1992.
53. Ganser, *NATO's Secret Armies,* 142–43, 146.
54. Ibid., 143, quoting Phil Davison, "A Very Right-Wing Coup Plot Surfaces in Belgium," *Independent*, January 24, 1990.
55. Ganser, *NATO's Secret Armies,* 27, quoting the Portuguese newspaper *Expresso*, November 24, 1990. According to the Spanish newspaper *El Pais*, November 26, 1990, Wörner added that SHAPE's coordination of Gladio had been confirmed by U.S. General John Galvin, who was then the Supreme Allied Commander Europe (Ganser, *NATO's Secret Armies*, 26).
56. Ganser, *NATO's Secret Armies*, 21, 22.

57. This memorandum can be found at the National Security Archive, April 30, 2001 (http://www.gwu.edu/~nsarchiv/news/20010430). It was revealed to U.S. readers by James Bamford in *Body of Secrets: Anatomy of the Ultra-secret National Security Agency* (2001; New York: Anchor Books, 2002), 82–91.

58. See the discussion of the testimony of Paul O'Neill and Richard Clarke in the section, "The Attack on Iraq," in chap. 6, below.

59. See David Ray Griffin, *The 9/11 Commission Report: Omissions and Distortions* (Northampton, MA: Interlink, 2005), chap. 10.

60. *The 9/11 Commission Report: Final Report of the National Commission on Terrorist Attacks upon the United States,* authorized ed. (New York: W. W. Norton, 2004), 116.

61. "Terrorist Stag Parties," *Wall Street Journal,* October 10, 2001 (http://www.opinionjournal.com/best/?id=95001298).

62. *The 9/11 Commission Report,* 248.

63. I have summarized 115 such problems in "The 9/11 Commission Report: A 571-Page Lie," 9/11 Visibility Project, May 22, 2005 (http://www.septembereleventh.org/newsarchive/2005-05-22-571pglie.php).

64. The flight manifest for American Airlines Flight 11 that was published by CNN can be seen at www.cnn.com/SPECIALS/2001/trade.center/victims/AA11.victims.html. The manifests for the other flights can be located by simply changing that part of the URL. The manifest for United Airlines Flight 93, for example, is at www.cnn.com/SPECIALS/2001/trade.center/victims/ua93.victims.html.

65. *The 9/11 Commission Report,* 19–20.

66. David Bamford, "Hijack 'Suspect' Alive in Morocco," BBC News, Sept. 22, 2001 (http://news.bbc.co.uk/1/hi/world/middle_east/1558669.stm). Several other alleged hijackers were reported to be alive in David Harrison, "Revealed: The Men with Stolen Identities," *Telegraph,* September 23, 2001 (www.portal.telegraph.co.uk/news/ main.jhtml?xml=/news/2001/09/23/widen23.xml). At least one of these claims, that involving Ahmed al-Nami, was based on a confusion. The al-Nami contacted by Harrison was 33, whereas the man of that name who was allegedly on Flight 93, which supposedly crashed in Pennsylvania, was only 21. See Christine Lamb, "The Six Sons of Asir," *Telegraph,* September 15, 2002 (http://www.portal.telegraph.co.uk/news/main.jhtml?xml=/news/2002/09/15/wdoss215.xml). But no such explanation seems possible with Waleed al-Shehri, since the photograph is clearly of a still-living man of that name.

67. Associated Press, October 5, 2001; *Boston Globe,* September 18, 2001; *Independent,* September 29, 2001. Another version has the bags found in Portland.

68. *The 9/11 Commission Report,* 1–2.

69. Ibid., chap. 1, n. 1.

70. The trip likewise provided the opportunity for security video frames showing Mohamed Atta and Abdullah al-Omari, also said to have been on Flight 11, at the Portland airport. Strangely, however, there were no photos of them at Boston's Logan Airport, which as a major international airport surely was better equipped with security cameras. Both issues are discussed in Rowland Morgan and Ian Henshall, *9/11 Revealed: The Unanswered Questions* (New York: Carroll & Graf, 2005), 180–83.

71. Richard Labevière, "CIA Agent Allegedly Met Bin Laden in July," *Le Figaro,* October 31, 2001. This story was also reported in Anthony Sampson, "CIA Agent Alleged to Have Met Bin Laden in July," *Guardian,* November 1, and

Adam Sage, "Ailing bin Laden 'Treated for Kidney Disease,'" *London Times*, November 1, 2001.

72. See Labeviere, "CIA Agent Allegedly Met Bin Laden in July," and Craig Unger, "Unasked Questions: The 9/11 Commission Should Ask Who Authorized the Evacuation of Saudi Nationals in the Days Following the Attacks," *Boston Globe*, April 11, 2004. For more on the "black sheep" issue, see Nafeez Ahmed, *The War on Freedom: How and Why America Was Attacked September 11, 2001* (Joshua Tree, CA: Tree of Life, 2002), 178–79.

73. *Telegraph*, February 23, 2002; Griffin, *The 9/11 Commission Report: Omissions and Distortions*, 60.

74. See the discussion in the section, "The Attack on Afghanistan," in chap. 6, below.

75. See "The Fake bin Laden Video" (http://www.whatreallyhappened.com/ osamatape.html).

76. *The 9/11 Commission Report*, 39.

77. "PAVE PAWS, Watching North America's Skies, 24 Hours a Day" (www.pavepaws.org).

78. Russ Wittenberg, who flew large commercial airliners for thirty-five years after serving in Vietnam as a fighter pilot, says that it would have been impossible for Flight 77 to have "descended 7,000 feet in two minutes, all the while performing a steep 270-degree banked turn before crashing into the Pentagon's first-floor wall without touching the lawn." It would, he adds, have been "totally impossible for an amateur who couldn't even fly a Cessna to maneuver the jetliner in such a highly professional manner" (Greg Szymanski, "Former Vietnam Combat and Commercial Pilot Firm Believer 9/11 Was Inside Government Job," Lewis News, Sunday, Jan. 8, 2006 [http://www.lewisnews.com/article. asp?ID=106623]). Hanjour's incompetence was reported by the *New York Times*, May 4, 2002, and CBS News, May 10, 2002. *The 9/11 Commission Report* sometimes acknowledges that Hanjour was known to be a "terrible pilot" (225–26, 242), but it elsewhere calls him "the operation's most experienced pilot" (530n147).

79. Won-Young Kim and Gerald R. Baum, "Seismic Observations during September 11, 2001, Terrorist Attack" (http://www.mgs.md.gov/esic/publications/ download/911pentagon.pdf).

80. Karen Kwiatkowski, who was then an air force lieutenant colonel employed at the Pentagon, writes of "a strange lack of visible debris on the Pentagon lawn, where I stood only moments after the impact . . . I saw . . . no airplane metal or cargo debris" ("Assessing the Official 9/11 Conspiracy Theory," in David Ray Griffin and Peter Dale Scott, eds., *9/11 and the American Empire: Intellectuals Speak Out*). For a more technical discussion of the debris, see "The Missing Wings" (http://www.physics911.net/missingwings.htm), in which A. K. Dewdney and G. W. Longspaugh argue that the absence of wing debris alone is sufficient to disprove the claim that an airliner hit the Pentagon. With regard to debris *inside* the building, both Ed Plaugher, the county fire chief, and Lee Evey, the head of the renovation project, reported seeing, immediately after the strike, no big pieces from an airplane (DoD News Briefings, September 12 and 15, 2001).

81. Photographs show that the façade of the west wing remained standing for thirty minutes after the strike and that, during this time, the hole in this façade was too small to have accommodated a 757. See Eric Hufschmid, *Painful Questions: An Analysis of the September 11th Attack* (Goleta, CA: Endpoint Software, 2002), chap. 9, and Dave McGowan, "September 11, 2001 Revisited: The

Series: Act II," Center for an Informed America (www.davesweb.cnchost.com/nwsltr68.html).

82. Ralph Omholt, "9-11 and the Impossible: Part One of an Online Journal of 9-11" (http://www.physics911.net/omholt.htm).

83. Karen Kwiatkowski, who was working at the Pentagon that morning, reports that "any physical remains of the aircraft that hit the Pentagon were quickly carted away to some unknown location, so we have no physical evidence that the aircraft really was Flight 77 or even a Boeing 757" ("Assessing the Official 9/11 Conspiracy Theory"). Photographic evidence of this removal can be seen on Eric Hufschmid's video, *Painful Deceptions* (available at www.EricHufschmid.net).

84. A photograph showing this literal cover-up can be seen in Omholt, "9-11 and the Impossible."

85. On the confiscation of the film from the Citgo gas station and a nearby hotel, respectively, see Bill McKelway "Three Months On, Tension Lingers Near the Pentagon," *Richmond Times-Dispatch*, December 11, 2001 (http://news.nationalgeographic.com/news/2001/12/1211_wirepentagon.html), and Bill Gertz and Rowan Scarborough, "Inside the Ring," *Washington Times*, September 21, 2001.

86. Scott Bingham, who has tried to get videos of the Pentagon strike released under the Freedom of Information Act, has his lawsuit and the official response posted on his Web site (http://www.flight77.info). See also "Government Responds to Flight 77 FOAI Request," 911Truth.org, August 2005 (http://www.911truth.org/article.php?story=20050824131004151).

Chapter 2—Explosive Testimony: Revelations about the Twin Towers in the 9/11 Oral Histories

1. Jim Dwyer, "City to Release Thousands of Oral Histories of 9/11 Today," *New York Times*, August 12, 2005. As Dwyer explained, the oral histories "were originally gathered on the order of Thomas Von Essen, the city fire commissioner on Sept. 11, who said he wanted to preserve those accounts before they became reshaped by a collective memory."

2. Jim Dwyer, "Vast Archive Yields New View of 9/11," *New York Times*, August 13, 2005.

3. These oral histories are available at a NYT Web site (http://graphics8.nytimes.com/packages/html/nyregion/20050812_WTC_GRAPHIC/met_WTC_histories_full_01.html).

4. Matea Gold and Maggie Farley, "Terrorists Attack New York, Pentagon," *Los Angeles Times*, September 12, 2001 (available at http://bernie.house.gov/documents/articles/20010912170838.asp).

5. "Special Report: Terrorism in the US," *Guardian,* September 12, 2001.

6. Greg Szymanski, "WTC Basement Blast and Injured Burn Victim Blows 'Official 9/11 Story' Sky High," Arctic Beacon.com, June 24, 2005.

7. Greg Szymanski, "Second WTC Janitor Comes Forward with Eye-Witness Testimony of 'Bomb-Like' Explosion in North Tower Basement," Arctic Beacon.com, July 12, 2005.

8. "We Will Not Forget: A Day of Terror," *The Chief Engineer*, July 2002.

9. Christopher Bollyn, "New Seismic Data Refutes Official Explanation," American Free Press, updated April 12, 2004 (http://www.americanfreepress.net/09_03_02/NEW_SEISMIC_/new_seismic_.html).

10. Quoted in Dennis Smith, *Report from Ground Zero: The Story of the Rescue Efforts at the World Trade Center* (New York: Penguin, 2002), 18.

11. "911 Tapes Tell Horror of 9/11," part 2, "Tapes Released for First Time," NBC TV, June 17, 2002 (www.wnbc.com/news/1315651/detail.html).

12. Greg Szymanski, "NY Fireman Lou Cacchioli Upset that 9/11 Commission 'Tried to Twist My Words,'" Arctic Beacon.com, July 19, 2005. Although the oral histories that were released on Aug. 12 did not include one from Cacchioli, the fact that he was on duty is confirmed on page 4 of Thomas Turilli's oral history.

13. Dean E. Murphy, *September 11: An Oral History* (New York: Doubleday, 2002), 9–15.

14. BBC Radio, September 11, 2001.

15. Quoted in Susan Hagen and Mary Carouba, *Women at Ground Zero: Stories of Courage and Compassion* (Indianapolis: Alpha Books, 2002), 65–66, 68.

16. John Bussey, "Eye of the Storm: One Journey Through Desperation and Chaos," *Wall Street Journal*, September 12, 2001 (http://online.wsj.com/public/resources/documents/040802pulitzer5.htm).

17. Alicia Shepard, Cathy Trost, and Newseum, *Running toward Danger: Stories behind the Breaking News of 9/11*, foreword by Tom Brokaw (Lanham, MD: Rowman & Littlefield, 2002), 87.

18. Quoted in Judith Sylvester and Suzanne Huffman, *Women Journalists at Ground Zero* (Lanham, MD: Rowman & Littlefield, 2002), 19.

19. For the video of this conversation, see "Evidence of Demolition Charges in WTC 2, What Really Happened" (http://www.whatreallyhappened.com/wtc2_cutter.html).

20. See "9/11 Revisited: Were Explosives Used?" (http://youtube.com/watch?v=psP_9RE0V2I).

21. Oral History of John Sudnik, 4 (for where to read the 9/11 oral histories of the FDNY, see n. 3, above).

22. Oral History of Timothy Julian, 10.

23. Oral History of Michael Ober, 4.

24. Oral History of Frank Cruthers, 4.

25. Oral History of Lonnie Penn, 5.

26. Oral History of Paul Curran, 11.

27. Oral History of Bradley Mann, 5–7.

28. Oral History of Kevin Darnowski, 8.

29. Oral History of Gregg Brady, 7.

30. Oral History of Thomas Turilli, 4.

31. Oral History of Craig Carlsen, 5–6.

32. Oral History of Joseph Meola, 5.

33. Oral History of Daniel Rivera, 9.

34. Oral History of Timothy Burke, 8–9.

35. Oral History of Edward Cachia, 5.

36. Oral History of James Walsh, 15.

37. Oral History of Stephen Gregory, 14–16.

38. Oral History of Karin Deshore, 15.

39. Ibid.

40. Oral History of Richard Banaciski, 3–4.

41. Oral History of Thomas Fitzpatrick, 13–14.

42. Oral History of Jay Swithers, 5.

43. Oral History of James Curran, 10–11.

44. Oral History of Brian Dixon, 15. Like many others, Dixon indicated that he

later came to accept the official interpretation, adding: "Then I guess in some sense of time we looked at it and realized, no, actually it just collapsed. That's what blew out the windows, not that there was an explosion there but that windows blew out."

45. See, for example, Eric Hufschmid's *Painful Questions: An Analysis of the September 11th Attack* (Goleta, CA: Endpoint Software, 2002); Jim Hoffman's Web site (http://911research.wtc7.net/index.html); and Jeff King's Web site (http://home.comcast.net/~jeffrey.king2/wsb/html/view.cgi-home.html-.html), especially "The World Trade Center Collapse: How Strong Is the Evidence for a Controlled Demolition?"

46. Oral History of Stephen Viola, 3.

47. Oral History of Angel Rivera, 7.

48. Oral History of William Wall, 9.

49. Oral History of Louis Cook, 8, 35.

50. The demolition of the Kingdome can be viewed at the Web site of Controlled Demolition, Inc. (http://www.controlled-demolition.com/default.asp?reqLocId=7&reqItemId=20030317140323), that of the Reading Grain Facility at ImplosionWorld.com (http://implosionworld.com/reading.html). I am indebted to Jim Hoffman for help on this and several other issues.

51. See the writings of Hufschmid, Hoffman, and King mentioned in note 45.

52. For a calculation of the energy required simply for the expansion of one of the resulting dust clouds, see Jim Hoffman, "The North Tower's Dust Cloud" (http://911research.wtc7.net/papers/dustvolume/volume.html). Hoffman concludes that gravitational energy would have been far from sufficient.

53. Oral History of Dominick DeRubbio, 5. DeRubbio, at least professing to accept the official interpretation, added, "but I guess it was just the floors starting to pancake one on top of the other."

54. Oral History of Kenneth Rogers, 3–4.

55. Oral History of Christopher Fenyo, 6–7.

56. Oral History of William Reynolds, 8.

57. Dwyer, "City to Release Thousands of Oral Histories of 9/11 Today."

58. Randy Lavello, "Bombs in the Building," Prison Planet.com (http://www.prisonplanet.com/analysis_lavello_050503_bombs.html).

59. Szymanski, "NY Fireman Lou Cacchioli Upset that 9/11 Commission 'Tried to Twist My Words.'"

60. Szymanski, "WTC Basement Blast and Injured Burn Victim Blows 'Official 9/11 Story' Sky High."

61. See MSNBC, "Officer: 9/11 Panel Didn't Pursue Atta Claim," August 17, 2005 (http://www.msnbc.msn.com/id/8985244&&CM=EmailThis&CE=1), and Philip Shenon, "Navy Officer Affirms Assertions about Pre-9/11 Data on Atta," *New York Times*, August 22, 2005.

62. For other items, see David Ray Griffin, *The 9/11 Commission Report: Omissions and Distortions* (Northampton, MA: Interlink, 2005).

63. Szymanski, "WTC Basement Blast and Injured Burn Victim Blows 'Official 9/11 Story' Sky High."

64. See Kevin Ryan, "Propping Up the War on Terror: Lies about the WTC by NIST and Underwriters Laboratories," in David Ray Griffin and Peter Dale Scott, eds., *9/11 and the American Empire: Intellectuals Speak Out* (Northampton, MA: Interlink Books, 2006), and Jim Hoffman, "Building a Better Mirage: NIST's 3-Year $20,000,000 Cover-Up of the Crime of the Century" (http://911research.wtc7.net/essays/nist/index.html).

65. Oral History of Timothy Julian, 10.

66. Oral History of James Drury, 12.

67. Liz Else, "Baltimore Blasters," *New Scientist* 183, no. 2457 (July 24, 2004): 48 (http://archive.newscientist.com/secure/article/article.jsp?rp=1&id=mg18324 575.700).

68. I could not have written this chapter without the amazingly generous help of Matthew Everett, who located and passed on to me most of the statements in the 9/11 oral histories quoted herein.

Chapter 3—The Destruction of the World Trade Center: Why the Official Account Cannot Be True

1. President George W. Bush, Address to the General Assembly of the United Nations, November 10, 2001. His more complete statement was: "We must speak the truth about terror. Let us never tolerate outrageous conspiracy theories concerning the attacks of 11 September—-malicious lies that attempt to shift the blame away from the terrorists themselves, away from the guilty." Excellent advice.

2. Thomas Hansen, "Outrageous Conspiracy Theories: Report on a Conversation with Philip Zelikow," 9/11 Visibility Project, June 7, 2005 (http://www.septembereleventh.org/newsarchive/2005-06-07-outrageous.php).

3. This report was prepared by the American Society of Civil Engineers (ASCE) on behalf of the Federal Emergency Management Agency (FEMA). See FEMA Report #403, *World Trade Center Building Performance Study*, May 2002 (www.fema.gov/library/wtcstudy.shtm). The public was exposed to this theory early on, with CNN saying shortly after 9/11: "The collapse, when it came, was caused by fire. . . . The fire weakened that portion of the structure which remained after the impact . . . to the point where it could no longer sustain the load" (CNN, Sept. 24, 2001).

4. *Final Report of the National Construction Safety Team on the Collapses of the World Trade Center Towers* (Draft), June 2005 (henceforth called the NIST Report).

5. NIST describes the collapses of the towers as instances of "progressive collapse," which happens when "a building or portion of a building collapses due to disproportionate spread of an initial local failure" (NIST Report, 200). NIST thereby falsely implies that the total collapses of the three WTC buildings were specific instances of a general category with other instances. NIST even claims that the collapses were "inevitable." For a good critique, see Jim Hoffman, "Building a Better Mirage: NIST's 3-Year $20,000,000 Cover-Up of the Crime of the Century," 911 Research, Dec. 8, 2005 (http://911research.wtc7.net/essays/nist/index.html). As Hoffman says: "The fact that there is not a single example of total top-down progressive collapse outside of the alleged examples of the Twin Towers makes it entirely unscientific to presuppose that the alleged phenomenon was operative here."

6. On Skilling, see Eric Nalder, "Twin Towers Engineered to Withstand Jet Collision," *Seattle Times,* February 27, 1993; partially quoted in James Glanz and Eric Tipton, *City in the Sky: The Rise and Fall of the World Trade Center* (New York: Times Books/Henry Holt, 2003), 138. On Robertson, see "The Fall of the World Trade Center," BBC2, March 7, 2002 (http://www.bbc.co.uk/science/horizon/2001/worldtradecentertrans.shtml).

7. Quoted in Christopher Bollyn, "Some Survivors Say 'Bombs Exploded Inside WTC,'" American Free Press, October 22, 2001 (http://www.americanfree

press.net/10_22_01/Some_Survivors_Say__Bombs_Expl/some_survivors_say
__bombs_expl.html).

8. Thomas Eagar and Christopher Musso, "Why Did the World Trade Center Collapse? Science, Engineering, and Speculation," *JOM: Journal of the Minerals, Metals & Materials Society* 53, no. 12 (2001): 8–11.

9. The NIST Report claims, "The towers withstood the impacts and would have remained standing were it not for the dislodged insulation (fireproofing) and the subsequent multifloor fires" (xliii and 171).

10. Sheila Barter, "How the World Trade Center Fell," BBC News, September 13, 2001 (http://news.bbc.co.uk/1/hi/world/americas/1540044.stm). Supported by these authorities, the show went on to claim that "as fires raged in the towers, driven by aviation fuel, the steel cores in each building would have eventually reached 800°C [1472°F]—hot enough to start buckling and collapsing."

11. In *The New Pearl Harbor: Disturbing Questions about 9/11 and the Bush Administration* (Northampton, MA: Interlink Books, 2004), 12–13, I cite Professor Thomas Eagar's acknowledgment of this fact.

12. Given that the claim that the fires in the towers melted its steel is about as absurd, from a scientific point of view, as a claim could be, it is amazing to see that some scientific journals seemed eager to rush into print with this claim. On the day after 9/11, for example, *New Scientist* published an article that claimed, "Each tower [after it was struck] remained upright for nearly an hour. Eventually raging fires melted the supporting steel struts" (Eugenie Samuel and Damian Carrington, "Design Choice for Towers Saved Lives," *New Scientist*, September 12, 2001 [http://www.newscientist.com/article.ns?id=dn1281]). The article's title reflects the equally absurd claim—attributed to "John Hooper, principal engineer in the company that provided engineering advice when the World Trade Center was designed"—that "most buildings would have come down immediately."

13. Stating this obvious point could, however, be costly to employees of companies with close ties to the government. On November 11, 2004, Kevin Ryan, the site manager of Environmental Health Laboratories, which is a division of Underwriters Laboratories, wrote an e-mail letter to Dr. Frank Gayle, deputy chief of the Metallurgy Division, Material Science and Engineering Laboratory, at the National Institute of Standards and Technology (NIST). In this letter, Ryan stated: "We know that the steel components were certified to ASTM E119. The time temperature curves for this standard require the samples to be exposed to temperatures around 2000°F for several hours. And as we all agree, the steel applied met those specifications. Additionally, I think we can all agree that even un-fireproofed steel will not melt until reaching red-hot temperatures of nearly 3000°F. Why Dr. Brown would imply that 2000°F would melt the high-grade steel used in those buildings makes no sense at all." After Ryan allowed his letter to become public, he was fired. His letter is available at http://www.septembereleventh.org/newsarchive/2004-11-11-ryan.php.

14. One well-known attempt to defend the official account has tried to use the absurdity of the steel-melting claim *against* those who reject the official account. In its March 2005 issue, *Popular Mechanics* magazine published a piece entitled "9/11: Debunking the Myths" (http://www.popularmechanics.com/science/defense/1227842.html?page=1&c=y). This article sets out to debunk what it alleges to be "16 of the most prevalent claims made by conspiracy theorists." One of these claims, according to *Popular Mechanics*, results from these "conspiracy theorists" having created a straw-man argument—pretending that the

official theory claims that the buildings came down because their steel melted—which the conspiracy theorists can then knock down. *Popular Mechanics* "refutes" this straw-man argument by instructing us that "jet fuel burns at 800° to 1500°F, not hot enough to melt steel (2750°F). However, experts agree that for the towers to collapse, their steel frames didn't need to melt, they just had to lose some of their structural strength." As we have seen, however, the idea that the towers collapsed because their steel melted was put into the public consciousness by some early defenders of the official theory. For critics of this theory to show the absurdity of this claim is not, therefore, to attack a straw man. The idea that the official theory is based on this absurd claim is, in any case, *not* one of the "16 most prevalent claims" of those who reject the official theory.

15. Even Shyam Sunder, the lead investigator for the NIST study, said, "The jet fuel probably burned out in less than 10 minutes"; quoted in Andy Field, "A Look Inside a Radical New Theory of the WTC Collapse," Firehouse.com, February 7, 2004 (http://cms.firehouse.com/content/article/article.jsp?section Id=46&id=25807). The NIST Report itself says, "The initial jet fuel fires themselves lasted at most a few minutes" (179).

16. Thomas Eagar, "The Collapse: An Engineer's Perspective," part of "Why the Towers Fell," *Nova,* April 30, 2002 (www.pbs.org/wgbh/nova/wtc/collapse.html).

17. Eric Hufschmid, *Painful Questions: An Analysis of the September 11th Attack* (Goleta, CA: Endpoint Software, 2002), 40.

18. The NIST Report, 88.

19. Ibid.

20. The NIST Report, trying to argue that steel is very vulnerable unless it is protected by insulation, says: "Bare structural steel components can heat quickly when exposed to a fire of even moderate intensity. Therefore, some sort of thermal protection, or insulation, is necessary" (68). As Hoffman points out, however: "These statements are meaningless, because they ignore the effect of steel's thermal conductivity, which draws away heat, and the considerable thermal mass of the 90,000 tons of steel in each Tower" ("Building a Better Mirage").

21. Quoted in "WTC 2: There Was No Inferno," What Really Happened (http://www.whatreallyhappened.com/wtc2_fire.html).

22. Quoted in "Tape Sheds Light on WTC Rescuers," CNN, August 4, 2002 (www.cnn.com/2002/US/08/04/wtc.firefighters). The voices of the firefighters reportedly "showed no panic, no sense that events were racing beyond their control" (Jim Dwyer and Ford Fessenden, "Lost Voices of Firefighters, Some on 78th Floor," *New York Times,* August 4, 2002 [available at http://www.mishalov.com/wtc_lostvoicesfiredept.html]).

23. As Eric Hufschmid says: "A fire will not affect steel unless the steel is exposed to it for a long . . . period of time" (*Painful Questions,* 33).

24. CNN, September 24, 2001.

25. FEMA, "Interstate Bank Building Fire, Los Angeles, California," 1988 (http://www.lafire.com//famous_fires/880504_1stInterstateFire/FEMA-TecReport/FEMA-report.htm).

26. FEMA, "High-Rise Office Building Fire One Meridian Plaza Philadelphia, Pennsylvania" (http://usfa.fema.gov/fire-service/techreports/tr049.shtm).

27. "Fire Practically Destroys Venezuela's Tallest Building" (http://www.whatreally happened.com/venezuela_fire.html).

28. FEMA Report #403, *World Trade Center Building Performance Study,* May 2002 (www.fema.gov/library/wtcstudy.shtm), appendix A.

29. Kevin Ryan, in his letter to Frank Gayle (see n. 13, above), wrote in criticism

of NIST's preliminary report: "This story just does not add up. If steel from those buildings did soften or melt, I'm sure we can all agree that this was certainly not due to jet fuel fires of any kind, let alone the briefly burning fires in those towers. . . . Please do what you can to quickly eliminate the confusion regarding the ability of jet fuel fires to soften or melt structural steel."

30. Norman Glover, "Collapse Lessons," *Fire Engineering*, October 2002 (http://fe. pennnet.com/Articles/Article_Display.cfm?Section=Archi&Subsection=Display &P=25&ARTICLE_ID=163411&KEYWORD=norman%20glover).

31. See, for example, Eric Hufschmid's *Painful Deceptions* (available at www.EricHufschmid.net); Jim Hoffman's Web site (http://911research.wtc7. net/index.html); and Jeff King's Web site (http://home.comcast.net/ ~jeffrey.king2/wsb/html/view.cgi-home.html-.html), especially "The World Trade Center Collapse: How Strong Is the Evidence for a Controlled Demolition?"

32. Liz Else, "Baltimore Blasters," *New Scientist* 183, no. 2457 (July 24, 2004): 48 (http://archive.newscientist.com/secure/article/article.jsp?rp=1&id=mg18324 575.700). (The reason for the title is that Controlled Demolition's office is near Baltimore.) Incredibly, after explaining how precisely explosives must be set to ensure that a building comes straight down, Loizeaux said that upon seeing the fires in the Twin Towers, he knew that the towers were "going to pancake down, almost vertically. It was the only way they could fail. It was inevitable." Given the fact that fire had never before caused steel-frame buildings to collapse, let alone in a way that perfectly mimicked controlled demolition, Loizeaux's statement is a cause for wonder. His company, incidentally, was hired to remove the steel from the WTC site after 9/11.

33. Knight Ridder, "Towers' Quick Collapse Surprises Engineers," September 12, 2001 (http://www.leadertelegram.com/specialreports/attack/storydetail.asp? ID=14). The fire theory is rendered even more unlikely if the first two characteristics are taken together. For fire to have induced a collapse that began suddenly and was entirely symmetrical, so that it went straight down, the fires would have needed to cause all the crucial parts of the building to fail simultaneously, even though the fires were not spread evenly throughout the buildings. As Jim Hoffman has written: "All 287 columns would have to have weakened to the point of collapse at the *same instant*" ("The Twin Towers Demolition," 9-11 Research.wtc7.net, n.d. [http://911research.wtc7.net/ talks/towers/slides .html]).

34. *The 9/11 Commission Report: Final Report of the National Commission on Terrorist Attacks upon the United States*, authorized ed. (New York: W. W. Norton, 2004), 305. That statement is probably a slight exaggeration, as the videos, according to most viewers, seem to suggest that the collapses took a few seconds longer. But they would still have occurred close to free-fall speed through the air.

35. As physicist Steven Jones puts it, "The Towers fall very rapidly to the ground, with the upper part falling nearly as rapidly as ejected debris which provide free-fall references. . . . Where is the delay that must be expected due to conservation of momentum—one of the foundational Laws of Physics? That is, as upper-falling floors strike lower floors—and intact steel support columns—the fall must be significantly impeded by the impacted mass. . . . [B]ut this is not the case. . . . How do the upper floors fall so quickly, then, and still conserve momentum in the collapsing buildings? The contradiction is ignored by FEMA, NIST and 9/11 Commission reports where conservation of momen-

tum and the fall times were not analyzed." See Steven E. Jones, "Why Indeed Did the WTC Buildings Collapse?" in David Ray Griffin and Peter Dale Scott, eds., *9/11 and the American Empire: Intellectuals Speak Out* (Northampton, MA: Interlink, 2006); also available at http://www.physics.byu.edu/research/energy/htm7.html.

36. Dave Heller, "Taking a Closer Look: Hard Science and the Collapse of the World Trade Center," *Garlic and Grass*, 6 (http://www.garlicandgrass.org/issue 6/Dave_Heller.cfm).

37. Each column, besides being at least thirty-six by sixteen inches, had walls that were at least four inches thick at the base, then tapered off in the upper floors, which had less weight to support. Pictures of columns can be seen on page 23 of Hufschmid's *Painful Questions*. (The reason for the qualification "at least" in these statements is that Jim Hoffman has recently concluded that some of them were even bigger. With reference to his article "The Core Structures: The Structural System of the Twin Towers," 9-11 Research.wtc7.net, n.d. [http://911research.wtc7.net/wtc/arch/core.html], Hoffman has written (e-mail letter of October 26, 2005): "Previously I've been saying that the core columns had outside dimensions of 36" x 16", but I now think that at least 1/3 of them had dimensions of 54" x 22", based on early articles in the *Engineering News Record* and photographs I took of close-up construction photos on display at the Skyscraper Museum in Manhattan. . . . Also, according to the illustration in the *Engineering News Record*, the thickness of the steel at the bases was 5", not 4"."

38. *The 9/11 Commission Report*, 541n.1.

39. NIST Report, 28, 143.

40. As Hoffman says ("Building a Better Mirage"), NIST's claim about these tremendously hot fires in the core is especially absurd given the fact that the core "had very little fuel; was far from any source of fresh air; had huge steel columns to wick away the heat; [and] does not show evidence of fires in any of the photographs or videos." All the evidence, in other words, suggests that none of the core columns would have reached the temperatures of some of the perimeter columns.

41. NIST rests its theory largely on the idea that collapse began with the failure of the trusses. Being much smaller and also less interconnected, trusses would have been much easier to heat up, so it is not surprising that the NIST Report focuses on them. To try to make its theory work, however, NIST claims that the trusses became much hotter than their own evidence supports. That is, although NIST found no evidence that any of the steel had gotten hotter than 1112°F (600°C) (176–77), it claims that some of the steel trusses were heated up to 1292°F (700°C). A supposedly scientific argument cannot arbitrarily add 180°F just because it happens to need it. In any case, besides the fact that this figure is entirely unsupported by any evidence, NIST's theory finally depends on the claim that the core columns failed as "a result of both splice connection failures and fracture of the columns themselves," because they were "weakened significantly by . . . thermal effects" (88, 180). But there is no explanation of how these massive columns would have been caused to "fracture," even if the temperatures had reached to those heights. As a study issued in the United Kingdom put it: "Thermal expansion and the response of the whole frame to this effect has *not* been described [by NIST] as yet" (B. Lane and S. Lamont, "ARUP Fire's Presentation regarding Tall Buildings and the Events of 9/11," ARUP Fire, April 2005 [http://www.arup.com/DOWNLOADBANK/download353.pdf]).

42. The RDX quotation is in Tom Held, "Hoan Bridge Blast Set Back to Friday," www.jsonline.com (*Milwaukee Journal Sentinel*), December 19, 2000 (http://www.jsonline.com/news/metro/dec00/hoan20121900a.asp). The DREXS quotation is in Hufschmid's video, *Painful Deceptions* (www.EricHufschmid.net).

43. Hoffman, "Your Eyes Don't Lie: Common Sense, Physics, and the World Trade Center Collapses," 9-11 Research.wtc7.net, 2004 (http://911research.wtc7.net/talks/radio/youreyesdontlie/index.html). In that statement, he said that most of the sections seemed to be no more than thirty feet long. He later revised this, saying that, judging from an aerial image taken twelve days after the attacks, most of the pieces seemed to be between twenty-four and forty-eight feet long, with only a few over fifty feet. He also noted that "the lengths of the pieces bear little resemblance to the lengths of the steel parts known to have gone into the construction," which means that one could not reasonably infer that the pieces simply broke at their joints (e-mail letter, September 27, 2005).

44. Jim Hoffman, "The North Tower's Dust Cloud: Analysis of Energy Requirements for the Expansion of the Dust Cloud Following the Collapse of 1 World Trade Center," Version 3, 9-11Research.wtc7.net, Oct. 16, 2003 (http://911research.wtc7.net/papers/dustvolume/volume.html). The available evidence, Hoffman says in this paper, suggests that the dust particles were very small indeed—on the order of ten microns.

45. *The World Trade Center: Rise and Fall of an American Icon,* The History Channel, September 8, 2002.

46. Hoffman ("The Twin Towers Demolition") says that the clouds expanded to five times the diameter of the towers in the first ten seconds. The demolition of the Kingdome can be viewed at the Web site of Controlled Demolition, Inc. (http://www.controlled-demolition.com/default.asp?reqLocId=7&reqItemId=20030317140323). The demolition of the Reading Grain Facility can be seen at ImplosionWorld.com (http://implosionworld.com/reading.html).

47. Hoffman, "The North Tower's Dust Cloud."

48. Hoffman, "The Twin Towers Demolition."

49. Jeff King, "The WTC Collapse: What the Videos Show," Indymedia Webcast News, Nov. 12, 2003 (http://ontario.indymedia.org/display.php3?article_id=7342&group=webcast).

50. Quoted in *Popular Mechanics*, "9/11: Debunking the Myths."

51. Don Paul and Jim Hoffman, *Waking Up from Our Nightmare: The 9/11/01 Crimes in New York City* (San Francisco: Irresistible/Revolutionary, 2004), 7.

52. For visual evidence of this and the preceding characteristics (except sliced steel), see Hufschmid's *Painful Questions*; Hufschmid's video *Painful Deceptions* (available at www.EricHufschmid.net); Jim Hoffman's Web site (http://911research.wtc7.net/index.html); and Jeff King's Web site (http://home.comcast.net/~jeffrey.king2/wsb/html/view.cgi-home.html-.html), especially "The World Trade Center Collapse: How Strong Is the Evidence for a Controlled Demolition?"

53. Both statements are quoted in Christopher Bollyn, "New Seismic Data Refutes Official Explanation," American Free Press, updated April 12, 2004 (http://www.americanfreepress.net/09_03_02/NEW_SEISMIC_/new_seismic_.html). Bollyn stated (e-mail letter of October 27, 2005) that these statements were made to him personally during telephone interviews with Tully and Loizeaux, probably in the summer of 2002. (Bollyn added that although he is not positive about the date of the telephone interviews, he is always "very precise about quotes.")

54. Quoted in James L. Williams, "WTC a Structural Success," *SEAU News: The*

Newsletter of the Structural Engineers Association of Utah, October 2001 (http://www.seau.org/SEAUNews-2001-10.pdf).

55. Jennifer Lin, "Recovery Worker Reflects on Months Spent at Ground Zero," Knight Ridder, May 29, 2002 (http://www.messenger-inquirer.com/news/attacks/4522011.htm).

56. Trudy Walsh, "Handheld APP Eased Recovery Tasks," *Government Computer News,* 21, no. 27a, September 11, 2002 (http://www.gcn.com/21_27a/news/19930-1.html).

57. Professor Allison Geyh of Johns Hopkins, who was part of a team of public health investigators who visited the site shortly after 9/11, wrote: "In some pockets now being uncovered they are finding molten steel" (*Magazine of Johns Hopkins Public Health,* Late Fall, 2001). Dr. Keith Eaton, who somewhat later toured the site with an engineer, said that he was shown slides of "molten metal, which was still red hot weeks after the event" (*The Structural Engineer*, September 3, 2002, 6). William Langewiesche, the only journalist who had unrestricted access to Ground Zero, wrote of descending to "areas where underground fires still burned and steel flowed in molten streams" (*American Ground: Unbuilding the World Trade Center* [New York: North Point Press, 2002], 31). Herb Trimpe, an Episcopalian deacon who served as a chaplain at Ground Zero, said, "The fires burned, up to 2,000 degrees, underground for quite a while. . . . I talked to many contractors and they said . . . beams had just totally melted because of the heat" ("The Chaplain's Tale," *Times-Herald Record,* September 8, 2000 [http://www.recordonline.com/adayinseptember/trimpe.htm]). James L. Williams, president of the Structural Engineers Association of Utah, wrote that "as of 21 days after the attack, the fires were still burning and molten steel was still running" ("WTC a Structural Success").

58. *Popular Mechanics*, "9/11: Debunking the Myths," March 2005 (http://www.popularmechanics.com/science/defense/1227842.html?page=1&c=y). This is, to be blunt, a spectacularly bad article. Besides the problems mentioned here and in n. 14, the article makes this amazing claim: "In the decade before 9/11, NORAD intercepted only one civilian plane over North America: golfer Payne Stewart's Learjet, in October 1999." In reality, as genuine 9/11 researchers know, the FAA reported in 2002 that it had scrambled fighters 67 times between September 2000 and June 2001 (FAA News Release, August 9, 2002), and the *Calgary Herald* (October 13, 2001) reported that NORAD scrambled fighters 129 times in 2000. By extrapolation, we can infer that NORAD had scrambled fighters over 1,000 times in the decade prior to 9/11. The claim by *Popular Mechanics* could be true only if in all of these cases, except for the Payne Stewart incident, the fighters were called back to base before they actually intercepted the aircraft in question. This is a most unlikely possibility, especially in light of the fact that Major Mike Snyder, a NORAD spokesperson, reportedly told the *Boston Globe* a few days after 9/11 that "[NORAD's] fighters routinely intercept aircraft" (Glen Johnson, "Otis Fighter Jets Scrambled Too Late to Halt the Attacks," *Boston Globe*, September 15, 2001 [http:// nl.newsbank.com/nl-search/we/Archives?p_action=print]).

As to why *Popular Mechanics* would have published such a bad article, one clue is perhaps provided by the fact that the article's "senior researcher" was twenty-five-year-old Benjamin Chertoff, cousin of Michael Chertoff, the new head of the Department of Homeland Security (see Christopher Bollyn, "9/11 and Chertoff: Cousin Wrote 9/11 Propaganda for PM," Rumor Mill News, March 4, 2005 [http://www.rumormillnews.com/cgi-bin/forum.cgi

?bem=66176]). Another relevant fact is that this article was published shortly after a coup at this Hearst-owned magazine, in which the editor-in-chief was replaced (see Christopher Bollyn, "The Hidden Hand of the C.I.A. and the 9/11 Propaganda of *Popular Mechanics*," American Free Press, March 19, 2005 [http://www.rense.com/general63/brutalpurgeofPMstaff.htm]). Young Chertoff's debunking article has itself been effectively debunked by many genuine 9/11 researchers, such as Jim Hoffman, "Popular Mechanics' Assault on 9/11 Truth," *Global Outlook* 10 (Spring–Summer 2005), 21–42 (which was based on Hoffman, "*Popular Mechanics*' Deceptive Smear Against 9/11 Truth," 911Review.com, February 15, 2005 [http://911review.com/pm/markup/index.html]), and Peter Meyer, "Reply to *Popular Mechanics* re 9/11," www.serendipity.li/wot/pop_mech/reply_to_popular_mechanics.htm. To be sure, these articles by Hoffman and Meyer, while agreeing on many points, take different approaches in response to some of the issues raised. But both articles demonstrate that *Popular Mechanics* owes its readers an apology for publishing such a massively flawed article on such an important subject.

59. Even if we were generous to a fault and allowed that there might be a one-in-ten chance that any one of the eleven features would occur without explosives, the chance that all eleven of them would occur together would be one in one hundred billion. This calculation assumes, to be sure, that the eleven features are independent of each other. (If only six were independent, so that five of them were correlated to others, the chance that all eleven would occur would still be one in a million.) If the eleven features are independent and we say, a little more realistically, that there is a 1-in-100 chance for each to occur without explosives, the chance that all eleven would occur would be one in 10^{22}. Were we to add in the idea that all these features would occur in three buildings on the same day, the probability would become so vanishingly small as to be virtually indistinguishable from zero. (That would still be the case if only six of the features were considered independent.) But if explosives were used in the buildings, there would be a high probability that all eleven features would have occurred in all three buildings. (For this argument, I am indebted to James Fetzer, who inspired it, and to Paul Zarembka, who helped with the final formulation.)

60. The official investigators found that they had less authority than the cleanup crews, a fact that led the Science Committee of the House of Representatives to report that "the lack of authority of investigators to impound pieces of steel for examination before they were recycled led to the loss of important pieces of evidence" (see the report at http://www.house.gov/science/hot/wtc/charter.htm).

61. "Baosteel Will Recycle World Trade Center Debris," Eastday.com, January 24, 2002 (http://www.china.org.cn/english/2002/Jan/25776.htm).

62. This removal was, moreover, carried out with the utmost care, because "the loads consisted of highly sensitive material." Each truck was equipped with a Vehicle Location Device, connected to GPS. "The software recorded every trip and location, sending out alerts if the vehicle traveled off course, arrived late at its destination, or deviated from expectations in any other way. . . . One driver . . . took an extended lunch break of an hour and a half. . . . [H]e was dismissed" (Jacqueline Emigh, "GPS on the Job in Massive World Trade Center Clean-Up," July 1, 2002 [http://securitysolutions.com/ar/security_gps _job_massive]).

63. *New York Times*, December 25, 2001. This protest was echoed by Professor Abolhassan Astaneh-Asl, professor of civil engineering at the University of Cal-

ifornia at Berkeley, who said: "Where there is a car accident and two people are killed, you keep the car until the trial is over. If a plane crashes, not only do you keep the plane, but you assemble all the pieces, take it to a hangar, and put it together. That's only for 200, 300 people, when they die. In this case, you had 3,000 people dead. You had a major . . . manmade structure. My wish was that we had spent whatever it takes. . . . Get all this steel, carry it to a lot. Instead of recycling it . . . After all, this is a crime scene and you have to figure out exactly what happened" (CBS News, March 12, 2002).

64. Francis L. Brannigan, Glenn P. Corbett, and Vincent Dunn, "WTC 'Investigation'? A Call to Action," *Fire Engineering*, January 2002 (http://fe .pennnet.com/Articles/Article_Display.cfm?Section=ARCHI&ARTICLE_ID= 133211&VERSION_NUM=1&p=25).

65. Bill Manning, "Selling Out the Investigation," *Fire Engineering*, January 2002 (http://fe.pennnet.com/Articles/Article_Display.cfm?Section=ARCHI&ART ICLE_ID=133237&VERSION_NUM=1).

66. Bloomberg was thereby recommending precisely what Bill Manning, the editor of *Fire Engineering*, had warned *against* when he wrote: "As things now stand . . . , the investigation into the World Trade Center fire and collapse will amount to paper- and computer-generated hypotheticals" (Manning, "Selling Out the Investigation"). What Bloomberg desired and Manning feared is exactly what we got with the NIST Report. It is, in fact, even worse. Physicist Steven Jones, after pointing out that there are "zero examples of fire-caused high-rise collapses" and that even NIST's "actual [computer] models fail to collapse," asks: "So how does the NIST team justify the WTC collapses?" He answers: "Easy, NIST concocted computer-generated hypotheticals for very 'severe' cases," and then these cases are further modified to get the desired result. The NIST Report, Jones adds, admits this, saying on page 142: "The more severe case . . . was used for the global analysis of each tower. Complete sets of simulations were then performed for [these cases]. To the extent that the simulations deviated from the photographic evidence or eyewitness reports [e.g., complete collapse occurred], the investigators adjusted the input" (Jones, "Why Indeed Did the WTC Buildings Collapse?").

67. "Baosteel Will Recycle World Trade Center Debris."

68. Bill Manning wrote: "The structural damage from the planes and the explosive ignition of jet fuel in themselves were not enough to bring down the towers. *Fire Engineering* has good reason to believe that the 'official investigation' blessed by FEMA . . . is a half-baked farce that may already have been commandeered by political forces whose primary interests, to put it mildly, lie far afield of full disclosure. Except for the marginal benefit obtained from a three-day, visual walk-through of evidence sites conducted by ASCE investigation committee members—described by one close source as a 'tourist trip'—no one's checking the evidence for anything" ("Selling Out the Investigation").

69. FEMA Report, appendix C (http://www.fema.gov/library/wtcstudy.shtm).

70. Quoted in Joan Killough-Miller, "The 'Deep Mystery' of Melted Steel," WPI Transformations, Spring 2002 (http://www.wpi.edu/News/Transformations/ 2002Spring/steel.html).

71. Quoted in James Glanz, "Engineers Are Baffled over the Collapse of 7 WTC; Steel Members Have Been Partly Evaporated," *New York Times*, November 29, 2001.

72. See the section headed "The ASCE's Disclosures of Steel Sulfidation" in Hoffman's "Building a Better Mirage."

73. FEMA Report, chap. 2. For visual evidence, see Jim Hoffman, "North Tower Collapse Video Frames: Video Evidence of the North Tower Collapse," 9-11 Research.wtc7.net, n.d. (http://911research.wtc7.net/wtc/evidence/videos/wtc1_close_frames.html).

74. James Glanz and Eric Lipton, "Towers Withstood Impact, but Fell to Fire, Report Says," *New York Times*, March 29, 2002.

75. Paul and Hoffman, *Waking Up from Our Nightmare*, 34 (see note 51, above).

76. Jones, "Why Indeed Did the WTC Buildings Collapse?"

77. Quoted in Else, "Baltimore Blasters."

78. See Margie Burns, "Secrecy Surrounds a Bush Brother's Role in 9/11 Security," *American Reporter* 9, no. 2021 (January 20, 2003). Marvin Bush's role in the company is mentioned in Craig Unger, *House of Bush, House of Saud: The Secret Relationship between the World's Two Most Powerful Dynasties* (New York & London: Scribner, 2004), 249.

79. Curtis L. Taylor and Sean Gardiner, "Heightened Security Alert Had Just Been Lifted," *New York Newsday*, September 12, 2001 (http://www.nynewsday.com/news/local/manhattan/wtc/ny-nyaler122362178sep12,0,6794009.story).

80. Scott Forbes's statement is posted at www.apfn.org/apfn/patriotic.htm.

81. Quoted in "Hell on Earth," *People*, September 24, 2001.

82. For Giuliani's complete statement, see "Who Told Giuliani the WTC Was Going to Collapse on 9/11?" (http://www.whatreallyhappened.com/wtc_giuliani.html). The statement can be heard at www.wireonfire.com/donpaul.

83. *The 9/11 Commission Report*, 302.

84. As pointed out in the previous chapter, these oral histories are available on a *New York Times* Web site (http://graphics8.nytimes.com/packages/html/nyregion/20050812_WTC_GRAPHIC/met_WTC_histories_full_01.html).

85. As Hufschmid points out, "Photos show the spectacular flames vanished quickly, and then the fire . . . slowly diminished" (*Painful Questions*, 38).

86. "If the . . . intention was to blame the collapse on the fires," Peter Meyer has written, "then the latest time at which the towers could be collapsed would be just as the fires were dying down. Since the fire in the South Tower resulted from the combustion of less fuel . . . , the fire in the South Tower began to go out earlier. . . . Those controlling the demolition thus had to collapse the South Tower before they collapsed the North Tower" ("Did the Twin Towers Collapse on Demand?" a section in Peter Meyer, "The World Trade Center Demolition and the So-Called War on Terrorism" [www.serendipity.li/wtc.html]).

87. Emergency Medical Services (EMS) division chief John Peruggia said that he was told that the "north tower was in danger of a near imminent collapse" (Oral History of John Peruggia, 17). Medical technician Richard Zarrillo, evidently a liaison between the OEM and EMS, said that he was told that "the buildings . . . are going to collapse" (Oral History of Richard Zarrillo, 5). Fire Marshal Stephen Mosiello and Deputy Assistant Chief of Safety Albert Turi also used the plural ("buildings") in reporting what they heard from Zarrillo in their oral histories. Turi reported that when Zarrillo was asked, "Where are we getting these reports?" his reply was, "You know, we're not sure, OEM is just reporting this." (For the location of the 9/11 Oral Histories, see chap. 2, n. 3, above.)

88. In "A Brief History of New York City's Office of Emergency Management," we read: "1996: By executive order, the Mayor's Office of Emergency Management is created. The Director reports directly to the Mayor, and serves as the local Director of Civil Defense" (http://www.nyc.gov/html/oem/html/other/oem_history.html).

89. "The city . . . initially refused access to the records to investigators from . . . the 9/11 Commission" but "relented when legal action was threatened" (Jim Dwyer, "City to Release Thousands of Oral Histories of 9/11 Today," *New York Times*, Aug. 12, 2005).

90. NIST Report, 80n, 140.

91. Jones, "Why Indeed Did the WTC Buildings Collapse?"

92. Besides being inherently implausible, this story came in at least two versions. According to the first version, which is referred to in the text, al-Sugami's passport was found after the collapses. (The FBI told CNN a week after 9/11 that the passport was found near the WTC after a "grid search"; ABC News said that it was found September 12.) According to the second version, provided by CBS the following January and perhaps thought to be less ridiculous, the passport was found "minutes after" the attack (Rowland Morgan and Ian Henshall, *9/11 Revealed: The Unanswered Questions* [New York: Carroll & Graf, 2005], 68).

93. James Glanz, "Engineers Are Baffled over the Collapse of 7 WTC; Steel Members Have Been Partly Evaporated," *New York Times*, November 29. 2001. Glanz wrote that "experts said no building like it, a modern, steel-reinforced high-rise, had ever collapsed because of an uncontrolled fire."

94. For photographs and discussion, see Hufschmid, *Painful Questions*, 62–65, and the section entitled "The 'Raging' Fires at WTC Tower Seven," in "The World Trade Center Fires (Not So Hot Eh?)," Global Research, September 27, 2004 (http://globalresearch.ca.myforums.net/viewtopic.php?t=523).

95. See FEMA, *World Trade Center Building Performance Study*, chap. 5, sec. 6.2, "Probable Collapse Sequence," which I discuss in *The New Pearl Harbor*, 22.

96. Hufschmid, *Painful Questions*, 64. The collapse of Building 7 also had all the other features of conventional demolitions, such as beginning suddenly and then going down at virtually free-fall speed—which in this case meant under seven seconds. This similarity to conventional implosions was mentioned by Dan Rather. Showing a video of the collapse of Building 7 on CBS that very evening, Rather said that it was "reminiscent of those pictures we've all seen too much on television before, when a building was deliberately destroyed by well-placed dynamite to knock it down" (CBS News, September 11, 2001). Videos of the collapse of Building 7, which have seldom appeared on mainstream television, can be viewed at various Web sites, including www.geocities.com/kill town/wtc7.html and www.whatreallyhappened.com/wtc7.html. Particularly good for this purpose is Eric Hufschmid's DVD *Painful Deceptions* (available at www.EricHufschmid.net).

97. Implosion World (http://www.implosionworld.com/dyk2.html).

98. Steven Jones, personal e-mail communication, October 10, 2005.

99. See nn. 103 and 113, below.

100. Oral History of Decosta Wright, 11–12.

101. Chief Frank Fellini said that the collapse zone was established "five or six hours" before the building came down, which would have been around noon (Oral History of Frank Fellini, 3). This time fits with the testimony of a firefighter who said he "heard reports all day long of 7 World Trade possibly coming down" (Oral History of Christopher Patrick Murray, 12) and of another who said: "We hung out for hours waiting for seven to come down" (Oral History of Vincent Massa, 17-18).

102. Oral History of Frank Fellini, 3.

103. Captain Chris Boyle, quoted in *Firehouse Magazine*, August 2002 (www.fire house.com/terrorist/911/magazine/gz/boyle.html).

104. *Popular Mechanics*, "9/11: Debunking the Myths."

105. Deputy Chief Peter Hayden (interview), "WTC: This Is Their Story," *Firehouse Magazine*, April 2002 (http://www.firehouse.com/terrorist/911/magazine/gz/hayden.html).

106. Oral History of Chief Daniel Nigro, 10.

107. Quoted in Dennis Smith, *Report from Ground Zero: The Heroic Story of the Rescuers at the World Trade Center* (New York: Penguin Putnam, 2002), 160.

108. Oral History of Tiernach Cassidy, 22.

109. Oral History of Decosta Wright, 11.

110. Oral History of Thomas McCarthy, 10–11.

111. Terry Schmidt's photograph can be seen on page 63 of Hufschmid's *Painful Questions* or on Schmidt's Web site (http://www.nycwireless.net/Images/wtc2/). Schmidt reports that he took this photograph between 3:09 and 3:16 p.m. (personal correspondence, January 8, 2006).

112. Even earthquakes, which have produced some partial collapses, have never produced the total collapse of a steel-frame high-rise building.

113. John Norman, "Search and Rescue Operations," *Fire Engineering*, October 2002.

114. See the previous chapter.

115. "Federal investigators concluded that it had been primarily the impact of the planes and, more specifically, the extreme fires that spread in their wake, that had caused the buildings to fall. . . . After the planes hit, . . . much of the spray-on fireproofing in the impact zone was dislodged, leaving the structural steel exposed and mortally vulnerable to the intense heat" (Jim Dwyer and Kevin Flynn, *102 Minutes: The Untold Story of the Fight to Survive inside the Twin Towers* [New York: Times Books, 2005], 252). Dwyer and Flynn even endorse NIST's totally unsupported claim (see Hoffman's "Mirage") that the collapses became "inevitable" (253).

116. Ibid., 258.

117. Dwyer has, in fact, written an article entitled "Vast Archive Yields New View of 9/11," *New York Times*, August 13, 2005 (http://www.nytimes.com/2005/08/13/nyregion/nyregionspecial3/13records.html?ex=1131339600&en=e619ef623287178f&ei=5070), but he did not mention the "new view" that would be suggested by the testimonies about explosions.

118. Silverstein's statement has been quoted in many places, including Rowland Morgan and Ian Henshall, *9/11 Revealed: The Unanswered Questions* (New York: Carroll & Graf, 2005). A critique of this book, put out by the U.S. State Department ("9/11 Revealed? New Book Repeats False Conspiracy Theories" [http://usinfo.state.gov/media/Archive/2005/Sep/16-241966.html]), claims that "the property owner was referring to pulling a contingent of firefighters out of the building in order to save lives because it appeared unstable." But that is hardly a plausible interpretation, especially given the following sentence—"And they made that decision to pull and we watched the building collapse"—plus the fact that elsewhere during the documentary (see the next note), one can hear "pull" used to mean "bring the building down."

119. *America Rebuilds*, PBS documentary, 2002 (www.pbs.org/americarebuilds). Silverstein's statement can be viewed (www.infowars.com/Video/911/wtc7_pbs.WMV) or heard on audio file (http://VestigialConscience.com/PullIt.mp3). For a discussion, see Jeremy Baker, "PBS Documentary: Silverstein, FDNY Razed WTC 7," Infowars.com (www.infowars.com/print/Sept11/FDNY.htm).

120. Dean E. Murphy, *September 11: An Oral History* (New York: Doubleday), 175–76. Currid, incidentally, was reelected president in 2002 (http://www.uniondemocracy.com/UDR/34-NYC%20Public%20Employees.htm).
121. Letter to the *LA Times Magazine*, September 18, 2005, by William Yarchin of Huntington Beach, California, in response to an interview with me in that magazine, conducted by Mark Ehrman, entitled "Getting Agnostic about 9/11," published August 28, 2005 (http://www.latimes.com/features/printedition/magazine/la-tm-crgriffin35aug28,1,3835884.story?coll=la-headlines-magazine).
122. Olivier Uyttebrouck, "Explosives Planted in Towers, N.M. Tech Expert Says," *Albuquerque Journal*, September 11, 2001 (http://www.public-action.com/911/jmcm/ABQjournal).
123. See John Fleck, "Fire, Not Extra Explosives, Doomed Buildings, Expert Says," *Albuquerque Journal*, September 21, 2001 (http://www.abqjournal.com/terror/anniversary/pmvan09-21-01.htm).
124. Romero reportedly claimed later that he did not change his stance. Rather, he told *Popular Mechanics*, he had been misquoted in the first story (by Uyttebrouck). "I was misquoted in saying that I thought it was explosives that brought down the building. I only said that that's what it *looked* like" ("9/11: Debunking the Myths," *Popular Mechanics,* March 2005 [http://www.popularmechanics.com/science/defense/1227842.html?page=1&c=y]). If that were the truth, however, it is strange that the second story, written by Fleck, did not say this but instead said that Romero had changed his mind. It seems that Romero was being less than truthful. He clearly did change his mind—or, to be more precise, his public stance.
125. "Tech Receives $15M for Anti-Terrorism Program" (http://infohost.nmt.edu/mainpage/news/2002/25sept03.html).
126. *Popular Mechanics*, "9/11: Debunking the Myths."

Chapter 4—Flights of Fancy: The 9/11 Commission's Incredible Tales of Flights 11, 175, 77, and 93

1. David Ray Griffin, *The 9/11 Commission Report: Omissions and Distortions* (Northampton, MA: Interlink, 2005), henceforth *Omissions and Distortions*.
2. Illarion Bykov and Jared Israel, "Guilty for 9-11: Bush, Rumsfeld, Myers, Section 1: Why Were None of the Hijacked Planes Intercepted?" (www.emperorsclothes.com/indict/911page.htm). This essay is listed in the table of contents under "Evidence of high-level government conspiracy in the events of 9-11."
3. "NORAD's Response Times," September 18, 2001 (available at www.standdown.net/noradseptember182001pressrelease.htm).
4. That this alleged phone call took eight minutes is an inference from the fact that, supposedly, NEADS was notified about Flight 11 shortly before 8:38 and the scramble order was not given until 8:46 (*The 9/11 Commission Report*, 20).
5. *The 9/11 Commission Report* (chap. 1, n. 103) cites a Pentagon document entitled "Aircraft Piracy (Hijacking) and Destruction of Derelict Airborne Objects," which was issued June 1, 2001. This document in turn cites Directive 3025.15, issued in 1997, which contains the statement quoted in the text. The idea that no standard procedures should prevent immediate responses in emergency situations is also stated in other places in the document of June 1, 2001. Section 4.4, after saying that the secretary of defense retains approval authority for various types of support, concludes by saying, "Nothing in this Directive prevents a commander from exercising his or her immediate emergency

response authority as outlined in DoD Directive 3025.1." And Section 4.5 begins with these words: "With the exception of immediate responses under imminently serious conditions, as provided in paragraph 4.7.1, below. . . ." I have discussed this issue at greater length in the afterword to the second edition of David Ray Griffin, *The New Pearl Harbor: Disturbing Questions about the Bush Administration and 9/11* (Northampton, MA: Interlink Books, 2004).

6. Tom Flocco, "Rookie in the 9-11 Hot Seat?" tomflocco.com, June 17, 2004 (http://tomflocco.com/modules.php?name=News&file=article&sid=65). Flocco adds that Laura Brown later e-mailed him to say that that teleconference had not started until about 8:45, but Flocco suspects that her earlier statement, made to him while they were both present at the first hearing of the 9/11 Commission, was closer to the truth than her later statement, which she made "after returning to her office and conferring with superiors." Flocco's belief that the 8:20 time was correct was, he says, reinforced by a source in the Department of Transportation who told him that phone bridges, linking officials from NORAD, the Secret Service, the Department of Defense, and the Department of Transportation, were established at 8:20 (Tom Flocco, "9-11 Probe Continues to Bypass Executive Branch Testimony," tomflocco.com, October 13, 2003 (http://tomflocco.com/modules.php?name=News&file=article&sid=10). See my discussion in *Omissions and Distortions,* 187.

7. This memo is available at www.911truth.org/article.php?story=2004081 200421797.

8. National Commission on Terrorist Attacks upon the United States, May 23, 2003 (http://www.911commission.gov/archive/hearing2/9-11Commission _Hearing_2003-05-23.htm).

9. Leslie Filson, *Air War over America: Sept. 11 Alters Face of Air Defense Mission,* foreword by Larry K. Arnold (Tyndall Air Force Base Public Affairs Office, 2003).

10. Still another problem is that earlier, when the Commission was explaining why no fighters were scrambled in time to intercept Flight 11, it said that NEADS had to call General Arnold to get permission. But this time, we are told, NEADS simply issued the order, without calling General Arnold, which undermines the Commission's claim that the call to Arnold was necessary in relation to the earlier flight.

11. Quoting Laura Brown, "FAA Communications with NORAD on September 11, 2001" (available at http://www.911truth.org/article.php?story=2004 081200421797).

12. National Commission on Terrorist Attacks upon the United States, May 23, 2003 (http://www.911commission.gov/archive/hearing2/9-11Commission _Hearing_2003-05-23.htm).

13. The idea that military officials knew about Flight 77 long before the Pentagon was struck is also supported by a *New York Times* story published four days after 9/11, which began, "During the hour or so that American Airlines Flight 77 was under the control of hijackers, up to the moment it struck the west side of the Pentagon, military officials in a command center on the east side of the building were urgently talking to . . . air traffic control officials about what to do" (Matthew Wald, "After the Attacks: Sky Rules; Pentagon Tracked Deadly Jet but Found No Way to Stop It," *New York Times,* September 15, 2001).

14. Quoting "Statement of Secretary of Transportation Norman Y. Mineta before the National Commission on Terrorist Attacks upon the United States, May

23, 2003" (available at www.cooperativeresearch.org/timeline/2003/commission testimony052303.htm).

15. Page 9 of *The 9/11 Commission Report* says 9:34. But 9:36 is the time given on pages 27 and 34, and it is the time that allows the Commission to claim that the military "had at most one or two minutes to react to the unidentified plane approaching Washington" (34).

16. Still another thing ignored by the report is the U.S. military's prodigious radar systems. The Web site for one of these systems, called PAVE PAWS, says that it is "capable of detecting and monitoring a great number of targets that would be consistent with a massive SLBM [Submarine Launched Ballistic Missile] attack" ("PAVE PAWS, Watching North America's Skies, 24 Hours a Day" (www.pavepaws.org). The PAVE PAWS system is surely not premised on the assumption that those SLBMs would have transponders. The claim that the military did not know about an aircraft approaching the Pentagon is, accordingly, absurd. After the strikes on the WTC, the U.S. military, if the attacks of 9/11 had genuinely been surprise attacks carried out by foreigners, would have been on the highest state of alert and would not have hesitated to shoot down any unauthorized and unidentified aircraft approaching Washington.

17. *The 9/11 Commission Report*, 30, 31, 34, 38, 44.

18. The Commission's professed inability to discover the identity of the Pentagon participants, along with its neglect of Clarke's account, may have something to do with the fact that it endorsed General Myers's quite different account of his whereabouts, according to which he was up on Capitol Hill at the time. The Commission also endorsed an account of Rumsfeld's movements that is quite different from Clarke's account (*Omissions and Distortions* 217–19).

19. "Statement of Secretary of Transportation Norman Y. Mineta before the National Commission on Terrorist Attacks upon the United States, May 23, 2003."

20. The *Calgary Herald* (October 13, 2001) reported that NORAD scrambled fighters 129 times in 2000; the FAA reported 67 scrambles between September 2000 and June 2001 (FAA News Release, August 9, 2002).

21. See Griffin "The 9/11 Commission Report: A 571-Page Lie," 9/11 Visibility Project, May 22, 2005 (http://www.septembereleventh.org/newsarchive/2005-05-22-571pglie.php).

Chapter 5—Bush Administration Responsibility for 9/11: From a *Prima Facie* to a Conclusive Case

1. David Ray Griffin, *The New Pearl Harbor: Disturbing Questions about the Bush Administration and 9/11* (Northampton, MA: Interlink, 2004), xxiii.

2. See chap. 3, n. 1, above.

3. David Ray Griffin, *The 9/11 Commission Report: Omissions and Distortions* (Northampton, MA: Interlink, 2005), 285–95.

4. The fact that Zelikow was "involved in the drafting" of this document was revealed on PBS in *Frontline*'s "Interview with Barton Gellman" on January 29, 2003, shortly after Zelikow had become executive director of the 9/11 Commission. According to Gellman, a staff writer for the *Washington Post*, Zelikow had told him this during a telephone conversation the previous day. The fact that Zelikow was the *primary* drafter of *NSS 2002* was revealed in James Mann, *Rise of the Vulcans: The History of Bush's War Cabinet* (New York: Viking, 2004). According to Mann, after Rice saw the first draft of this document (which had

been prepared by Richard Haass, the director of policy planning in Colin Powell's State Department), she "ordered the document be completely rewritten. She thought the Bush administration needed something bolder. . . . Rice turned the writing over to her old colleague, . . . Philip Zelikow" (316). Mann later adds that "the hawks in the Pentagon and in Vice President Cheney's office hadn't been closely involved, even though the document incorporated many of their key ideas. They had left the details and the drafting in the hands of Rice and Zelikow, along with Rice's deputy, Stephen Hadley" (331).

5. Kean and Hamilton, in the preface, say: "The professional staff, headed by Philip Zelikow, . . . conducted the exacting investigative work upon which the Commission has built" (*The 9/11 Commission Report: Final Report of the National Commission on Terrorist Attacks upon the United States*, authorized ed. [New York: W. W. Norton, 2004], xvi–xvii).

6. These statements are quoted in Peter Lance, *Cover Up: What the Government Is Still Hiding about the War on Terror* (New York: Harper-Collins/ReganBooks, 2004), 139–40.

7. David Ray Griffin, "The 9/11 Commission Report: A 571-Page Lie," 9/11 Visibility Project, May 22, 2005 (http://www.septembereleventh.org/newsarchive/2005-05-22-571pglie.php).

8. *The 9/11 Commission Report*, 541 n. 1.

9. *San Francisco Chronicle*, September 29, 2001.

10. *The 9/11 Commission Report*, 499 n. 130.

Chapter 6—Imperial Motives for a "New Pearl Harbor"

1. Stefan Halper and Jonathan Clarke, *America Alone: The Neo-Conservatives and the Global Order* (Cambridge: Cambridge University Press, 2004), 4. (Halper and Clarke, identifying with the Reagan presidency, criticize the ideological agenda of the neocons from what they call a "center-right" perspective [5–7].)

2. Stephen J. Sniegoski, "Neoconservatives, Israel, and 9/11: The Origins of the U.S. War on Iraq," in *Neoconned Again: Hypocrisy, Lawlessness, and the Rape of Iraq*, ed. D. L. O'Huallachain and J. Forrest Sharpe (Vienna, VA: IHS Press, 2005), 81–109.

3. Gary Dorrien, *Imperial Designs: Neoconservatism and the New Pax Americana* (New York: Routledge, 2004), 16.

4. Dorrien's examples, some of whom may no longer be neocons, are "William Bennett, Peter Berger, Francis Fukuyama, Zalmay Khalilzad, Jeane Kirkpatrick, Ernest Lefever, James Nuechterlein, Daniel Patrick Moynihan, Michael Novak, Richard John Neuhaus, George Weigel, and James Q. Wilson" (ibid., 15).

5. Michael Lind, "A Tragedy of Errors," *The Nation*, February 23, 2004, online; quoted in Justin Raimondo, "A Real Hijacking: The Neoconservative Fifth Column and the War in Iraq," in O'Huallachain and Sharpe, eds., *Neoconned Again*, 112–24, at 123.

6. Norman Podhoretz, "After the Cold War," *Commentary* 92 (July 1991), and "Neoconservatism: A Eulogy," *Commentary* 101 (March 1996); both cited in Andrew J. Bacevich, *The New American Militarism: How Americans Are Seduced by War* (Oxford: Oxford University Press, 2005), 80.

7. Irving Kristol, *Wall Street Journal*, March 3, 1986; quoted in Gary Dorrien, *The Neoconservative Mind: Politics, Culture, and the War of Ideology* (Philadelphia: Temple University Press, 1993), 117.

8. Charles Krauthammer, "Universal Dominion: Toward a Unipolar World," *National Interest*, Winter 1989, 47–49.

9. Charles Krauthammer, "The Unipolar Moment," *Foreign Affairs* 70, no. 1 (1990–91).

10. Charles Krauthammer, "Bless Our Pax Americana," *Washington Post*, March 22, 1991.

11. Department of Defense, "Defense Planning Guidance," February 18, 1992. Although Libby is usually considered the author of this draft, Dorrien says that it was actually written by Wolfowitz's aide Zalmay Khalilzad, who had been briefed on what it should say by Wolfowitz and Libby—with additional input from Andrew Marshall, Richard Perle, and Albert Wohlstetter (*Imperial Designs*, 39).

12. Andrew J. Bacevich, *American Empire: The Realities and Consequences of U.S. Diplomacy* (Cambridge: Harvard University Press, 2002), 44.

13. Patrick E. Tyler, "U.S. Strategy Plan Calls for Ensuring No Rivals Develop: A One Superpower World," *New York Times*, March 8, 1992 (http://work.colum.edu/~amiller/wolfowitz1992.htm); Barton Gellman, "Keeping the U.S. First: Pentagon Would Preclude a Rival Superpower," *Washington Post*, March 11, 1992 (http://www.yale.edu/strattech/92dpg.html).

14. Editorial, *Wall Street Journal*, March 16, 1992.

15. Quoted in Barton Gellman, "Aim of Defense Plan Supported by Bush," *Washington Post*, March 12, 1992.

16. Quoted in Gellman, "Keeping the U.S. First."

17. Bacevich, *American Empire*, 45.

18. Paul Wolfowitz, "Remembering the Future," *National Interest*, Spring 2000 (http://www.findarticles.com/p/articles/mi_m2751/is_2000_Spring/ai_61299040).

19. Dorrien, *Imperial Designs*, 39.

20. David Armstrong, "Dick Cheney's Song of America," *Harper's*, October 2002.

21. Dorrien, *Imperial Designs*, 142.

22. Nicholas Lemann, "The Next World Order: The Bush Administration May Have a Brand-New Doctrine of Power," *New Yorker*, April 1, 2002 (http://www.newyorker.com/fact/content/articles/020401fa_FACT1). Lemann further reported that the first major product of this new thinking was a brief prepared by Wolfowitz to be presented to Cheney on May 21, 1990, at which time Cheney was also supposed to hear Colin Powell's proposal for revising U.S. foreign policy but did not. Cheney then, on the basis of Wolfowitz's proposal, briefed President Bush, who delivered a major foreign policy address on August 2 (the day that Iraq invaded Kuwait).

23. Brinkley's statement is quoted in "Cheney Is Power Hitter in White House Lineup," *USA Today*, August 28, 2002, which is quoted in Halper and Clarke, *America Alone*, 120.

24. Dorrien, *Imperial Designs*, 42.

25. "Defense Strategy of the 1990s," Department of Defense, 1992.

26. Lemann, "The Next World Order."

27. "Defense Strategy for the 1990s," Department of Defense, January 1993. Lemann, in "The Next World Order," reported that although this was an unclassified and hence "scrubbed" version of the official document, "it contained the essential ideas of 'shaping,' rather than reacting to, the rest of the world, and of preventing the rise of other superpowers."

28. Zalmay Khalilzad, *From Containment to Global Leadership? America and the World after the Cold War* (Santa Monica, CA: Rand Corporation, 1995).

29. Bacevich, *The New American Militarism*, 81.
30. Robert Kagan, "American Power: A Guide for the Perplexed," *Commentary* 101 (April 1996).
31. William Kristol and Robert Kagan, "Foreign Policy and the Republican Future," *Weekly Standard*, October 12, 1998.
32. Robert Kagan, "The Clinton Legacy Abroad," *Weekly Standard*, January 15, 2001; quoted in Bacevich, *The New American Militarism*, 85.
33. Halper and Clarke, *America Alone*, 110.
34. Ibid., 126.
35. Dorrien, *Imperial Designs*, 68, 130.
36. Project for the New American Century, "Statement of Principles," June 3, 1997 (http://www.newamericancentury.org/statementofprinciples.htm).
37. Project for the New American Century (henceforth PNAC), *Rebuilding America's Defenses: Strategy, Forces and Resources for a New Century*, September 2000 (www.newamericancentury.org).
38. Dorrien, *Imperial Designs*, 142–43; Sniegoski, "Neoconservatives, Israel, and 9/11," 94–95.
39. Dorrien, *Imperial Designs*, 168, citing Kristol and Kagan, "Time for an Investigation," *Weekly Standard*, May 27, 2002: 9–10, and Kagan and Kristol, "Still Time for an Investigation," *Weekly Standard*, June 10, 2002: 9–10.
40. Krauthammer, "The Bush Doctrine," *Time*, March 5, 2001 (http://edition.cnn.com/ALLPOLITICS/time/2001/03/05/doctrine.html).
41. Krauthammer's statements, originally published in Emily Eakin, "All Roads Lead to D.C.," *New York Times*, Week In Review, March 31, 2002, are quoted in Jonathan Freedland, "Is America the New Rome?" *Guardian*, September 18, 2002.
42. Robert Kaplan, "Supremacy by Stealth: Ten Rules for Managing the World," *Atlantic Monthly*, July/August 2003.
43. See John McMurtry, "9/11 and the 9/11 Wars: Understanding the Supreme Crimes," in *9/11 and the American Empire: Intellectuals Speak Out*, ed. David Ray Griffin and Peter Dale Scott (Northampton, MA: Interlink Books, 2006).
44. Paul Kennedy, *The Rise and Fall of Great Powers: Economic Change and Military Conflict from 1500 to 2000* (New York: Vintage Books, 1987).
45. Paul Kennedy, "The Eagle Has Landed," *Financial Times*, February 22, 2002.
46. Bacevich, *American Empire*, 244.
47. This distancing is especially evident in Bacevich's later book, *The New American Militarism*.
48. Claes Ryn, "The Ideology of American Empire," in O'Huallachain and Sharpe, eds., *Neoconned Again*, 63–79, at 65.
49. Norman Podhoretz, "The Reagan Road to Détente," *Foreign Affairs* 63 (1984): 452; "The Neo-Conservative Anguish over Reagan's Foreign Policy," *New York Times Magazine*, May 2, 1982; both quoted in Bacevich, *The New American Militarism*, 74.
50. Bacevich, *The New American Militarism*, 133.
51. "Joint Vision 2010" (http://www.dtic.mil/jv2010/jvpub.htm).
52. General Howell M. Estes III, USAF, United States Space Command, "Vision for 2020," February 1997 (http://www.fas.org/spp/military/docops/usspac/visbook.pdf).
53. "Joint Vision 2020" (http://www.dtic.mil/jointvision/jvpub2.htm).
54. Bacevich, *American Empire*, 127.
55. PNAC, *Rebuilding America's Defenses*, 4.

56. Ibid., 38, 54, 30.
57. Ibid., iv, 6, 50, 51, 59.
58. Ibid., 62.
59. Ibid., 51.
60. Dorrien, *Imperial Designs*, 45.
61. Ibid., 44–46; Bacevich, *The New American Militarism*, 152–64, 167–73. Richard Perle, who also became a Wohlstetter disciple at a young age, said of Wolfowitz: "Paul thinks the way Albert thinks" (Dorrien, *Imperial Designs*, 46).
62. "Andrew Marshall," Source Watch, Center for Media & Democracy (http://www.sourcewatch.org/index.php?title=Andrew_Marshall).
63. *Report of the Commission to Assess U.S. National Security Space Management and Organization* (http://www.defenselink.mil/pubs/spaceabout.html), 7.
64. Ibid., 15.
65. This according to the *Washington Post*, January 27, 2002.
66. Robert Kagan, "We Must Fight This War," *Washington Post*, September 12, 2001; Henry Kissinger, "Destroy the Network," *Washington Post*, September 11, 2001 (http://washingtonpost.com); Lance Morrow, "The Case for Rage and Retribution," *Time*, September 11, 2001.
67. "Secretary Rumsfeld Interview with the New York Times," *New York Times*, October 12, 2001.
68. Nicholas Lemann, "The Next World Order: The Bush Administration May Have a Brand-New Doctrine of Power," *New Yorker*, April 1, 2002 (http://www.newyorker.com/fact/content/articles/020401fa_FACT1). The phrase in the inside quotation marks is a direct quote from Rice; the rest of the statement is Lemann's paraphrase.
69. "Remarks by National Security Adviser Condoleezza Rice on Terrorism and Foreign Policy," April 29, 2002 (www.whitehouse.gov).
70. Bob Woodward, *Bush at War* (New York: Simon & Schuster, 2002), 32.
71. "September 11, 2001: Attack on America: Remarks by the President in Telephone Conversation with New York Mayor Giuliani and New York Governor Pataki 11:00 A.M. EDT; September 13, 2001," available at http://www.yale.edu/lawweb/avalon/sept_11/president_009.htm; "Bush Vows to 'Whip Terrorism,'" Reuters, September 14, 2001.
72. Lemann, "The Next World Order."
73. Department of Defense News Briefing on Pentagon Attack, 6:42 PM, Sept. 11, 2001 (available at http://www.yale.edu/lawweb/avalon/sept_11/dod_brief 02.htm). According to the transcript, the question was asked by Secretary Rumsfeld. But the flow of the discussion suggests that it came from a reporter. In either case, the 9/11 attacks were interpreted to mean that greater military spending was needed, "especially for missile defense."
74. Bacevich, *The New American Militarism*, 173; the second phrase in quotation marks was taken by Bacevich from Thomas E. Ricks, "For Rumsfeld, Many Roadblocks," *Washington Post*, August 7, 2001.
75. Ibid., 173.
76. Perle's statement is quoted by Bacevich (ibid., 173–74) from Neil Swidey, "The Mind of the Administration," *Boston Globe*, May 18, 2003.
77. *The National Security Strategy of the United States of America*, September 2002, henceforth *NSS 2002* (www.whitehouse.gov/nsc/nss.html), 29–30.
78. *NSS 2002*, 28.
79. In using this hyphenated term, I follow the precedent of Catherine Keller in "Omnipotence and Preemption," in David Ray Griffin, John B. Cobb Jr.,

Richard Falk, and Catherine Keller, *The American Empire and the Commonwealth of God* (Louisville, KY: Westminster John Knox Press, 2006).

80. Barton Gellman, "Keeping the U.S. First: Pentagon Would Preclude a Rival Superpower"; cited in Halper and Clarke, *America Alone*, 141.

81. Institute for Advanced Strategic and Political Studies, "A Clean Break: A New Strategy for Securing the Realm," June 1996 (http://www.israeleconomy.org/strat1.htm).

82. PNAC, "Statement of Principles," 1997 (http://www.newamericancentury.org/statementofprinciples.htm).

83. PNAC, Letter to President Clinton on Iraq, May 29, 1998 (http://www.new americancentury.org/iraqclintonletter.htm).

84. Bacevich, *The New American Militarism*, 91.

85. "President Bush Delivers Graduation Speech at West Point," June 1, 2002 (http://www.whitehouse.gov/news/releases/2002/06/20020601-3.html).

86. *NSS 2002*, cover letter.

87. Ibid., 6, 15.

88. Ibid., 15.

89. Halper and Clarke, *America Alone*, 142.

90. Max Boot, "Think Again: Neocons," *Foreign Policy*, January/February 2004 (http://www.cfr.org/publication/7592/think_again.html), 18.

91. James Mann, *Rise of the Vulcans: The History of Bush's War Cabinet* (New York: Viking, 2004), 316, 331. Haass, interestingly, had in 2000 given an address called "Imperial America," in which he called on Americans to "re-conceive their global role from one of a traditional nation-state to an imperial power" (Richard N. Haass, "Imperial America," delivered November 11, 2000, Brookings Institution [http://www.brookings.edu/dybdocroot/views/articles/haass/2000imperial.htm]). Haass's foreign policy suggestions, however, were very different from those of the neocons. He said that "primacy is not to be confused with hegemony" and that "an effort to assert U.S. hegemony is . . . bound to fail." He called for accepting the fact that the world in coming decades "will be a world more multipolar than the present one." He said that "an imperial foreign policy is not to be confused with imperialism," which involves exploitation, and that "imperial America is not to be confused with either hegemonic America or unilateral America." In the new world order he envisaged, "The United States would need to relinquish some freedom of action," so it "would be more difficult to carry out preventive or preemptive strikes on suspect military facilities." And he suggested that "coercion and the use of force would normally be a last resort." The United States would instead rely primarily on "persuasion," "consultation," and "global institutions," especially the U.N. Security Council. One can see why Rice, who had shared the responsibility of giving Bush foreign policy advice during the campaign with Paul Wolfowitz and who was now working in the Bush-Cheney White House, would have, after seeing Haass's draft, wanted the document to be "completely rewritten," as Mann reports (*Rise of the Vulcans*, 316).

92. Ashton Carter, John Deutch, and Philip Zelikow, "Catastrophic Terrorism: Tackling the New Danger," *Foreign Affairs*, November/December 1998, 80–94 (available at http://cryptome.quintessenz.at/mirror/ct-tnd.htm).

93. "President Addresses the Nation in Prime Time Press Conference," April 13, 2004 (http://www.whitehouse.gov/news/releases/2004/04/20040413-20.html).

94. "Statement by the President in His Address to the Nation," September 11, 2001 (http://www.whitehouse.gov/news/releases/2001/09/20010911-16.html).

95. "Bin Laden Is Wanted: Dead or Alive, Says Bush," *Telegraph*, September 18,

2001 (http://www.telegraph.co.uk/news/main.jhtml?xml=/news/2001/09/18/wbush18.xml).

96. "White House Warns Taliban: 'We Will Defeat You'" (CNN.com, September 21, 2001).

97. Kathy Gannon, Associated Press, "Taliban Willing to Talk, but Wants U.S. Respect" (http://www.suburbanchicagonews.com/focus/terrorism/archives/1001/w01taliban.html).

98. For the various kinds of evidence, see Griffin, *New Pearl Harbor*, chap. 8, or *The 9/11 Commission Report: Omissions and Distortions*, chap. 6.

99. Francis Boyle, "No Proof, No Investigation, No Accountability, No Law" (http://www.ratical.org/ratville/CAH/fab051702.html). Boyle points out that a White Paper, entitled "Responsibility for the Terrorist Atrocities in the United States," *was* provided by British Prime Minister Tony Blair on October 4, 2001. But it began with the disclaimer that it "does not purport to provide a prosecutable case against Usama Bin Laden in a court of law."

100. Zbigniew Brzezinski, *The Grand Chessboard: American Primacy and Its Geostrategic Imperatives* (New York: Basic Books, 1997), 35–36.

101. Ibid., 36.

102. Ibid., 212.

103. Ibid., 212, 24–25.

104. See Ahmed Rashid, *Taliban: Militant Islam, Oil and Fundamentalism in Central Asia* (New Haven, CT: Yale University Press, 2001), chaps. 12 and 13, entitled "Romancing the Taliban: The Battle for Pipelines."

105. Ibid., 75–79, 175.

106. Julio Godoy, "U.S. Taliban Policy Influenced by Oil," Inter Press Service, November 16, 2001.

107. This according to Niaz Naik, the highly respected Pakistani representative at the meeting, as reported in George Arney, "U.S. 'Planned Attack on Taleban,'" BBC News, September 18, 2001. In a story in the *Guardian* entitled "Threat of U.S. Strikes Passed to Taliban Weeks Before NY Attack" (September 22, 2001), one of the American representatives was quoted as confirming that this discussion of military action did occur.

108. *The Frontier Post*, October 10, 2001, cited in Nafeez Mosaddeq Ahmed, *The War on Freedom: How and Why America Was Attacked September 11, 2001* (Joshua Tree, CA: Tree of Life, 2002), 227.

109. Chalmers Johnson, *The Sorrows of Empire: Militarism, Secrecy, and the End of the Republic* (New York: Metropolitan Books, 2004), 178–79.

110. On his career, see "Zalmay Khalilzad," Source Watch (http://www.sourcewatch.org/index.php?title=Zalmay_Khalilzad).

111. *Chicago Tribune*, March 18, 2002, quoting from the Israeli newspaper *Ma'ariv*.

112. Johnson, *Sorrows of Empire*, 182–83.

113. That Wolfowitz made this comment in a statement to the Commission was reported by Commissioner Jamie Gorelick. The statements by Gorelick and Rumsfeld are quoted in "Day One Transcript: 9/11 Commission Hearing," *Washington Post*, March 23, 2004 (http://www.washingtonpost.com/wp-dyn/articles/A17798-2004Mar23.html).

114. Sniegoski, "Neoconservatives, Israel, and 9/11," 86–87, citing Arnold Beichman, "How the Divide over Iraq Strategies Began," *Washington Times*, November 27, 2002.

115. Albert Wohlstetter, "Help Iraqi Dissidents Oust Saddam," *Wall Street Journal*, August 25, 1992.

116. Albert Wohlstetter, "Meeting the Threat in the Persian Gulf," *Survey* 25 (Spring 1981): 128–88; discussed in Bacevich, *The New American Militarism*, 191.
117. Arnaud de Borchgrave, "All in the Family," *Washington Times*, September 13, 2004, online.
118. Paul D. Wolfowitz and Zalmay M. Khalilzad, "Saddam Must Go," *Weekly Standard*, December 1997.
119. William Kristol and Robert Kagan, "Bombing Iraq Isn't Enough," *New York Times*, January 30, 1998.
120. "Prepared Testimony of Paul D. Wolfowitz," House National Security Committee, U.S. Congress, September 16, 1998; Wolfowitz, "Iraqi Rebels with a Cause," *New Republic*, December 7, 1998.
121. PNAC, Letter to President Clinton on Iraq, January 26, 1998 (http://www.newamericancentury.org/iraqclintonletter.htm). PNAC, Letter to Gingrich and Lott on Iraq, May 29, 1998 (http://www.newamericancentury.org/iraqletter1998.htm).
122. PNAC, *Rebuilding America's Defenses*, 14.
123. O'Neill is quoted to this effect in Ron Susskind, *The Price of Loyalty: George W. Bush, the White House, and the Education of Paul O'Neill* (New York: Simon & Schuster, 2004). O'Neill repeated this point in an interview on CBS's *60 Minutes* in January 2004. Susskind, whose book also draws on interviews with other officials, said that in its first weeks the Bush administration was discussing the occupation of Iraq and the question of how to divide up its oil (www.cbsnews.com/stories/2004/01/09/60minutes/main592330.shtml).
124. Richard Clarke, *Against All Enemies: Inside America's War on Terror* (New York: Free Press, 2004), 264.
125. Quoted in Elizabeth Drew, "The Neocons in Power," *New York Review of Books* 50, no. 10 (June 12, 2003).
126. Woodward, *Bush at War*, 83.
127. Reported by CBS News, September 4, 2002. This note, written by Rumsfeld's top aide, Stephen Cambone (who participated in PNAC's project to produce *Rebuilding America's Defenses*), is now available online (http://www.outragedmoderates.org/2006/02/dod-staffers-notes-from-911-obtained.html).
128. Bob Woodward, *Bush at War*, 48–49.
129. Ibid., 49, 83–85.
130. Glenn Kessler, "U.S. Decision on Iraq Has Puzzling Past," *Washington Post*, January 12, 2003 (http://www.washingtonpost.com/wp-dyn/articles/A43909-2003Jan11.html).
131. Sniegoski, "Neoconservatives, Israel, and 9/11," 101.
132. Halper and Clarke, *America Alone*, 230.
133. Sniegoski, "Neoconservatives, Israel, and 9/11," 108–9.
134. "Remarks by the Vice President to the Veterans of Foreign Wars 103rd National Convention," August 26, 2002 (http://www.whitehouse.gov/news/releases/2002/08/20020826.html).
135. "Remarks by the President on Iraq," October 7, 2002 (http://www.whitehouse.gov/news/releases/2002/10/20021007-8.html).
136. Halper and Clarke, *America Alone*, 203; see also the entirety of their chap. 7, "The False Pretences."
137. Ibid., 210, 209.
138. Ibid., 201, 214.
139. Ibid., 218.
140. Quoted in Gustave Gilbert, *Nuremberg Diary* (New York: Farrar, Straus & Co.,

1947), 278. Gilbert was reporting a conversation he had with Hermann Göring on the evening of April 18, 1946, while the Nuremberg trials were going on.

141. President Ronald Reagan, "Remarks at the Annual Washington Conference of the American Legion," February 22, 1983; quoted in Bacevich, *The New American Militarism*, 185.

142. "President Bush Delivers Graduation Speech at West Point," June 1, 2002 (http://www.whitehouse.gov/news/releases/2002/06/20020601-3.html); Department of Defense press conference, April 23, 2003, quoted in Rahul Mahajan, *Full Spectrum Dominance: U.S. Power in Iraq and Beyond* (New York: Seven Stories Press, 2003), 9.

143. Max Boot, "American Imperialism? No Need to Run Away from Label," *USA Today*, May 6, 2003; available on the Web site of the Council on Foreign Relations (http://www.cfr.org/publication.html?id=5934).

144. Joseph S. Nye Jr., "American Power and Strategy after Iraq," *Foreign Affairs*, July/August 2003: 60; quoted in Halper and Clarke, *America Alone*, 256.

145. Bacevich, *American Empire*, 242 (quoting Charles Beard, *Giddy Minds and Foreign Quarrels* [1939], 87).

146. Bacevich, *American Empire*, 244.

Chapter 7—Jesus and the Roman Empire

1. Chalmers Johnson, *Blowback: The Costs and Consequences of American Empire* (New York: Henry Holt, 2000), 8.

2. Richard A. Horsley, *Jesus and Empire: The Kingdom of God and the New World Disorder* (Minneapolis: Fortress, 2003), 13.

3. Susan P. Mattern, *Rome and the Enemy: Imperial Strategy in the Principate* (Berkeley: University of California Press, 1999), 90.

4. See Mattern, *Rome and the Enemy*, and Edward N. Luttwak, *The Grand Strategy of the Roman Empire: From the First Century A.D. to the Third* (Baltimore: Johns Hopkins University Press, 1976).

5. Klaus Wengst, *Pax Romana and the Peace of Jesus Christ* (Philadelphia: Fortress, 1987), 9.

6. Horace, *Odes* 3.5.1–3; quoted in Wengst, *Pax Romana*, 14.

7. Horsley, *Jesus and Empire*, 20–23.

8. Quoted in ibid., 23–24. The Greek word *euangelion* is, of course, the term used in the New Testament for "good news" or "gospel."

9. Quoted in Wengst, *Pax Romana*, 7.

10. Horsley, *Jesus and Empire*, 197.

11. Tacitus, *Agricola* 14.1; quoted in Horsley, *Jesus and Empire*, 31.

12. Mattern, *Rome and the Enemy*, 22, 117. This centrality of perception was central to Luttwak's well-known study, *The Grand Strategy of the Roman Empire*, which said of the empire in the early part of the first century A.D.: "Client states great and small are . . . kept in subjection by their own perceptions of Roman power. . . . [T]he sphere of imperial control is limited only by the range at which others perceive Roman power as compelling obedience" (192).

13. Polybius, 10.15–17; quoted in Horsley, *Jesus and Empire*, 27.

14. Horsley, *Jesus and Empire*, 108.

15. Ibid., 117, 172.

16. Ibid., 27.

17. Ibid.

18. Pseudo-Quintilian, *Declamations* 274.

19. K. C. Hanson and Douglas E. Oakman, *Palestine in the Time of Jesus: Social Structures and Social Conflicts* (Minneapolis: Augsburg Fortress, 1998), 92.

20. Horsley, *Jesus and Empire*, 22.

21. Wengst, *Pax Romana*, 14.

22. Mattern, *Rome and the Enemy*, 214-15; Horsley, *Jesus and Empire*, 24.

23. Mattern, *Rome and the Enemy*, 135.

24. Hanson and Oakman, *Palestine in the Time of Jesus*, 67.

25. Horsley, *Jesus and Empire*, 29, 34.

26. Ibid., 29.

27. Horsley, *Jesus and Empire*, 6, 15, 28; Richard A. Horsley and Neil Asher Silberman, *The Message and the Kingdom: How Jesus and Paul Ignited a Revolution and Transformed the Ancient World* (New York: Grosset/Putnam, 1997), 84–86.

28. Horsley, *Jesus and Empire*, 31–32; Horsley and Silberman, *The Message and the Kingdom*, 16–17.

29. Horsley and Silberman, *The Message and the Kingdom*, 17; Horsley, *Jesus and Empire*, 32, 85.

30. Horsley, *Jesus and Empire*, 15, 20, 30, 33, 46, 85; Richard A. Horsley, *Jesus and the Spiral of Violence: Popular Jewish Resistance in Roman Palestine* (San Francisco: Harper & Row, 1987), 286–87; Horsley and Silberman, *The Message and the Kingdom*, 78–79.

31. Horsley and Silberman, *The Message and the Kingdom*, 83.

32. Horsley, *Jesus and Empire*, 41, 99.

33. Horsley and Silberman, *The Message and the Kingdom*, 4.

34. Ibid., 17; Horsley, *Jesus and Empire*, 32.

35. Quoted in Hanson and Oakman, *Palestine in the Time of Jesus*, 115.

36. Horsley, *Jesus and Empire*, 61; Horsley and Silberman, *The Message and the Kingdom*, 26.

37. Marcus Borg, *Jesus: A New Vision* (San Francisco: HarperSanFrancisco, 1991), 95; Richard A. Horsley and John S. Hanson, *Bandits, Prophets, and Messiahs: Popular Movements in the Time of Jesus* (San Francisco: Harper & Row, 1987), 54–56.

38. Horsley and Silberman, *The Message and the Kingdom*, 26–29.

39. Ibid., 129.

40. Marcus Borg offers two major arguments against this view. First, some of the material that clearly implies a literal end of the world is understandable as originating after the resurrection of Jesus, which was interpreted by some Christians as the beginning ("first fruits") of the end. Also, some of this material is best understood as originating only after the destruction of Jerusalem in 70 C.E., which, given the association in some traditions of the destruction of Jerusalem with the beginning of the end time, led some Christians to believe that the (literal) end of the world was near (Marcus Borg, *Conflict, Holiness and Politics in the Teachings of Jesus* [New York & Toronto: Edwin Mellen, 1984], 216). Borg's second argument is that, although there are a few "apocalyptic" sayings that are best understood as originating with Jesus himself and that do seem, if taken literally, to be predicting the near end of the world, taking them literally involves a failure to appreciate the metaphorical nature of apocalyptic imagery. For example, now that most of the "imminent expectation" passages have been dated after the death of Jesus, much of the weight for the claim that Jesus expected an imminent end of the world, in a cosmic cataclysm effected by a supernatural act of God, is borne by Mark 13:24–27, which reads: "But in those days, after that suffering, the sun will be darkened, and the moon will

not give its light, and the stars will be falling from heaven. . . . Then they will see the 'Son of Man coming in clouds' with great power and glory." However, much precedent existed for using the language of the darkening of the sun and the moon and the falling of stars to refer metaphorically to the "day of Yahweh" as a judgment upon a particular nation. This language is used, for example, with reference to Egypt in Ezek. 32:7, to Babylon in Isa. 13:10, to Gentile nations in Joel 3:15 and 4 Ezra 5:4–6, and to Israel in Amos 8:9 and Joel 2:10 and 2:30–31. Indeed, this latter prophecy in Joel, which refers to the sun's darkening and the moon's turning to blood, is cited in Acts 2:19–20 as having been fulfilled on the day of Pentecost (Borg, *Conflict, Holiness and Politics*, 216–17). The author of Luke-Acts certainly did not believe the world had literally come to an end some sixty years before he was writing his works. Finally, while it is Mark 13 in general, sometimes called the Little Apocalypse, that is the primary basis for thinking that Jesus expected a cataclysmic end of the world, Jesus in vv. 14–16 tells people that when these events come, they should flee to the mountains—a recommendation that implies that the mountains are *not* about to collapse. Jesus' advice, Borg suggests, is more consistent with the view, supported by other evidence, that he was predicting the destruction of Jerusalem (ibid., 177–96).

41. Horsley, *Jesus and Empire*, 81; Horsley and Silberman, *The Message and the Kingdom*, 53–54.
42. Horsley, *Jesus and Empire*, 174–75; Borg, *Conflict, Holiness and Politics*, 383n.
43. Horsley, *Jesus and the Spiral*, 170.
44. Ibid., 189. Horsley also points to Mark 3:27, which indicates that Satan's goods (demons) can be plundered only because Satan had been bound (*Jesus and Empire*, 102).
45. Horsley, *Jesus and Empire*, 101.
46. Ibid., 84.
47. Horsley, *Jesus and the Spiral*, 157.
48. Herman E. Daly makes this point in *Beyond Growth: The Economics of Sustainable Development* (Boston: Beacon, 1996), 208.
49. Isa. 65:17–23; cited in Horsley and Silberman, *The Message and the Kingdom*, 6, 14.
50. Matt. 21:33–46; Mark 12:1–12; Luke 20:9–19.
51. Mark 12:13–17; Luke 23:2; Horsley, *Jesus and the Spiral*, 307–14.
52. Mark 12:1–9 and parallels; see Horsley, *Jesus and the Spiral*, 305–6.
53. Horsley, *Jesus and the Spiral*, 282.
54. Mark 13:1–2; 14:57–58; 15:29; Matt. 26:60–61; John 2:18-22.
55. Horsley, *Jesus and the Spiral*, 299; E. P. Sanders, *Jesus and Judaism* (Philadelphia: Fortress, 1985), 69–70, 302.
56. Paula Fredriksen, *From Jesus to Christ: The Origins of the New Testament Images of Jesus* (New Haven, CT: Yale University Press, 1988), 120, 79.
57. Horsley, *Jesus and Empire*, 132.
58. Horsley and Silberman, *The Message and the Kingdom*, 227.
59. Ibid., 11.
60. Ibid., 157–58, 148, 203.
61. Some modern Christian theologians, in reaction to this otherworldly Christianity, have said that we need to preach a fully this-worldly salvation. I believe, however, that we both should and can reaffirm all four dimensions of salvation as understood in the New Testament: (1) the present deliverance from bondage to demonic power, (2) the expectation of a more complete salvation in a reign

of God on earth, (3) the expectation of an even more complete salvation—later called "sanctification" and "deification"—in a life after death, and (4) the fact that, in any case, our lives have permanent significance because they are known everlastingly by God. I have argued that this fourfold view is compatible with the kind of theology I have espoused, known as "process theology," in "Process Eschatology," in *The Handbook of Eschatology*, ed. Jerry Walls (Oxford: Oxford University Press, 2006). I have argued for the truth of the third and fourth dimensions in chap. 6 of my *Reenchantment without Supernaturalism: A Process Philosophy of Religion* (Ithaca, NY: Cornell University Press, 2001). One reason that the reaffirmation of these latter two dimensions is important is that people are more able to challenge the state when they have confidence that their identity does not depend entirely on their bodies, which are subject to being imprisoned and even executed by the state.

62. Horsley, *Jesus and the Spiral*, 307–14.
63. See Conrad Cherry, ed., *God's New Israel: Religious Interpretations of American Destiny*, rev. and updated ed. (Chapel Hill: University of North Carolina Press, 1997).
64. Anders Stephanson, *Manifest Destiny: American Expansion and the Empire of Right* (New York: Hill & Wang, 1995), 59.
65. See David Ray Griffin, *God, Power, and Evil: A Process Theodicy* (1976, 1991; Louisville, KY: Westminster John Knox, 2004 [with a new preface]); *Evil Revisited: Responses and Reconsiderations* (Albany: State University of New York Press, 1991); "Creation out of Nothing, Creation out of Chaos, and the Problem of Evil," in *Encountering Evil: Live Options in Theodicy*, ed. Stephen T. Davis, 2nd ed. (Louisville, KY: Westminster John Knox, 2001), 108–25.

Chapter 8—The Divine and the Demonic

1. Jeffrey Burton Russell, *The Devil: Perceptions of Evil from Antiquity to Primitive Christianity* (Ithaca, NY: Cornell University Press, 1977), 228, 248.
2. Jon D. Levenson, *Creation and the Persistence of Evil: The Jewish Drama of Divine Omnipotence* (San Francisco: Harper & Row, 1988), 5, 121, 157n.12.
3. Ibid., 7–18.
4. Ibid., xiii, 49, 50.
5. Ibid., 12, 26, 122–23.
6. Plato, *The Timaeus*, 30A.
7. Gerhard May, *Creatio Ex Nihilo: The Doctrine of "Creation out of Nothing" in Early Christian Thought*, trans. A. S. Worrall (Edinburgh: T. & T. Clark, 1994).
8. Ibid., xi–xii, 7.
9. Ibid., 7–8, 21.
10. Ibid., 11, 16.
11. Ibid., xi.
12. Ibid., viii, xii, 25–26, 77, 161, 174.
13. Ibid., 122.
14. Ibid., xiii, 61, 74.
15. Ibid., 40, 56.
16. Ibid., 56n, 152.
17. Ibid., 140, 142, 145.
18. Ibid., 141.
19. Ibid., 147, 151, 159, 178.
20. Ibid., 161.

21. Ibid., 167–68, 174, 177.

22. I have illustrated the insolubility of the problem of evil, given the traditional doctrine of divine omnipotence, in *God, Power, and Evil: A Process Theodicy* (Philadelphia: Westminster, 1976), and *Evil Revisited: Responses and Reconsiderations* (Albany: State University of New York Press, 1991).

23. St. Augustine, *Enchiridion*, trans. J. F. Shaw, in Whitney J. Oates, ed., *Basic Writings of St. Augustine*, 2 vols. (New York: Random House, 1978), 14.96; 24.95.

24. St. Augustine, *Grace and Free Will*, trans. P. Holmes, in Oates, *Basic Writings of St. Augustine*, 41; 42.

25. St. Augustine, *The Nature of the Good*, trans. John H. S. Burleigh, in *Augustine: Earlier Writings*, The Library of Christian Classics, vol. 6 (Philadelphia: Westminster, 1953), 32.

26. A basic understanding of this position can be derived from John B. Cobb Jr. and David Ray Griffin, *Process Theology: An Introductory Exposition* (Philadelphia: Westminster, 1976; reprinted by Westminster John Knox Press).

27. See Isa. 64:8, Jer. 18:4, and Rom. 9:20–21.

28. Some physical cosmologists, to be sure, believe in a big bang that was the very beginning of finite existence as such, so that prior to it there was no space or time. Most cosmologists, however, realize that this interpretation is simply a philosophical assumption, with no possible evidence to back it up. That is, if there was a big bang (and the "if" should be emphasized), there would be no evidence about the conditions prior to it. In any case, regardless of whether these big-bang cosmologists believe that time and space in some sense have always existed, they all seem to agree that there always had to be energy.

29. Alan H. Guth can serve as a representative of this version of the mainstream view. Guth, who sometimes speaks of a "vacuum" and sometimes "a repulsive-gravity material," says: "It may seem strange to see the words 'vacuum' and 'material' used to describe the same thing, but keep in mind that this stuff is *strange*. The word 'vacuum' is used to emphasize that it is different from ordinary matter, while I am calling it a material to emphasize that it is different from an ordinary vacuum!" He also, for this reason, sometimes calls it a "false vacuum." Alan Guth, "Eternal Inflation," in *Cosmic Questions*, ed. James B. Miller, Annals of the New York Academy of Sciences, Vol. 950 (New York: The New York Academy of Sciences, 2001), 66–82, at 81 n. 7.

30. Nicolas Berdyaev, *The Destiny of Man* (New York: Harper & Row, 1960), 22–35; *Truth and Revelation* (New York: Collier Books, 1962), 124.

31. There are, to be sure, different ways to interpret the principle of indeterminacy. But one possible way, which cannot be ruled out experimentally, is that the indeterminacy is a reflection of self-determinacy.

32. Julius Adler and Wing-Wai Tse, "Decision-Making in Bacteria," *Science* 184 (1974): 1292–94; A. Goldbeter and D. E. Koshland Jr., "Simple Molecular Model for Sensing Adaptation Based on Receptor Modification with Application to Bacterial Chemotaxis," *Journal of Molecular Biology* 161, no. 3 (1982): 395–416.

33. Charles Hartshorne reported that he heard Millikan say this.

34. For a much longer discussion of this point, see my *Unsnarling the World-Knot: Consciousness, Freedom, and the Mind-Body Problem* (Berkeley: University of California Press, 1998), chap. 9, "Compound Individuals and Freedom."

35. Alfred North Whitehead, *Adventures of Ideas* (1933; New York: Free Press, 1967), 166.

36. For a more extensive discussion of this point, see my *God, Power, and Evil,* 291–97; *Evil Revisited,* 26–29; or *Process Theology* (coauthored with John Cobb), 69–75.

37. Assuming, at least, that life did not appear elsewhere much earlier than it appeared on our planet almost 4 billion years ago.

38. I have briefly discussed this period, more generally known as the "Cambrian explosion," in my *Religion and Scientific Naturalism: Overcoming the Conflicts* (Albany: State University of New York Press, 2000), 280–81.

39. This distinction is implicit in Whitehead's thought but was not emphasized. He spoke simply of creativity and was intent on distinguishing it from God, because it was that distinction that explained creaturely freedom and thereby avoided the traditional problem of evil. Most of Whitehead's discussion of creativity, therefore, focuses on creativity as embodied in creatures. He does make clear, nevertheless, that creativity is embodied in God as well, referring to God as the "aboriginal instance" and "primordial exemplification" of creativity (Alfred North Whitehead, *Process and Reality,* corrected ed., ed. David Ray Griffin and Donald W. Sherburne [New York: Free Press, 1978], 225, 344).

40. For the way in which process theism affirms divine omniscience without denying the ultimate reality of time, see my *Reenchantment without Supernaturalism: A Process Philosophy of Religion* (Ithaca, NY: Cornell University Press, 2001), 158–59.

41. Abraham Joshua Heschel, *The Prophets* (Philadelphia: Jewish Publication Society of America, 1962), 26, 224, 231, 314.

42. Marcus Borg, *Jesus: A New Vision* (San Francisco: HarperSanFrancisco, 1991), 108–11.

43. See Charles Hartshorne, *Man's Vision of God and the Logic of Theism* (New York: Harper & Row, 1941), 174–87, or *Omnipotence and Other Theological Mistakes* (Albany: State University of New York Press, 1984), 52–62. I have discussed the idea of God as soul of the universe in *Reenchantment without Supernaturalism,* 140–42.

44. A perceptive reader of the manuscript for this book asked if this idea, that God loves all creatures, implies that God loves the demonic, which I have called a creature. No, because the statement that God loves all creatures refers to individual creatures, meaning those with experience and hence intrinsic value. Only they have feelings that can be felt with sympathy or compassion. But the demonic is (by hypothesis) not an individual, but a complex abstraction or structure. It is the creativity of a society, and thereby the individuals that make it up, as in-formed by a set of symbols, habits, dispositions, beliefs, values, and so on. I refer to the demonic as a creature in order to emphasize the fact that it is not eternal, being instead a byproduct of God's persuasive creation of beings with the kind of high-level experience, and hence the kind of high-level power, that human beings have. God (by hypothesis) wants to overcome the demonic, because it is destructive of the experience of individual beings, whom God loves.

45. Henry David Aiken, "God and Evil: A Study of Some Relations between Faith and Morals," *Ethics* 68, no. 2 (January 1958): 77–97, at 82; P. H. Nowell-Smith, "Morality: Religious and Secular," in *Christian Ethics and Contemporary Philosophy,* ed. Ian T. Ramsey (London: SCM Press, 1966), 95–112, at 97.

46. J. Brenton Stearns, "The Naturalistic Fallacy and the Question of the Existence of God," *Religious Studies* 8, no. 3 (September 1972): 207–20, at 212–13.

47. This language of the "creative love" and "responsive love" of God was intro-

duced in Cobb and Griffin, *Process Theology*, chap. 3, "God as Creative-Responsive Love." Unfortunately, as we explained, classical Christian theologians, such as St. Anselm and St. Thomas Aquinas, did not attribute responsive love to God because they took some Greek philosophers, with their insistence that the divine reality must be "impassible" (emotionally unaffected by the world), as more definitive on this topic than the New Testament. This led Anselm to ask, in a prayer to God: "how art thou . . . compassionate, and, at the same time, passionless. For, if thou art passionless, thou dost not feel sympathy for the wretched; but this it is to be compassionate" (*Proslogium* VII, in *Proslogium; Monologium; An Appendix, In Behalf of the Fool, by Gaunilon; and Cur Deus Homo*, trans. S. N. Deane [LaSalle: Open Court, 1945], 13–14). Anselm's attempted resolution was the same as that later offered by St. Thomas, who said: "To sorrow . . . over the misery of others belongs not to God, but it does most properly belong to Him to dispel that misery" (*Summa Theologica* 1, a.21, a.3, ans). One problem with this answer is that, according to these theologians, God did *not* dispel the misery of all human beings, but even increased the misery of many by foreordaining them to eternal punishment in hell. This horrible doctrine of traditional theism was brought out even more explicitly by John Calvin, who explicitly affirmed "double predestination," according to which God predestined some people to heaven and others to hell, and not because God had foreknowledge of how they would act but solely because God chose to do so (see my exposition of Calvin's position in chap. 10 of *God, Power, and Evil*). This doctrine was only the most horrible implication of the acceptance of *creatio ex nihilo*, which implies that every detail of our world is the way it is because God willed it to be that way. If Aiken, Nowell-Smith, and Stearns had simply pointed out that traditional theists did not conclude from the metaphysical uniqueness of God that God is necessarily and perfectly good, their claim would have been correct. But Stearns, for example, goes beyond this to claim that "given any metaphysical description of God, God's goodness is logically contingent" ("The Naturalistic Fallacy," 214). This is wrong, because from the metaphysical description of God given by process theology, God is good necessarily, not contingently.

48. I have developed this notion of the "immanent trinity" (along with two versions of the "economic trinity") in "A Naturalistic Trinity," in *Trinity in Process: A Relational Theology of God*, ed. Joseph A. Bracken and Marjorie Hewitt Suchocki (New York: Continuum, 1997), 23–40. One of the virtues of this way of understanding God as trinitarian is that it is a conception that can be accepted by Jews, Muslims, and other unitarians.

49. Matthew Fox, *Original Blessing* (Sante Fe, NM: Bear & Co., 1983).

50. Andrew Bard Schmookler, *The Parable of the Tribes: The Problem of Power in Social Evolution* (Boston: Houghton Mifflin, 1986). Schmookler's view of the central importance of the war-system in shaping the direction taken by civilization over the past several millennia has been reinforced for me by William H. McNeill's *The Pursuit of Power: Technology, Armed Force, and Society since A.D. 1000* (Chicago: University of Chicago Press, 1982).

51. The question of whether the war-system was more of a cause or more of a result of the settled agricultural communities is one we need not take a position on.

52. We also need not take a position on the question of when the first "truly human" beings arose.

53. Schmookler, *The Parable of the Tribes*, 45.

54. For example, in an essay in a volume entitled *The Perils of Anarchy: Contemporary*

Realism and International Security, ed. Michael E. Brown, Sean M. Lynn-Jones, and Steven E. Miller (Cambridge: MIT Press, 1995), Christopher Layne writes: "International politics is an anarchic, self-help realm. 'Anarchy,' rather than denoting chaos or rampant disorder, refers in international politics to the fact that there is no central authority capable of making and enforcing rules of behavior on the international system's units (states)" (293).

55. As David Held says, "Realism posits that the system of sovereign states is inescapably anarchic in character; and that this anarchy forces all states, in the inevitable absence of any supreme arbiter to enforce moral behaviour and agreed international codes, to pursue power politics in order to attain their vital interests" (*Democracy and the Global Order: From the Modern State to Cosmopolitan Governance* [Stanford, CA: Stanford University Press, 1995], 74–75).

56. The term "anarchy" has, of course, a quite different valence in the philosophical-political theory known as "anarchism." But I am here restricting the discussion to the way the term is used in the discourse of political realists.

57. These statements from Thucydides are quoted in Schmookler, *The Parable of the Tribes*, 70.

58. Brown, Lynn-Jones, and Miller, eds., *The Perils of Anarchy*, ix.

59. Georg Schwarzenberger, *Power Politics: An Introduction to the Study of International Relations and Post-War Planning* (London: J. Cape, 1941), 430, 339.

60. Frederick L. Schuman, "Toward a World State," in H. D. Gideonse, R. B. Frosdick, W. F. Ogburn, and F. L. Schuman, *The Politics of Atomic Energy* (New York: Woodrow Wilson Foundation, 1946), 35–55; *The Commonwealth of Man: An Inquiry into Power Politics and World Government* (London: Robert Hale, 1954).

61. I am ignoring here the question of where the first system that can be called "capitalist" arose.

62. Gerda Lerner, *The Creation of Patriarchy* (New York: Oxford University Press, 1986), 35.

63. Arthur C. McGill, *Suffering: A Test of Theological Method* (Philadelphia: Westminster, 1982), 51, 88, 99, 116, 129, 131.

64. Ernest Becker, "Bunuel and the Demonic," in Ernest Becker, *Angel in Armor: A Post-Freudian Perspective on the Nature of Man* (New York: George Braziller, 1969), 111.

65. McGill, *Suffering*, 117.

66. Schmookler suggests that the selection for power would have also operated with regard to religious ideologies (*The Parable of the Tribes*, 73, 80), but he does not develop this idea at length.

67. See Walter Rauschenbusch, *A Theology for the Social Gospel* (New York: Macmillan, 1918), especially the chapters on "The Supra-Personal Forces of Evil" and "The Kingdom of Evil."

68. See David Frum and Richard Perle, *An End to Evil: How to Win the War on Terror* (New York: Random House, 2004).

Chapter 9—The American Empire, Demonic Evil, and 9/11

1. See Conrad Cherry, ed., *God's New Israel: Religious Interpretations of American Destiny*, rev. and updated ed. (Chapel Hill: University of North Carolina Press, 1997).

2. Anders Stephanson, *Manifest Destiny: American Expansion and the Empire of Right* (New York: Hill & Wang, 1995), xi.

3. Richard Van Alstyne, *The Rising American Empire* (1960; New York, Norton, 1974), 159.

4. Stephanson, *Manifest Destiny*, 19.

5. Andrew J. Bacevich, *American Empire: The Realities and Consequences of U.S. Diplomacy* (Cambridge: Harvard University Press, 2002), 30. For some examples, see Van Alstyne, *The Rising American Empire*; Noam Chomsky, *American Power and the New Mandarins* (1967; New York: Vintage Books, 1969), and *Rogue States: The Rule of Force in World Affairs* (Cambridge: South End Press, 2000); Richard Falk, "Imperialism in Crisis," an introduction to Mansour Farhang, *U.S. Imperialism: From the Spanish-American War to the Iranian Revolution* (Boston: South End Press, 1981); Lloyd C. Gardner, Walter F. LaFeber, and Thomas J. McCormick, *Creation of the American Empire* (Chicago: Rand McNally, 1973); Walter LaFeber, *The New Empire: An Interpretation of American Expansion 1860–1898* (1963; Ithaca, NY: Cornell University Press, 1998); Harry Magdoff, *The Age of Imperialism: The Economics of U.S. Foreign Policy* (New York: Monthly Review, 1966, 1969); Michael Parenti, *Against Empire* (San Francisco: City Lights, 1995); William Appleman Williams, *The Tragedy of American Diplomacy* (1959; New York: Norton, 1988), and *Empire as a Way of Life: An Essay on the Causes and Character of America's Present Predicament* (Oxford: Oxford University Press, 1980); Howard Zinn, *A People's History of the United States* (New York: Harper & Row, 1980, 1990).

6. Ronald Steel, *Pax Americana* (New York: Viking Press, 1967), 15, 14.

7. Ibid., 16–17, 18, vii.

8. See Ronald Steel, *Temptations of a Superpower* (Cambridge: Harvard University Press, 1995).

9. Charles Krauthammer, "The Unipolar Moment," *Foreign Affairs* 70, no. 1 (1990–91): 295–306, at 304–5.

10. Ben Wattenberg, *The First Universal Nation: Leading Indicators and Ideas about the Surge of America in the 1990s* (New York: Free Press, 1991), 202; quoted in Gary Dorrien, *Imperial Designs: Neoconservatism and the New Pax Americana* (New York: Routledge, 2004), 91.

11. William Kristol and Robert Kagan, "Toward a Neo-Reaganite Foreign Policy," *Foreign Affairs* 75 (July/August 1996): 18–32, at 20, 27; quoted in Dorrien, *Imperial Designs*, 126, 128.

12. Robert Kagan, "The Benevolent Empire," *Foreign Policy* (Summer 1998): 24–35 (http://www.carnegieendowment.org/publications/index.cfm?fa=view&id=275).

13. Charles Krauthammer, "The Unipolar Moment Revisited: United States World Dominance," *The National Interest*, Winter 2002 (available at http://www.find articles.com/p/articles/mi_m2751/is_2002_Winter/ai_95841625); republished as "The Unipolar Era," in *The Imperial Tense: Prospects and Problems of American Empire*, ed. Andrew J. Bacevich (Chicago: Ivan R. Dee, 2003), 47–65; see 59 for the quoted material.

14. Dinesh D'Souza, "In Praise of an American Empire," *Christian Science Monitor*, April 26, 2002.

15. Max Boot, "What Next? The Foreign Policy Agenda beyond Iraq," *Weekly Standard*, May 5, 2003 (http://www.weeklystandard.com/Content/Public/Articles/000/000/002/606hotoc.asp?pg=2).

16. Joshua Muravchik, *Exporting Democracy: Fulfilling America's Mission* (Washington, DC: American Enterprise Institute, 1991), 227; Wattenberg, *The First Universal Nation*, 196.

17. Dorrien, *Imperial Designs*, 80.
18. George W. Bush, "Address of the President to the Nation," September 7, 2003 (http://www.whitehouse.gov/news/releases/2003/09/20030907-1.html).
19. Bush, "State of the Union Address," January 28, 2003 (http://www.cnn.com/2003/ALLPOLITICS/01/28/sotu.transcript).
20. Bush, "Second Inaugural Address," January 20, 2005 (http://www.white house.gov/inaugural).
21. Charles Krauthammer, "Tomorrow's Threat," *Washington Post*, January 21, 2005 (http://www.washingtonpost.com/wp-dyn/articles/A25279-2005Jan 20.html).
22. Quoted and discussed in Ray McGovern, "God on Their Side," TomPaine.com, December 30, 2003 (http://www.tompaine.com/feature 2.cfm/ID/9678/view/print).
23. During the Cold War, Bacevich says, he had assumed that American foreign policy was actually guided by its stated objectives, which were "quite limited—to protect our homeland, to preserve our values, to defend our closest allies." However, after Bacevich saw that after the Cold War ended, America did not greatly decrease its military spending, weapons systems, and overseas bases, he looked at the historical evidence again and decided that some left-wing critics of American foreign policy, such as Charles Beard and William Appleman Williams, had been basically right all along. See Bacevich, *American Empire*, viii, 11.
24. Ibid., 46, 4.
25. Ibid., 133, 52.
26. Ibid., 115, 196.
27. Chalmers Johnson, *The Sorrows of Empire: Militarism, Secrecy, and the End of the Republic* (New York: Henry Holt, 2004), 4.
28. Noam Chomsky, *Hegemony or Survival: America's Quest for Global Dominance* (New York: Metropolitan Books, 2003).
29. Richard Falk, "Will the Empire Be Fascist?" *Global Dialogues*, 2003; "Resisting the Global Domination Project: An Interview with Prof. Richard Falk," *Frontline* 20, no. 8 (April 12–25, 2003); "Slouching toward a Fascist World Order," in David Ray Griffin, John B. Cobb Jr., Richard Falk, and Catherine Keller, *The American Empire and the Commonwealth of God* (Louisville, KY: Westminster John Knox, 2006).
30. I agree that atheism (in the broad sense, meaning that there is nothing in the universe that provides a home for moral ideals) does imply relativism, which is one of the main reasons that the defense of theism (in the broad sense) is important; see Griffin, "Theism and the Crisis in Moral Theory: Rethinking Modern Autonomy," in *Nature, Truth, and Value: Exploring the Thought of Frederick Ferré*, ed. George Allan and Merle Allshouse (Lanham, MD: Lexington Books, 2005), 199–220.
31. I have sought to contribute to this discussion in various places, especially *Reenchantment without Supernaturalism: A Process Philosophy of Religion* (Ithaca, NY: Cornell University Press, 2001). I emphasize that I am endorsing a view that is theistic in the *broad* sense partly in order to include some religious traditions, such as some forms of Hinduism and Buddhism, that do not accept theism as dominantly understood in Christianity, Islam, and Judaism, and also because I myself reject traditional theism, especially insofar as it affirms divine omnipotence, which has created an insoluble problem of evil—as I have argued in *God, Power, and Evil: A Process Theodicy* (1976: Louisville, KY: Westminster John

Knox, 2004) and *Evil Revisited: Responses and Reconsiderations* (Albany: State University of New York Press, 1991).

32. For essays by theologians from various religious traditions who accept some common norms while holding that religions really do differ, and not just superficially, see David Ray Griffin, ed., *Deep Religious Pluralism* (Louisville, KY: Westminster John Knox, 2005).

33. Hans Küng, *A Global Ethic for Global Politics and Economics* (New York: Oxford University Press, 1998), 98–99. The discussion of common moral principles in the various religious traditions has been carried forward by other philosophers and theologians. For examples, see Leonard Swidler, ed., *For All Life: Toward a Universal Declaration of a Global Ethic: An Interreligious Dialogue* (Ashland, OR: White Cloud Press, 1998); Daniel C. Maguire, *Sacred Energies: When the World's Religions Sit Down to Talk about the Future of Human Life and the Plight of This Planet* (Minneapolis: Fortress, 2002); and Paul F. Knitter and Chandra Muzaffar, eds., *Subverting Greed: Religious Perspectives on the Global Economy* (Maryknoll, NY: Orbis, 2002).

34. See—in addition to Michael Walzer, who is discussed in the text—Charles Taylor, "The Politics of Recognition," in Charles Taylor et al., *Multiculturalism: Examining the Politics of Recognition*, ed. Amy Gutmann (Princeton, NJ: Princeton University Press, 1994), 59, 61; Michael Sandel, *Democracy's Discontent: America in Search of a Public Philosophy* (Cambridge: Harvard University Press, 1996), 341–42; Amitai Etzioni, *The New Golden Rule: Community and Morality in a Democratic Society* (New York: Basic Books, 1996), 218–33, 248.

35. Michael Walzer, *Thick and Thin: Moral Argument at Home and Abroad* (Notre Dame, IN: University of Notre Dame Press, 1994), x, xi.

36. Ibid., 17.

37. Ibid., 6.

38. Ibid., 10.

39. Henry Shue, *Basic Rights: Subsistence, Affluence, and U.S. Foreign Policy*, 2nd ed. (Princeton, NJ: Princeton University Press, 1996), 19.

40. Ibid., 23.

41. Available at http://www.un.org/Overview/rights.html.

42. James Nickel, *Making Sense of Human Rights: Philosophical Reflections on the Universal Declaration of Human Rights* (Berkeley: University of California Press, 1987), 51.

43. Gene Outka and John P. Reeder Jr., eds., *Prospects for a Common Morality* (Princeton, NJ: Princeton University Press, 1993), 3.

44. Laurence H. Shoup and William Minter, *Imperial Brain Trust: The Council on Foreign Relations and United States Foreign Policy* (New York: Monthly Review Press, 1977), 135.

45. Ibid., 140, 142.

46. Ibid., 145.

47. Ibid., 146.

48. Walter LaFeber, Richard Polenberg, and Nancy Woloch, *The American Century: A History of the United States since 1941*, 5th ed. (Boston: McGraw-Hill, 1998), 385.

49. William Blum, *Killing Hope: U.S. Military and CIA Interventions since World War II* (Monroe, ME: Common Courage, 1995), 70.

50. Ibid., 71.

51. Audrey R. Kahin and George McT. Kahin, *Subversion as Foreign Policy: The Secret*

Eisenhower and Dulles Debacle in Indonesia (Seattle: University of Washington Press, 1995), 4.

52. Blum, *Killing Hope*, 69.
53. Walter LaFeber, *The American Age: U.S. Foreign Policy since 1750*, 2nd ed. (New York: Norton, 1993), 518.
54. Blum, *Killing Hope*, 70.
55. Noam Chomsky, *Deterring Democracy*, 2nd ed. (New York: Hill & Wang, 1992), 50 (quoting the *New York Times*, August 6, 1954).
56. LaFeber, *The American Age*, 518.
57. Blum, *Killing Hope*, 72.
58. William Rivers Pitt, *War on Iraq* (New York: Context Books, 2002), 17.
59. Piero Gleijeses, *Shattered Hope: The Guatemalan Revolution and the United States, 1944–1954* (Princeton, NJ: Princeton University Press, 1991), 3.
60. Ibid., 150.
61. Ibid., 152, 155–60, 163.
62. Ibid., 135, 160.
63. Ibid., 257, 262, 298.
64. Ibid., 78–79, 140–41, 143–46, 182, 190, 192, 216, 233–34; Nick Cullather, *Secret History: The CIA's Classified Account of Its Operations in Guatemala, 1952–1954* (Stanford, CA: Stanford University Press, 1999), 142. (Cullather's study, which draws on both Gleijeses's book and CIA files, was originally intended only for internal CIA use.)
65. Cullather, *Secret History*, 107–8.
66. This was actually the Eisenhower administration's second attempt to overthrow Arbenz. After the first attempt, Arbenz discovered and published evidence of American involvement. The U.S. State Department called the accusations "ridiculous and untrue," adding, "It is the policy of the United States not to interfere in the internal affairs of other nations" (Blum, *Killing Hope*, 78). What it meant, however, is that it is the policy of the United States not to get caught and then, if it does, to lie.
67. Gleijeses, *Shattered Hope*, 246–47, 254, 256, 305, 313, 335, 338–39, 341, 365, 375, 380; Cullather, *Secret History*, 60, 64, 68, 82, 84–85, 89.
68. Blum, *Killing Hope*, 82.
69. Noam Chomsky, *Year 501: The Conquest Continues* (Boston: South End, 1993), 174–76.
70. David F. Schmitz, *Thank God They're on Our Side: The United States and Right-Wing Dictatorships, 1921–1965* (Chapel Hill: University of North Carolina Press, 1999), 173.
71. Gleijeses, *Shattered Hope*, 235 (citing Dwight D. Eisenhower, *Mandate for Change, 1953–1956* [Garden City, NJ: Doubleday, 1963], 421–27, 573–75).
72. Blum, *Killing Hope*, 216.
73. Ibid., 218.
74. Ibid., 215, 220.
75. Kahin and Kahin, *Subversion as Foreign Policy*, 32, 40, 42–43, 50–51; Noam Chomsky, *Powers and Prospects: Reflections on Human Nature and the Social Order* (Boston: South End, 1996), 190. It was only with the publication of the book by the Kahins in 1995 that the information about America's 1965 intervention was made public. It had been kept secret for thirty years and is still unknown to most Americans.
76. Kahin and Kahin, *Subversion as Foreign Policy*, 91, 92, 93, 126, 161.
77. Ibid., 10, 15, 74, 84, 87–88.

78. Ibid., 149–51; cf. 124.

79. Ibid., 86, 99, 102, 119–20, 128, 132, 134, 136, 138, 140, 150–51, 158, 161, 186, 216.

80. Ibid., 193–94, 208.

81. Ibid., 225.

82. On arms, see Chomsky, *Year 501*, 126, and Gabriel Kolko, *Confronting the Third World: United States Foreign Policy 1945–1980* (New York: Pantheon, 1988), 181. On shooting lists, see Kathy Kadane, *San Francisco Examiner*, May 20, 1990. For additional evidence of U.S. responsibility, see Kahin and Kahin, *Subversion as Foreign Policy*, 123, 225, and Blum, *Killing Hope*, 195–97.

83. Kahin and Kahin, *Subversion as Foreign Policy*, 227–28; Noam Chomsky and Edward S. Herman, *Washington Connection and Third World Fascism* (Montreal: Black Rose, 1979), 207.

84. Kahin and Kahin, *Subversion as Foreign Policy*, 227–28; Noam Chomsky, *Rogue States: The Rule of Force in World Affairs* (Cambridge: South End Press, 2000), 6, 144; Chomsky and Herman, *The Washington Connection*, 208–19, 228; John Stockwell, *The Praetorian Guard: The U.S. Role in the New World Order* (Boston: South End, 1991), 72.

85. Kahin and Kahin, *Subversion as Foreign Policy*, 194, 217; Chomsky and Herman, *The Washington Connection*, 209–10.

86. Kolko, *Confronting the Third World*, 185; Chomsky and Herman, *Washington Connection*, 209–10.

87. Ralph W. McGehee, *Deadly Deceits: My 25 Years in the CIA* (New York: Sheridan Square Publications, 1983), 57–58; Stockwell, *The Praetorian Guard*, 72–73.

88. Blum, *Killing Hope*. See also Anthony Arnove, ed., *Iraq under Siege: The Deadly Impact of Sanctions and War*, updated ed. (Cambridge: South End, 2002); Phyllis Bennis, *Before and After: US Foreign Policy and the September 11th Crisis* (New York: Olive Branch, 2003); Chomsky, *Deterring Democracy, Year 501, Rogue States: The Rule of Force in World Affairs*, and *Fateful Triangle: The United States, Israel, and the Palestinians*, updated ed., foreword by Edward Said (Cambridge: South End, 1999); Dilip Hiro, *Iraq: In the Eye of the Storm* (New York: Nation Books, 2002); Chalmers Johnson, *The Sorrows of Empire: Militarism, Secrecy, and the End of the Republic* (New York: Henry Holt, 2004); Peter Kornbluh, *Nicaragua: The Price of Intervention: Reagan's Wars against the Sandinistas* (Washington, DC: Institute for Policy Studies, 1987); Jonathan Kwitny, *Endless Enemies: The Making of an Unfriendly World* (New York: Penguin Books, 1986); Richard Labevière, *Dollars for Terror: The United States and Islam* (New York: Algora, 2000); Walter LaFeber, *Inevitable Revolutions: The United States in Central America*, 2nd ed. (New York: Norton, 1993); George McT. Kahin, *Intervention: How America Became Involved in Vietnam* (New York: Anchor, 1987); Schmitz, *Thank God They're on Our Side*; John Tirman, *Spoils of War: The Human Cost of America's Arm Trade* (New York: Free Press, 1997); Marilyn B. Young, *The Vietnam Wars: 1945–1990* (New York: Harper-Perennial, 1991).

89. Stefan Halper and Jonathan Clarke, *America Alone: The Neo-Conservatives and the Global Order* (Cambridge: Cambridge University Press, 2004), 219, citing Kaplan and Kristol, *War over Iraq*, 95–99.

90. Robert Dreyfuss, "Oil-Control Formula," July 18, 2005 (http://www.tompaine.com/articles/20050718/oilcontrol_formula.php).

91. Adam Horowitz, "Iraq: U.S. Plans to Reshape the Iraqi Economy," *Z Magazine*,

September 1, 2003 (www.corpwatch.org/article.php?id=11154), citing a report in the *Wall Street Journal*, May 1, 2003.

92. Naomi Klein, "Baghdad: Year Zero," *Harper's*, September 24, 2004 (http://harpers.org/BaghdadYearZero.html).

93. Ibid. See also Antonia Juhasz, *The Bush Agenda* (New York: Regan, 2006).

94. Greg Palast, "Secret US Plans for Iraq's Oil," BBC Newsnight, March 17, 2005 (http://news.bbc.co.uk/2/hi/programmes/newsnight/4354269.stm).

95. See Klein, "Baghdad"; Center for Economic and Social Rights, "Beyond Torture: U.S. Violations of Occupation Law in Iraq," June 10, 2004 (http://cesr.org/node/view/227), esp. "Violation X: Fundamentally Changing the Economic Structure."

96. Dorrien, *Imperial Designs*, 242–44, citing Wesley K. Clark, *Winning Modern Wars: Iraq, Terrorism, and the American Empire* (New York: Public Affairs, 2003), 120, 130.

97. See, for example, Ray McGovern, "The Intelligence Made Them Do It," March 18, 2005 (www.tompaine.com/articles/the_intelligence_made_them_do_it.php); Justin Raimondo, "'Dead Wrong'—or Outright Deception? Iraqi WMD: Someone Threw Us a Curveball," April 1, 2005 (http://www.antiwar.com/justin/?articleid=5423); and Maureen Dowd, "Curveball the Goofball," *New York Times*, April 3, 2005 (http://www.nytimes.com/2005/04/03/opinion/04dowd.html?th&emc=th), who pointed out that none of the investigations have answered the basic question: "How did the White House and Pentagon spin the information and why has no one gotten in trouble for it?"

98. David Manning, "The Secret Downing Street Memo: Secret and Strictly Personal—UK Eyes Only," *Sunday Times* (London), May 1, 2005 (http://www.timesonline.co.uk/article/0,,2087-1593607,00.html). For discussion, see Ray McGovern, "Proof the Fix Was In," Antiwar.com, May 5, 2005 (http://www.antiwar.com/mcgovern/index.php?articleid=5844); Greg Palast, "Impeachment Time: Facts Were Fixed," May 5, 2005 (www.GregPalast.com/detail.cfm?artid=426&row=0); and John Prados, "Iraq: When Was the Die Cast?" May 3, 2005 (www.tompaine.com/articles/iraq_when_was_the_die_cast.php).

99. "Remarks by the Vice President to the Veterans of Foreign Wars 103rd National Convention," August 26, 2002 (http://www.whitehouse.gov/news/releases/2002/08/20020826.html).

100. "Remarks by the President on Iraq," October 7, 2002 (http://www.whitehouse.gov/news/releases/2002/10/20021007-8.html).

101. "U.S. Secretary of State Colin Powell Addresses the U.N. Security Council," February 5, 2003 (http://www.whitehouse.gov/news/releases/2003/02/20030205-1.html).

102. "Powell Regrets UN Speech on Iraq WMDs," ABC NewsOnline, September 9, 2005 (http://www.abc.net.au/news/newsitems/200509/s1456650.htm).

103. See Col. W. Patrick Lang (retired), "Drinking the Kool-Aid: Making the Case for War with Compromised Integrity and Intelligence," and Ray McGovern, "Sham Dunk: Cooking Intelligence for the President," in *Neoconned Again: Hypocrisy, Lawlessness, and the Rape of Iraq*, ed. D. L. O'Huallachain and J. Forrest Sharpe (Vienna, VA: IHS Press, 2005), 249–75 and 277–305, respectively.

104. Gernot Köhler, *Global Apartheid* (New York: Institute for World Order, 1978).

105. Ibid., 4.

106. Ibid., 2.

107. Ibid., 6. As we will see below, there is even greater disparity in the world today.
108. Ibid., 9.
109. Thomas C. Schelling, "The Global Dimension," in *Rethinking America's Security,* ed. Graham Allison and Gregory F. Treverton (New York: W. W. Norton, 1992), 196–210, at 200.
110. Richard Falk, "Democratizing, Internationalizing, and Globalizing: A Collage of Blurred Images," *Third World Quarterly* 12, no. 4 (1993): 627–40, at 629.
111. Schelling, "The Global Dimension," 200.
112. Titus Alexander, *Unraveling Global Apartheid: An Overview of World Politics* (Cambridge: Polity Press, 1996), 9, 246.
113. Ibid., 257.
114. Ibid., 176, 7.
115. Quoted in Robert Heilbroner, *Twenty-First-Century Capitalism* (New York: W. W. Norton, 1993), 55–56.
116. Colin Parkins, "North-South Relations and Globalization after the Cold War," in *Global Politics: An Introduction,* ed. Charlotte Bretherton and Geoffrey Ponton (Cambridge, MA, & Oxford: Blackwell, 1996), 49–73, at 50–51.
117. Ibid., 51.
118. George F. Kennan, "PPS/23: Review of Current Trends in U.S. Foreign Policy." First published in *Foreign Relations of the United States,* vol. 1 (1948):509–29, it has been reprinted in Thomas H. Entzold and John Lewis Gaddis, eds., *Containment: Documents on American Policy and Strategy, 1945–1950* (New York: Columbia University Press, 1978), 226–28; the quoted passage is at 226–27. Kennan, speaking in this secret memo with the kind of frankness that is never found in public documents, continued: "To do so, we will have to dispense with all sentimentality and day-dreaming. . . . We need not deceive ourselves that we can afford today the luxury of altruism and world-benefaction. . . . The day is not far off when we are going to have to deal in straight power concepts. The less we are then hampered by idealistic slogans, the better."
119. So called because they were formally established at a meeting in 1944 in Bretton Woods, New Hampshire, although GATT was actually established at a subsequent meeting, after the originally planned International Trade Organization was not ratified. In any case, as John Cobb points out, although the establishment of the United Nations captured much more of the world's attention in 1944, "the actions taken at Bretton Woods would prove, in the long run, more fateful." See John B. Cobb Jr., *The Earthist Challenge to Economism: A Theological Critique of the World Bank* (London: Macmillan, 1999), 61.
120. David C. Korten, *When Corporations Rule the World* (San Francisco: Berrett-Koehler, and West Hartford, CT: Kumarian Press, 1995), 160.
121. Ibid., 172.
122. Ibid.
123. Walden Bello, *Dark Victory: The United States, Structural Adjustment, and Global Poverty* (London: Pluto Press, 1994); John B. Cobb Jr., "Imperialism in American Economic Policy," a chapter in Griffin, Cobb, Falk, and Keller, *The American Empire and the Commonwealth of God.*
124. John Perkins, *Confessions of an Economic Hit Man* (San Francisco: Berrett-Koehler, 2004).
125. Cobb, *The Earthist Challenge to Economism,* 83.
126. Devinder Sharma, "World Bank's Latest Passion," ZNet Commentary, December 20, 2004 (http://www.zmag.org/sustainers/content/2004-12/17 sharma.cfm).

127. United Nations Development Program, *Human Development Report: International Cooperation at a Crossroads: Aid, Trade, and Security in an Unequal World* (http://hdr.undp.org/reports/global/2005).

128. Reality of Aid 2004 (http://www.realityofaid.org/roareport.php?table=roa 2004&id=1); Barry Mason, "World Hunger Report: 852 Million Starve in the Midst of Plenty," December 19, 2003 (http://www.starvation.net/842million starveinthemidstofplenty.htm).

129. "Vision for 2020," February 1997 (http://www.fas.org/spp/military/docops/usspac/visbook.pdf).

130. Tim Weiner, "Air Force Seeks Bush's Approval for Space Weapons Programs," *New York Times*, May 18, 2005 (http://www.nytimes.com/2005/05/18/business/18space.html?th&emc=th).

131. Robert Kagan, "The Benevolent Empire," 24–35.

132. Dorrien, *Imperial Designs*, 18.

133. Ibid.

134. Ben J. Wattenberg, "Neo-Manifest Destinarianism," *National Interest* 21 (Fall 1990): 54; quoted in Dorrien, *Imperial Designs*, 80.

135. Although the phrase "global apartheid" was not allowed to appear in the Summit's final statement, Mbeki's use of it is quoted by Patrick Bond in "Politics, Poverty and Uneven Development in Theory and Practice," October 23, 2002 (http://www.nibr.no/content/download/1758/7643/file/NFU-Patrick-Bond-paper.doc).

136. See, for example, the National Council of Catholic Bishops, *The Challenge of Peace: God's Promise and Our Response* (Washington, DC: Office of Pub. Services, United States Catholic Conference, 1983); "The Morality of Nuclear Deterrence," issued on the fifteenth anniversary of *The Challenge of Peace* and signed by seventy-five U.S. Catholic Bishops and members of Pax Christi (http://www.ccnr.org/pax_christi.html); Robert Jay Lifton and Richard Falk, *Indefensible Weapons: The Political and Psychological Case against Nuclearism*, updated ed. (New York: Basic Books, 1991); Helen Caldicott, *The New Nuclear Danger: George W. Bush's Military-Industrial Complex*, rev. and updated ed. (New York: New Press, 2004).

137. Particularly good on this issue is Caldicott, *The New Nuclear Danger*.

138. "The Treaty on the Non-Proliferation of Nuclear Weapons" (available at http://www.un.org/events/npt2005/npttreaty.html).

139. President John F. Kennedy, "Address before the General Assembly of the United Nations," September 25, 1961; this passage contained in "JFK on Nuclear Weapons and Non-Proliferation," Waging Peace (http://www.wagingpeace.org/articles/2003/11/17_carnegie_jfk-nuclear.htm).

140. See Avner Cohen, *Israel and the Bomb* (New York: Columbia University Press, 1999); D. K. Palit and P. K. S. Namboodiri, *Pakistan's Islamic Bomb* (New Delhi: Vikas, 1979); Steve Weissman and Herbert Krosney, *The Islamic Bomb* (New York: Times Books, 1981).

141. Columnist Bob Herbert denounced this agreement in an op-ed piece called "Nuclear Madness," *New York Times,* March 6, 2006 (available at http://www.topplebush.com/oped2589.shtml).

142. "The Treaty on the Non-Proliferation of Nuclear Weapons" (available at http://www.un.org/events/npt2005/npttreaty.html).

143. For a highly authoritative discussion, see Sir John Houghton (who has been cochair of the Scientific Assessment Working Group of the IPCC [Intergovernmental Panel on Climate Change], *Global Warming: The Complete Briefing*, 3rd

ed. (Cambridge: Cambridge University Press, 2004). For books that are especially good on the destructive influence of the United States and the oil lobby, see Jeremy Leggett, *The Carbon Era: Global Warming and the End of the Oil Era* (New York: Routledge, 2001), and Ross Gelbspan, *Boiling Point: How Politicians, Big Oil and Coal, Journalists and Activists Are Fueling the Climate Crisis—And What We Can Do to Avert Disaster* (New York: Basic Books, 2004). On the possibility of runaway global warming, see Leggett's book.

144. See Griffin, *Reenchantment without Supernaturalism,* chap. 6, and "Process Eschatology," in *The Handbook of Eschatology,* ed. Jerry Walls (Oxford: Oxford University Press, 2006).

145. "Statement by the President in His Address to the Nation," 8:30 p.m., September 11, 2001 (http://www.whitehouse.gov/news/releases/2001/09/20010911-16.html).

146. This statement is in Weston's blurb for my book *The 9/11 Commission Report: Omissions and Distortions.*

147. Samuel P. Huntington, *The Clash of Civilizations and the Remaking of World Order* (New York: Simon & Schuster, 1998).

148. Chomsky, *Hegemony or Survival,* 9, 116, 193.

149. John Le Carré, "The United States Has Gone Completely Mad," *London Times,* January 15, 2003.

150. See Caldicott, *The New Nuclear Danger.*

151. David Ray Griffin, "9/11, the American Empire, and Common Moral Norms," in *9/11 and the American Empire: Intellectuals Speak Out,* ed. Griffin and Peter Dale Scott (Northampton, MA: Interlink, 2006).

Chapter 10—A Call to Reflection and Action

1. I have in mind especially my two previous books, *The New Pearl Harbor: Disturbing Questions about 9/11 and the Bush Administration* (Northampton, MA: Interlink Books, 2004), and *The 9/11 Commission Report: Omissions and Distortions* (Northampton, MA: Interlink Books, 2005), as well as *9/11 and the American Empire: Intellectuals Speak Out* (Northampton, MA: Interlink, 2006), which I edited with Peter Dale Scott. See also Kevin Barrett, John B. Cobb Jr., and Sandra Lubarsky, *9/11 and the American Empire: Christians, Jews, and Muslims Speak Out* (Northampton, MA: Interlink, 2006).

2. See Alan Cowell, "For Blair, Iraq Issue Just Won't Go Away," *New York Times,* May 2, 2005; Walter Pincus, "British Intelligence Warned Blair of War," *Washington Post,* May 13, 2005: A18; Mark Memmott, "'Downing Street Memo' Gets Fresh Attention," *USA Today,* June 8, 2005; David E. Sanger, "Prewar British Memo Says War Decision Wasn't Made," *New York Times,* June 13, 2005.

3. "While Editors Nationwide Call for Increased Scrutiny of Downing Street Memo, Biggest Editorial Pages Remain Silent," Media Matters for America, June 15, 2005 (http://mediamatters.org/items/printable/200506150003).

4. David Michael Green, "Stop the Crime of the Century," CommonDreams.org, May 13, 2005 (http://www.commondreams.org/views05/0513-20.htm).

5. Robert Dreyfuss, "A Memo and Two Catechisms," May 23, 2005 (http://www.tompaine.com/articles/20050523/a_memo_and_two_catechisms.php).

6. For an analysis of the memo and the press coverage of it, see Mark Danner, "Why the Memo Matters," *New York Review of Books,* July 14, 2005 (available at http://www.tomdispatch.com/index.mhtml?emx=x&pid=3602).

7. Mark Crispin Miller, "None Dare Call It Stolen," *Harper's*, August 2005.

8. Mark Crispin Miller, *Fooled Again* (New York: Basic Books, 2005).

9. Anita Miller, *What Went Wrong in Ohio: The Conyers Report on the 2004 Presidential Election*, introduction by Gore Vidal (Chicago: Academy Chicago Publishers, 2005).

10. Peter Phillips, "Another Year of Distorted Election Coverage," in *Censored 2006: The 25 Top Censored Stories,* ed. Peter Phillips (New York: Seven Stories, 2005). See also, in the same volume, Dennis Loo, "No Paper Trail Left Behind."

11. Gregory Palast, *The Best Democracy That Money Can Buy* (New York: Penguin, 2005).

12. See, for example, Dean Alger, *Megamedia: How Giant Corporations Dominate Mass Media, Distort Competition, and Endanger Democracy* (Lanham, MD: Rowman & Littlefield, 2000); Ben H. Bagdikian, *The New Media Monopoly* (Boston: Beacon Press, 2004); Edward S. Herman and Noam Chomsky, *Manufacturing Consent: The Political Economy of the Mass Media* (1988; New York: Pantheon, 2002); Robert W. McChesney, *The Problem of the Media: U.S. Communication Politics in the 21st Century* (New York: Monthly Review Press, 2004); and Kristina Borjesson, ed., *Into the Buzzsaw: Leading Journalists Expose the Myth of a Free Press*, rev. ed. (New York: Prometheus, 2004).

13. See Deborah Madsen, *American Exceptionalism* (Jackson: University of Mississippi Press, 1998).

14. Andrew J. Bacevich, *American Empire: The Realities and Consequences of U.S. Diplomacy* (Cambridge: Harvard University Press, 2002), 133.

15. Lord Acton, *Essays*, ed. Rufus F. Fears (Liberty Classics, 1985), 2:383. Acton's statement is quoted in Garry Wills, *Papal Sin: Structures of Deceit* (New York: Doubleday, 2000), 2.

16. Bacevich, *American Empire*, 127, 17.

17. Jurgen Brauer and Nicholas Anglewicz, "Two-Thirds on Defense," Tom Paine, June 10, 2005 (http://www.tompaine.com/articles/20050610/twothirds_on_defense.php).

18. See, for example, David Cay Johnson, "Corporate Wealth Share Rises for Top-Income Americans," *New York Times*, January 26, 2006 (www.nytimes.com/2006/01/29/national/29rich.html?emc=eta1), which reports that although in 1991, after the Reagan-Bush years, the top 1 percent of households already owned 38.7 percent of the country's wealth, by 2003 this figure had risen to 57.5 percent (up 4 percent from just the previous year). See also Achin Vanaik, "Unequal Gains: For the Elites, the Super-Rich Are the True Heroes of the Times," *Telegraph*, December 22, 2005 (http://www.globalpolicy.org/socecon/inequal/2005/1222inequgains.htm). Churches should especially study *Economic Apartheid in America: A Primer on Economic Inequality and Insecurity*, by Chuck Collins and Felice Yeskel with United for a Fair Economy and Class Action, rev. ed. (New York: The New Press, 2005).

19. See note 135 of chap. 9, above.

20. David Ray Griffin, "Global Government: Objections Considered," in *Toward Genuine Global Governance: Critical Reactions to "Our Global Neighborhood,"* ed. Errol E. Harris and James A. Yunker (Westport, CT: Praeger, 1999), 69–92; "Global Empire or Global Democracy: The Present Alternatives," in Griffin, Cobb, Falk, and Keller, *The American Empire and the Commonwealth of God*.

21. See Robert McAfee Brown, "1984: Orwell and Barmen," *Christian Century*,

August 15–22, 1984 (available at http://www.religion-online.org/show article.asp?title=1415).

22. Quoted in G. Clarke Chapman, *Facing the Nuclear Heresy: A Call to Reformation* (Elgin, IL: Brethren Press, 1986), 50. Chapman's book is a call for Christians to declare nuclear weapons a *status confessionis*. My own view is that nuclear weapons are now part and parcel of the world order based around sovereign states, so that the only way to eliminate the world of nuclear weapons is to overcome this world order through the creation of global democracy.

Index of Names